Homeland Insecurity

HOMELAND INSECURITY

The Rise and Rise of Global
Anti-Terrorism Law

Conor Gearty

polity

First published in 2024 by Polity Press

Polity Press
65 Bridge Street
Cambridge CB2 1UR, UK

Polity Press
111 River Street
Hoboken, NJ 07030, USA

ISBN-13: 978-1-5095-5371-6

A catalogue record for this book is available from the British Library.

Library of Congress Control Number: 2023952140

Typeset in 11.5 on 14pt Adobe Garamond
by Cheshire Typesetting Ltd, Cuddington, Cheshire
Printed and bound in Great Britain by CPI Group (UK) Ltd, Croydon

The publisher has used its best endeavours to ensure that the URLs for external websites referred to in this book are correct and active at the time of going to press. However, the publisher has no responsibility for the websites and can make no guarantee that a site will remain live or that the content is or will remain appropriate.

Every effort has been made to trace all copyright holders, but if any have been overlooked the publisher will be pleased to include any necessary credits in any subsequent reprint or edition.

For further information on Polity, visit our website:
politybooks.com

To Aoife, with love

Contents

Acknowledgements

This book has grown out of my engagement over many years with the subjects of terrorism, anti-terrorism law, human rights and civil liberties. Generations of students in my law and terrorism courses at King's College London and later the London School of Economics have kept me on my toes intellectually. Those who attended workshops on a draft of this book at Queen's University Belfast and at my own academic home LSE's Law School helped me to focus the argument at a critical time: I am very grateful to Richard English and Kieron McEvoy for arranging the first, and to my Law School Dean David Kershaw for encouraging me to hold the second. I am thankful to all those who made the time to come to these events, and especially to Fatima Ahdash, Diamond Ashiagbor, Michelle Hughes, Richard Martin and Ntina Tzouvalu for their prepared comments on specific chapters at the LSE event. Neil Duxbury read the whole manuscript from start to finish and made a range of suggestions which were immensely helpful. Aoife Nolan brought her superb editorial gaze to bear at critical moments in the book's evolution and eventual finalization. My editors at Polity, first Pascal Porcheron and later Julia Davies, have been supportive throughout, and the anonymous readers who reviewed first the proposal and then the book itself have improved it in many important ways. Polity's whole production team have been a delight to work with. It remains my book, and the mistakes are all mine, but there would have been more and the book would have been much less than it is without the generous assistance of all those mentioned above, as well as the countless others who have in various ways (often without their – or even me – knowing it) helped me to think through the subject in the way that you see laid out before you in this volume.

Introduction: Home and Away

Liberalism and political violence

In 1891, the Swiss authorities wanted the United Kingdom to send an anarchist revolutionary back to their jurisdiction for trial. Angelo Castioni had shot and killed a member of the Swiss state council while attacking an arsenal and municipal palace in one of the country's governing units (cantons). Three judges (Denman J., Hawkins J. and Stephen J.) refused to order his return.[1] Far from going against him, it was the political nature of Castioni's violent act that rendered him safe from extradition. The relevant British law, passed in 1870, had specifically excluded such conduct from its reach.[2] In those days in Britain, a high level of foreign-based political violence was tolerated, protected even where it occurred outside the UK's jurisdiction and 'in the course of a struggle for power between two parties in a State'.[3] As Mr Justice Hawkins observed, 'one cannot look too hardly and weigh in golden scales the acts of men hot in their political excitement'.[4] For his part, Stephen J. observed that 'the shooting on this occasion took place in a scene of very great tumult, at a moment when, if a man decided to use deadly violence, he had very little time to consider what was happening and to see what he ought to do, and that, therefore, he was committing an act greatly to be regretted'[5] – but not sufficiently regrettable as to deprive him of his protection from extradition.

It is hard to imagine a judge saying the same about a political killing today. Now people like Castioni would not have a chance; actions similar to his are excoriated as beyond the bounds of morality wherever they occur, a disease to be rooted out of our liberal body politic at all costs and regardless of motive, context or location. Of course, the contemporary political subversive has a far wider range of destructive tools at their disposal (and a greater capacity to wreak harm), than ever the likes of Castioni had. There may very well be several good reasons for why the contemporary 'terrorist' is treated differently, and we shall come to these in the course of this book. The political defence against extradition has, however, clearly faded away,[6] and, with it, its Victorian assumptions about liberty and freedom for the foreign fighter.

Even mere plotting against transparently pernicious regimes abroad now potentially attracts the hostile attention of local prosecutors. In one recent case in Britain, a person found to have been planning a violent revolt against Colonel Gaddafi in Libya could not rely on the purity of their ambitions: 'There is no exemption from criminal liability for terrorist activities which are motivated or said to be morally justified by the alleged nobility of the terrorist cause.'[7] For this English Court of Appeal, giving judgment in 2007, 'terrorism [was] an international modern scourge',[8] and so, while 'the call of resistance to tyranny and invasion evokes an echoing response down the ages',[9] there was 'nothing in the legislation' on terrorism which 'might support [the] distinction' argued for by the accused between resisting democratic states (wrong) and fighting authoritarian states (not wrong).[10] This new moralism does not stop at individuals who have engaged in or planned acts of violence: even if they do nothing themselves, members of 'terrorist groups' risk punishment by reason of their affiliation.[11] And anti-terrorism laws not only collude in the removal of people like Castioni into the hands of their enemies – they reach into domestic subversion as well, playing havoc with civil liberties and personal freedom under cover of a promiscuously defined national security.

In this book, I explore how this change in sentiment has come about and the effect it has had on our system of laws – indeed, on our liberal political culture as a whole.[12] The 'our' here reaches beyond the United Kingdom to encompass Europe, North America and democracies across the world. With the attacks of 11 September 2001 ('9/11'), the subject of 'terrorism' seems to have (literally and metaphorically) exploded onto the scene, with scores of violent disputes with power around the world (some justified, some not) being repackaged as part of a global movement of disorder rather than being seen as the discrete, locally based challenges to authority that they usually are. The world is this book's stage, albeit the driving force behind the changes in the law that it describes has been European and American in origin. The field of anti-terrorism law now extends beyond democratic borders to the wider world, where despots everywhere welcome it with open arms. The laws that these concerns about terrorism have generated are important, and their impact on civil liberties severe. I look at these legislative and executive acts (international, regional and national) closely, arguing that they have fundamentally affected the shape of our democratic culture, and that they are here to stay whether or not terrorist atrocity remains as a central source of anxiety.

Law and the study of (counter-)terrorism

I began this book thinking I was writing a book about the history of terrorism. I had done something similar over thirty years ago,[13] and it nagged me that I had never built properly on that early book with later editions in order to have a more consistent engagement in the field. I soon realized that any such project was a futile endeavour in the here and now. What had struck me as original in 1991 now seemed passé. New work had emerged, much of it original and critical in a way that made anything I might now want to say seem to be verging on the superfluous. More to the point, I had become too much of a lawyer in the decades since I had unwittingly engaged in what I now knew to have been an interdisciplinary endeavour, mixing history, international relations and politics with (just a dash of) law.

So I thought 'why not turn my disciplinary commitment into a strength?' This book on the rise and rise of anti-terrorism law is the result. There are many excellent treatises on the law of terrorism (international and national),[14] and important books too on the history of and policies behind counter-terrorism.[15] But few of the general treatments of the subject, no matter how compendious, have specific sections or chapters devoted to anti-terrorism law as such.[16] My particular interest here has led me to focus on the development of such laws rather than on their current substance – less a snapshot of the present than a reflection on how we got where we are today.

But this then created a further difficulty: what causes this or that particular law to be enacted is often a question requiring answers that go beyond law. This has particularly been the case with anti-terrorism law. The field encompassing this brand of law is no product of careful academic study or a law commission enquiry into this or that lacunae in the legislative status quo; it has been hurled onto the statute book by the waves of political, diplomatic and international energy that have already done so much to determine its shape before it arrives. Much of Part One of this book, on the origins of anti-terrorism law, is therefore light on legal detail – slightly disconcertingly perhaps, but in the circumstances of *this* branch of law I think inevitable. The law comes into its own when the subject of terrorism itself does: in the aftermath of the attacks on New York and the Pentagon on 11 September 2001.

Where does this volume fit in intellectual terms? There are deliberate echoes of Boukalas's work in my choice of title,[17] and I have found that author's well-argued disinclination to follow certain well-established politico-legal philosophers in this area to be very persuasive.[18] At very least my book is a contribution to the necessary 'historicisation of terrorism' that has been evident in recent years.[19] As my LSE colleague Audrey Alejandro and my research student (now Dr) Mattia Pinto wrote when considering Foucault's impact on the law: 'the construction of legal categories is an important vehicle for producing legal meanings'.[20] This is what I think this book is mainly doing: constructing a genealogy of a particularly important legal term ('terrorism') and as a result of doing so submitting the origins and growth of anti-terrorism law (its main focus) to close examination. As Charlotte Heath-Kelly has noted, '[t]hreats and crises are socially constructed, not objective realties',[21] and anti-terrorism law and practice have become the bridge between the construction of terrorism as a security crisis and its manifestation on the ground. My book fits within the literature as a contribution from a lawyer to the critical terrorism studies movement that has done so much to energize the field.[22]

Security versus liberty

Despite their immense power as a driver of what followed, the attacks of 11 September are not the start of our story. To get to the bottom of our subject, to understand how it has emerged and enjoyed the kind of success that I am describing here, we need to go behind that pivotal event. We need in particular to understand the political-cultural environment in which the post-9/11 laws have come to be enacted.[23] Many of those laws are self-evidently repressive. Of course, there are obvious answers, rooted in the public nature of the violence wrought by subversive politi-

4

cal actors, the disregard by such 'terrorists' of innocent bystanders, the arbitrariness of their actions, their lack of material self-interest – in sum, the immorality and incomprehensibility of their conduct.

But nagging doubts surely remain. How has a polity that loudly protests its commitment to freedom and equality (as liberal democracies invariably do) ended up so easily accommodating anti-terrorism laws and practices that – with their wide-ranging police powers, their acceptance of surveillance, their openness to extra-legal or barely legal actions like torture and assassination, their extended pre-trial detention, their discriminatory impact and much else – so obviously mock this stated commitment? What is it about the way that liberal democracy views the world that makes such a blatant double standard – we are a free society; we embrace coercive anti-terrorism laws – possible? How can freedom seem to be secured rather than fatally undermined by these active displays of state power? Or, to put the same point into the form of a different set of questions: How have illiberal anti-terrorism laws come to be so successful in a democratic culture which is supposedly devoted to individual freedom and civil liberties? Why has the 'global war on terror' met with so little resistance from democratic states? Why has that 'war' been so (relatively speaking) easy to justify, generating little pushback and surviving well past the original crisis which gave rise to it? We need to be able to answer these various questions in order to make sense of the origins and operation of the laws that we are about to examine, and to appreciate fully the changes they have wrought in how we understand ourselves and the political world in which we live.

There is an underbelly to liberal society that has always emphasized security rather than liberty, with some asserting that even efforts to balance the two are just part of liberal mythology.[24] This is where our subject feels at home. This book identifies the critical period for the growth of our anti-terrorism legal culture as being from 1968 until about 1983: a time of radical-Left violence in Europe and the United States, nationalist struggle in Spain, Ireland and elsewhere, and above all a period during which the militant determination of the Palestinian movement to resist Israeli power was at its highest. Without question, there were legitimate fears generated by these various arenas of political violence during this period, especially when concerns about 'Islamist extremism' could be added into the mix after 1979. Proponents of anti-terrorism laws did not make up the bombs, the kidnappings, the hijackings, the hostage-taking, the assassinations that afflicted democratic society during these years. The violence was nasty, theatrical and scary, terrifyingly capable of striking at the most normal of times in the most normal of places. But from a Western point of view – and quite unlike the impact of political violence on the Palestinian people, or the violence wrought on their citizens by the South American military leaders of the 1960s, or by US forces in Vietnam or Cambodia, or any other government for that matter with the capacity and inclination to kill its political opponents – there was hardly any of it. The chances of being caught up in a terrorist incident in the West have always been vanishingly small, even when terrorism has been at its supposed height. Despite this, the West allowed itself over the course of this period to become convinced that its way of life was being fundamentally threatened, and so felt obliged to mount the fierce legal fightback anticipated above and detailed in the pages that follow, a fightback which, after the end of the Cold War and the events of 9/11, has had long-term implications for the freedom that is enjoyed in our liberal democratic culture.

Explaining anti-terrorism law

How did all this happen? The book suggests two explanations for the successful embedding of anti-terrorism law in liberal democracy's collective mind-set, both going beyond the narrative just laid out. The first, and the deepest, draws on the West's experience as a colonial power. In the next chapter, I argue that the coercive response that was routinely deployed against local resistance to the rule of its various empires familiarized European liberal and later democratic culture as a whole with the idea that freedom could co-exist with (perhaps even needed) swingeing anti-subversive laws. Indeed, many of these laws were characterized even at the time as 'anti-terrorism' initiatives (among, it is true, other labels). It is worth recalling at this juncture that the image of empire is no long-lost memory beyond any living person's recall but rather continued via persistent French and (mainly) British control of overseas territories until well into the second half of the twentieth century (and in authoritarian Portugal into the 1970s).

Then, just as empire waned and sovereign nationhood became the new norm of international relations, a fresh reorganization of world power took place, organized this time along lines that pitted the great victors of the Second World War against each other, in an apparent fight to the death between communist and capitalist ways of looking at the world. This 'Cold War' is the second of our deep explanations for the hold that 'terrorism' has achieved on the world, and is the focal point of Chapter 2. Overlapping with the last years of colonialism, the Cold War generated large incentives for Western culture (an active United States as well as a tiring Western Europe) to support those post-colonial states that – choosing the American side – were inclined to deploy their inherited anti-subversive laws to destroy their radical domestic opponents, particularly (but not exclusively) those who threatened revolutionary change from within and who were not afraid to contemplate violence as a route to the achievement of their aims. As with its exercise of colonial power, the liberal West has had plenty of practice countering radical dissent within its own borders, usually anti-capitalist/socialist in character, and often in purported support of the very values (free speech, the rule of law, human rights, etc.) that such state coercion appeared to contradict.

The laws on anti-terrorism that we see today are descendants of the democratic common sense that was created by these two grand twentieth-century movements: the idea, first, that anti-insurgency laws are a way of retaining colonial possessions that, since it does not involve a challenge to domestic (colonizer) democratic values, over time comes to be treated as ordinary, or at least not exceptional. And, second, that any liberal democratic society (European, American, post-colonial) is perfectly entitled – indeed obliged – to use what powers it has at its disposal to protect what it claims is its democratic culture from radical change, from within or without, or (as indeed was often the case during the Cold War) from both at once acting in subversive combination. These two historical factors offer an explanation as to why the door was open to an anti-terrorism trope in the late 1960s and beyond: democratic society was much more used to this kind of law than it understood or assumed, so inured to gliding over contradictions in the application of its values on the ground that it could replace one set of contradictions with another without even noticing what it was doing.

This context might satisfactorily explain the openness of liberal society to an anti-terrorism turn, but it does not tell us exactly how it came about, or why it took the shape that it did. We know that after the attacks of 9/11, President Bush felt confident in the knowledge that people would understand his talk of an 'axis of evil' and a 'crusade' against global terrorism. The UK prime minister Tony Blair even used the word 'existential' to describe the threat both men saw as being posed by those who had masterminded the attacks. How had the fear of global terrorism thrown down such deep roots and been able to thrive as it did?[25] The soil may have been prepared by the underlying colonial and Cold War narratives, but that is not a sufficient explanation of the global dimension to what followed. I address this core point in Chapters 4, 5 and 6.

The first of these chapters concerns the efforts, briefly alluded to earlier, being made by sub-nationalist movements in Western Europe and North America to assert their freedom, against both authoritarian polities (the Basque group ETA in Franco's Spain) and democratic states (the IRA in the UK, the FLQ in Canada, and many others). Together with the radical ideologies engaged in political violence in Western Europe at the same time (the Red Army Faction, the Red Brigades and so on, discussed as part of the Cold War struggle in Chapter 2), these groups and their activities were important paving stones on the road that took democracies far away from tacit acceptance of subversive political violence abroad (epitomized by the *Castioni* case) and liberal acceptance that its proponents at home were entitled to traditional fair treatment. Colonial anti-insurgency violence had, of course, always been present abroad. But when such insurgency began showing up at home as well, threatening not just the colonial but the domestic political order – and doing so not in faraway places but right there in the state's own front yard – a more direct response could not be avoided. It became acceptable (essential even) to destroy such challenges to domestic authority, and through a use of force that felt right both to those who deployed it and to the democratic citizenry that now could not help but see it happening, right there in front of them, and so needed satisfactory explanations rather than simple denial. When we examine these various movements in Chapter 3, we will see how each in their different way stimulated coercive legislative responses, increasingly deployed in the late 1960s and taking clearer shape in the early 1970s in the language of terrorism. Domestic adherence to the rule of law remained strong, but in all of these domestic agitations (those recounted in Chapter 2 as well as Chapter 3) it was put under immense strain and sometimes collapsed completely.

Neither the radical Left's aspiring revolutionaries of the Cold War nor the 'pseudo-colonials'[26] within constitutional democracies were, however, the main event. The immediate cause of the upsurge of the 'global terrorist' phenomenon during this critical early phase 1968–74 was rooted in the Middle East. In Chapter 4, I explore the habit of mind that simmered up in Western culture from the late 1960s onwards: that of seeing Palestinian resistance as more than something in itself, as a manifestation of a global problem rather than a reaction to local oppression, a challenge to civilized living as a whole rather than a parochial crisis. It is clear that this way of thinking could not have happened through Palestine alone, however dramatic and international the violence of its defenders occasionally was. The occurrence of analogous violence elsewhere helped the framing, bringing things (as it were) to the boil. I see the Palestinian violence of 1968–74 as central, as the supplier of the core materials on the road to 'global terrorism', and therefore as a generator of the necessity for a set of generalized anti-terrorism responses, both policy-oriented and legal, that went beyond whatever were the local concerns of this or that democratic state. This anti-terrorism drive also went beyond law; indeed, in this early phase it was often uninterested in the law as a focus of counter-terrorist activity. It was during this time that efforts by various Palestinian factions loosely (and in some cases directly) affiliated with the mainstream Palestinian movement the Palestine Liberation Organization (PLO) were successfully redescribed by their opponents (principally the Israeli state and its supporters in the United States) in terms that no longer acknowledged their conventional status as freedom fighters in search of national self-determination, instead recasting them as key operatives in a terrorist war whose target was not only an 'occupier' Israel but Western civilization as a whole.

To this narrative thrust, already quite successful in terms of painting Palestinian resistance as an existential challenge to the democratic West, was then added an additional ingredient in the late 1970s/early 1980s: the risk to Western culture and freedom of thought posed by Islamist militancy. Here is the subject of Chapter 5, the final offering in our section on the roots of modern anti-terrorism law. Bubbling under the surface in the 1970s as a component of Palestinian resistance, this new threat came into its own after the 1979 overthrow of the regime of Mohammad Reza Pahlavi, the last Persian monarch, and his government's replacement the same year by a proudly named Islamic Republic of Iran. Led by the radical cleric Ayatollah Khomeini, Iran directly defied Western power, holding US diplomats and other American citizens hostage in Tehran for over fourteen months in 1979–81, and equipping military elements in Lebanon to resist Israeli incursions into its northern neighbour (where the Palestinian resistance had a presence irritating to its powerful antagonist). The US and French military engagement in Lebanon that followed the invasion of that country by Israel in 1982 was seen off a year later by Iran's proxy in the region, Hezbollah, whose two trucks loaded with bombs and driven with force at American and French military barracks killed 307 people in October 1983, the great majority of them US marines. With this dramatic and successful deployment of the 'suicide bomber', the embedding of this kind of violence as part of a global problem of terror was well and truly launched.

The 'invention of terrorism'[27] that I have just briefly described is what provided the initial stimulus for the array of anti-terrorism laws that are the primary focus of this book. A central point in what follows is that these laws did not suddenly spring from nowhere as solutions to specific problems that national policy experts, legislators and law enforcement personnel had independently concluded were needed. The world of problems they inhabited had been framed for them by powerful and influential actors in the field of international relations, actors who had been methodically driving their own agendas under cover of discourses ostensibly rooted in global ethics and civilizational struggle, and who in doing so were able to avail themselves of pre-set (and invariably supportive) colonial and Cold War narratives. In the second part of this book, I turn to the uncontrolled proliferation in law and administrative practice of the language of terrorism in the aftermath of the extraordinary attacks by Al-Qaeda on the United States on 11 September 2001.

Here I track the debilitating impact on national law (Chapter 6) and international law (Chapters 8 and 9) of the routinization of anti-terrorism law that has occurred since those attacks, and show how what was once a recherché piece of positioning by a few states with an interest in the matter has become a global free-for-all, with governments everywhere uniting in a dismal shared effort to cast many (and, in some authoritarian states, all) of their political opponents as 'terrorist' and thus creatures beyond the pale of political discourse. While the active engagement of more authentic liberal discourses, such as those rooted in respect for human rights and the rule of law (discussed in Chapter 9) have done good work in modifying the immediate excesses of anti-terrorism law, their very success has – depressingly – served only to embed these laws further in our democratic and legal vocabulary.

My bleak concluding chapter suggests that the point has now been reached where anti-terrorism law has made substantial and seemingly permanent inroads into what we used routinely to believe a democratic polity absolutely required by way of democracy and respect for human rights. I go so far as to say that anti-terrorism law no longer needs terrorism to survive: it has altogether successfully outgrown its rationale, expanding into an irrepressible bureaucracy of state power. This is where I tackle directly a point that appears obliquely throughout: the uncomfortable connection between terrorism and constructions of racial difference, the latter being a habit learnt in colonial times that has proved near-impossible to shed. Writing about migration law recently, Nadine El-Enany said of her subject that '[u]nderstanding migration law as a racial regime of power, as part of a colonial edifice, allows us to see the danger of accepting legal categories as given'.[28] I feel the same about our anti-terrorism laws.

In its deconstruction of how such an approach has been successfully embedded, this book also complements (while having a different focus) the work of Ntina Tzouvala, whose powerful critique of recent anti-terrorism laws draws strength from her understanding of a wider political economy that demands the delivery of profit to certain corporate actors whatever the wider cost.[29] There is no doubt in my mind that Tzouvala's argument explains the alacrity with which commercial actors in the US and Britain, and indeed further afield, grabbed their post-9/11 anti-terrorism moment, and why leading this charge were the various experts, consultants and developers of this or that piece of anti-terrorism kit that stood to make substantial financial gains from the stampede for new tools with which to protect their various homelands. To accept this is not however to diminish the influence of political leaders intent on using anti-terrorism to secure their own political interests (corporate, of course, but not exclusively so). The operation of both drivers at the same time has made the 'global war on terrorism' well-nigh impossible to resist.

In its essence, one could say that this book is about how liberal democracy first embraced, then slightly tamed and finally learnt to live with the 'war on terror'.

It was tempting to believe, writing in the early autumn of 2023, that we were coming to the end of the era of terrorism even if not of counter-terrorism laws. The invasion of Ukraine by Russia in early 2022 had reminded people of what real conflict looks like. With an ever-more assertive Russia and China and a sharp increase in conflicts in and near Europe itself (such as in Nagorno-Karabakh), it appeared that war was back for the West, supplanting our anxieties about less all-embracing forms of political violence.[30] But then apparently out-of-the-blue came the attacks on 7 October by Hamas in southern Israel and the brutal counter-terrorism reaction that these provoked on the part of the country affected. It is clear that the attention grabbed by terrorism as a world problem has dismal mileage left in it, its impact in terms of laws and the debilitation of freedom remaining as powerful as ever. The book's subtitle is 'rise and rise', not 'rise and fall'.

PART ONE

ROOTS

ONE

Imperium

Origins

The conventional way to start an historical account of terrorism is with various groups from the past that engaged in the sort of political violence that we would today recognize – and unhesitatingly describe – as 'terrorism'. This usually involves some attention being paid to the Assassins, a fairly obscure Muslim sect who killed their opponents with daggers back in the twelfth century CE, and whose eponymous modus operandi gave a new word to the English language.[1] Some scholars reach even further back to the Zealots, a Jewish group whose hostility to the Roman presence in Palestine during the first century CE manifested itself in violence, and whose provocations played no small part in the destruction of Jerusalem by imperial forces in 70 CE. Both supposed early paradigms of our contemporary terrorism problem have in them seductive aspects – violent Muslims, squabbles over Palestine – that resonate today and increase their appeal as suitable anticipators of where we are now.[2] It is the same for the nineteenth-century anarchists, some of them eccentric rejoicers in their labelling as 'terrorists', whose violence tried to be 'ethical' but was nevertheless aimed at securing radical change from a position of intense political and (it goes without saying) military weakness – Castioni, the killer from Switzerland whom we met in the Introduction, may not have called himself a terrorist, but many similarly disposed activists did.[3] A little earlier than the anarchists, the Paris of the period immediately after the French Revolution is also often irresistible to those in search of origins, the explicit use of the technique of terror by the leaders of France in 1793–94 being thought to be too good to miss.[4] As this last kind of violence was deployed by the state, it was both horribly more efficient than and radically different from that achievable by mere subversion. But it is exactly such violence by the antagonists (rather than the wielders) of state power that is the key ingredient making up what is commonly understood as terrorism today (and which explains the widespread appeal to the contemporary scholar of the Zealots, the Assassins and the anarchists).

I have done exactly this kind of history in the past myself,[5] but now believe that it gets our subject off to a false start, or rather (to mix the sporting metaphor) sends the runners down the wrong highways and byways of history, in search of illusionary connections that confuse more than they clarify. The element of the indefinable in terrorism seems to me to be unavoidable,[6] the range of conduct being too varied for the groups in question all to be plausibly grouped together under this single label. This is especially so when it is done without regard either to time or place, or to whether this contemporary label mattered when such groups were active. Even excellent studies (like that by Joshua Tschantret[7]) risk a flattening of the explanatory power of systematic political violence by sweeping all of it into a singular category called 'terrorist', and then foregrounding technical explanations (modernity, weaponry, better opportunities for communication) at the expense of a nuanced understanding of the wider political picture (which might include colonial oppression in some cases, authoritarian excesses in others). The reification of violent subversion as abstractedly wrong carries the risk that we miss altogether (or else downplay or exculpate) the proactive and then reactive violence of the state actors against whom the violence has been deployed. This wider picture can often reveal state violence productive of high levels of terror in those subject to it (even if it is not called 'terrorism'), and many of the states whose leaders resist 'terrorism' in the loudest possible manner are themselves often erected on exactly the kind of violence that they now all agree to abhor.

If it is neither ancient history nor an a priori supposition about the wrongness of all subversive violence everywhere, what is it that makes our current assumptions about 'terrorist' violence (and therefore the rightness of anti-terrorism law) so deeply rooted? Of course there was 9/11 and, in the preceding decades, various incidents of seemingly senseless civilian killings that we are surely right (both in context and as a plausible fact-specific moral generalization) to deplore and to deploy the law to counter: I discussed these events in general terms in the previous chapter, and will analyse them – and the reaction they provoked – in greater detail in later chapters.

For now though, we are concerned with the deeper origins of our subject, with how it has so successfully embedded itself in the way we think. This takes us to the first of the two informing influences of subversive political violence (today's terrorism) that were anticipated at the end of the last chapter: our (Europe's) colonial heritage. Looking back over the past 300 years or so, where do we find the clearest examples of the use of politically motivated violence by weak groups in opposition to the overwhelmingly superior force of a state whose authority they reject? In what arenas of power do we see such subversion condemned as utterly wrong, as beyond any capacity for exculpatory explanation, as often specifically declared to be terrorist? It is not with the anarchists or other analogous anti-despotic movements to which we have already made passing reference (and to which we will return, albeit briefly, in later chapters). The two questions posed as I have just posed them lead inevitably in each case to a clear answer: resistance to colonial control in response to the first; colonial narratives (as explanations for retaliatory violence) as the response to the second.

One of the central arguments in this book can now be baldly stated: the routine acceptance of anti-terrorism laws today is rooted in colonial power's reaction to challenges to its authority, and in particular in how that reaction – often extremely violent though it was – was able to be plausibly packaged for colonial power's domestic audiences as not inconsistent with (indeed as supported by) liberal values. Colonial violence has prepared us for the excesses of the 'war on terror', inured us to what our supposed values surely demand should be unthinkable.

Empire has not been an easy subject for those who concentrate on subversive violence. As current controversies about critical scholarship demonstrate, the subject of colonialism is painful for those among the citizens of the former colonial powers who treasure positive narratives about the power once wielded by their forebears, and for whom discussion of the causes of anti-colonial violence is to be avoided if at all possible. As Angela Woollacott has remarked of the grandest imperial project of all, '[t]his is not to suggest that the violence of empire has been completely expunged from historical memory in Britain. The evidence, particularly during moments of crisis, is simply too extensive to enable such forgetting. But . . . its visibility, like that of empire itself, is "a political artefact that has waxed and waned".'[8] What is at stake when it comes to empire, as Ann Stoler argues, is 'a dismembering, a difficulty speaking, a difficulty generating a vocabulary that associates appropriate words and concepts with appropriate things'.[9] As Deana Heath puts it, '[t]he violence of empire is rediscovered, according to Stoler, when it is deemed safe for public consumption and scholarly investigation'.[10] It is not surprising that the violence of empire has not played a prominent part in anti-terrorism studies, but it deserves a central place in any discussion of the origin of anti-terrorism law. The time to do this may not yet be safe, but undeniably it is right.

The work of Nasser Hussain is valuable here, showing as it does the importance of law in the process of securing plausible explanations for imperial violence. Hussain details how, as early as the late-eighteenth-century 'impeachment of colonial India's first governor-general, Warren Hastings, . . . government by law was already becoming the privileged basis for the conceptualization of the "moral legitimacy" of British colonialism'.[11] If legality was 'the preeminent signifier of state legitimacy and of "civilization"',[12] then it was a legality that was always accompanied by insistence on executive power hinging on the force of arms. While the British in India 'developed an elaborate and relatively strong judiciary, they equally insisted that certain "acts of state" would be beyond judicial inquiry'.[13] It was martial law that served to close this gap between law and raw power, dignifying the latter with the moral aura of the former. The disguising of brute colonial force as law allowed the state to act with impunity without troubling the consciences of its imperial supporters at home. Right from the start the difference between imperial and counter-imperialist violence was clear: the first was law, the second banditry.

Homeland

Law needs an idea of jurisdiction in order to work properly. Locating this is less easy for countries whose influence reaches beyond their own borders than for those hunkered down in a domestic space assigned them by international law and practice. In the former cases, where exactly was home? Where was abroad? Truly foreign places for sure, but from an imperial UK perspective (for example) was India part of home, or was it abroad? The evolution of counter-terrorism laws, and particularly the rigour with which they have been applied by liberal polities, has historically depended on at whom exactly the subversive challenge to authority has been aimed, whether to power at home or to authority far away. Until recently (and this is the change this book tracks) the remote mattered little: the Castionis of this world could do their destructive foreign work and still live unhindered in the domestic liberal state, plotting further revolution for all the authorities cared. This was as long as, of course, they did not threaten that state as well. Domestic challenges to what is clearly the homeland (whether that of an empire or an ordinary liberal state) have always been taken particularly seriously, counting as dangerous internal subversion. For the colonial powers, the 'home' that needed to be secured was never simply where (to coin a phrase) the hearth is. Jurisdiction was asserted well beyond the four corners of the territorial state. There were uncertain homelands like Ireland (for Britain) and Algeria (for France), but the point goes further than these. Much of 'abroad' was not truly abroad so far as these imperial sovereign powers were concerned; rather 'home' extended to places that they treated as 'possessions', territories beyond the constitutional parameters of their state, but which were controlled by them and ruled in their interests. This domestic/colonial/foreign distinction is central to the argument in this book. For those European powers (and they were invariably European) engaged in colonial aggrandisement, there always was a 'home-home' but then also as well a 'home-abroad' – an India, say, or the multiple other parts of Asia controlled by the Netherlands or France. Places like Ireland and (later) Algeria were stuck in the middle, not quite home-home, but not home-abroad either.

When looking at how anti-terrorism laws operate both today and (whatever they were called) in the imperial past, it is impossible not to see how they are and were invariably deployed differently depending on the location of the subjects of their power. Such laws function against 'the other' – that is to say, those who present as different from loyal citizens of the relevant sovereign power. This 'othering' was a commonplace in the colonial period, when the recalcitrant subjects asserting freedom were by definition different from the citizens of the home country and remained so even when yoked into the imperial polity as a matter of law (Ireland and Algeria being two of the clearest examples of this), or (as in later eras) brought to the homeland to do necessary work. The terrorists of old were the mindless savages challenging the rightness of this or that imperial project. Today they continue to fester in post-colonial 'safe-havens' or are part of a post-imperial power's local 'suspect community' – citizens perhaps, residents almost certainly, but not really, truly at home, not proper members of 'our home'. The subjects of anti-terrorism law are always different because they are not truly us. This racist impulse is the beating heart of our story, the impetus that has made possible both the invention of terrorism in the first place and thereafter its careful sustenance in our laws. Of course, there have been recent efforts to broaden the reach of anti-terrorism law, just as there are other sources of the laws I am looking at in this book: we come to all this in later chapters. But looked at through this original lens, anti-terrorism law is how colonialism is done in the twenty-first century. It has grown out of the difference between us and them (civilized v savage; Christian v pagan; white v non-white) that was an essential feature of the imperial control exercised by the old European powers. Those who resisted colonial power were disrupters of this order, the nastier elements of 'them' organizing challenges to 'our' decent power.

We exist today with the 'legacy of violence'[14] bequeathed us by that extraordinarily all-encompassing system of power – of home-abroad – that can be plausibly described as 'colonialism'. The national power that availed itself of its capacity to dominate the peoples of the globe on the largest scale was one that throughout the period of its domination saw itself as a liberal, free society: the United Kingdom. Whether or not Britain was truly the land of the free, it was able plausibly to present itself as such. But as Hussain has noted, even that pretence slipped so far as its colonial possessions were concerned. James Martel put it well when he observed that 'the disguise of normal law that one found in Britain itself was not engaged with in the colonies in part because it was felt that the perceived need to be continuously violent in the face of the ongoing resistance of local populations trumped any desire to promote the appearance of an orderly legal apparatus'.[15] It is through the approach of the British to the management of its empire that we find liberal democracy familiarizing itself with its capacity to think of itself as a free, open (and indeed good) society while being *at the same time* constituted by high levels of political violence against its opponents, whether in the home-abroad of the colonies or in the suspect home-home of Ireland. Where Britain led, other European countries followed, in later decades not allowing their own (gradual) democratization to interfere with continued dominion over their foreign fields. Britain's management of its empire is especially important to our story because it was during the years of its greatest global influence (the first sixty years of the twentieth century) that the mechanisms of control we would today think of (and, as we shall see, were thought of even then) as 'counter-terrorism' were put in place. The trick lay in exploiting the 'home-home'/'home-abroad' distinction so as to insulate the former from the actions necessary to keep the latter under control. Or, as one of the brilliant recent scholars engaged in colonial-related terrorism studies put it, quoting another pathbreaker in the field: 'the racialization of one's opponents is central to liberal counterinsurgency, as this racial differentiation is what "resolves the tensions between illiberal methods and liberal discourse"'.[16]

Plunder

Richard Reid has noted that, '[i]n the context of imperialism and the creation of the "new" European empires in the late nineteenth and early twentieth century, the term terrorism seems apposite in considering the actions of European state-level actors'.[17] The period from the mid-eighteenth century through to the last quarter of the twentieth century saw an unprecedented drive by a small number of European nations (first for control, then for retention of that control) over the world's sea and land resources. The enslavement of local people on a vast scale was also part, and a key part, of the subjugation project. Primary actors in the execution of this ambitious project included the United Kingdom, but also the Netherlands, Belgium, France, Spain, Portugal and (towards the end) Germany and Italy. It was not just a nineteenth-century 'scramble for Africa', as the schoolbooks used to put it, but during earlier eras a scramble for the whole world. Violent subjugation had long underpinned England's pacification of Ireland, from pre-colonial times right through until its absorption within the United Kingdom in 1801.[18] This entailed traditional military campaigns against local Irish leaders as well as extensive forced dispossession of land, and on occasion forms of brutal conquest that would today be described as 'ethnic cleansing'. As early as the start of the seventeenth century there was 'violent resistance across South and South East Asia in response to the arrival of Portuguese, Dutch, British and Spanish colonists'.[19] Settler communities from these imperial powers sometimes shook off (often violently) their colonial rulers, replacing one set of external controllers with another closer to home: the United States is one such example, the Afrikaner Boers another, and Ian Smith's Rhodesia (now Zimbabwe) a much more recent (but short-lived) third.

The level of violence required to achieve the success enjoyed by these colonizing European nations was not the less staggering because the battles in the early phases of each conflict were so one-sided. Superior weaponry and organization – the result of industrial and cultural changes in the colonizing nations that had not occurred elsewhere – ensured that this was the case.[20] Violence in British-run India, so extensive as control was being exerted in the eighteenth century, continued throughout the nineteenth. As Deana Heath observes in her excoriating account of 'torture and state violence in colonial India' during the years 1837–1901, there had been 'at least 228 armed conflicts across the British empire, many of which were punitive colonial campaigns designed to quell unrest'.[21] The distinguished Indian political scientist Professor Ranabir Samaddar notes that, '[i]n this war-torn century, empire making meant terror at every level and every step'.[22] In Africa, 'responses to colonial invasion took numerous forms', with 'anti-colonial insurgencies, while usually short-lived, [taking] on at least some of the attributes of "terrorism" and [these] were certainly seen as acts of illegitimate violence on the part of nascent colonial authorities'.[23] However aggressive the long-established local communities were in their defence, nothing can explain – much less justify – responses like those of Germany to resistance in German Southwest Africa (today's Namibia), of which one specialist historian has observed that, '[a]t a certain point, state terrorism becomes genocide, as it did in the case of the Nama, Herero and San: between 65,000 and 80,000 Africans were killed, and entire communities were simply wiped out'.[24] The Belgian engagement in the Congo in the 1890s and 1900s was so awful 'as to attract censure from other European powers – quite a feat in the age of violent imperialism'.[25]

Efforts at revolt in the form of uprisings by enslaved people or resistance by the wider community affected by colonial expansion were invariably brutally crushed across the British empire (as they were by other colonial powers as well, both during this period and by the late-

IMPERIUM

comers subsequently). The uprising in India in 1857, for example, initially
by Muslim members of the army expected to use cartridges rumoured
to be greased with beef and pork fat, but quickly growing into a wider
rejection of British rule, produced a clampdown by the Raj which was of
extreme brutality. Whole villages and towns were destroyed. In her recent
comprehensive history of the British empire, Caroline Elkins has this
verbatim account from one British officer: 'The order went out to shoot
every soul ... It was literally murder ... I have seen many bloody and
awful sights lately but such a one as I witnessed yesterday I pray I never
see again. The women were all spared but their screams on seeing their
husbands and sons butchered were most painful.'[26] The late-nineteenth-
century expansion of the British empire into Africa reproduced the same
techniques of control, both to secure territory and then to punish resistance. At the Battle of Omdurman, fought in 1898 as the culmination
of a campaign to avenge the death of General Gordon at the hands of
Sudanese Muslim opponents (the Mahdists), British forces killed at least
10,000 and wounded over 13,000 for the loss of just forty-seven soldiers
with another 382 wounded.[27] British efforts to extinguish Boer resistance
in South Africa in the late 1890s and early 1900s generated mass starva-
tion in the vast 'concentration camps' into which hundreds of thousands
of Afrikaners were herded.[28]

None of this extraordinarily brutal political violence, often deliberately intended to cause terror in those who witnessed it (as well as, of
course, its victims) fits within conventional terrorist narratives. It was war
fought between European powers and a diverse range of forces defending
their homelands in orthodox military ways, with the vast technological
superiority of the Europeans meaning that they invariably won. This
same asymmetry in favour of the imperial powers continued until well
into the first half of the twentieth century. The British were once again
to the fore, controllers (after the First World War) of a quarter of the
landmass of the globe and some 458 million people. Towns were razed
to the ground by brutal military forces recruited into Ireland in 1919–20,
specifically in order to make the Irish pay for not turning in those who
were at the time resisting London's power.[29] In the early 1920s, vastly
superior airpower was deployed by British forces to subjugate revolt
against British rule in Mesopotamia (later Iraq). The linkages with the
'counter-terrorism' of today can sometimes be very clear. As Joseph

McQuade has observed, drawing on the work of a leading cultural historian of the British empire:

> While the technology that has enabled the recent proliferation of unmanned drones is quite new, historian Priya Satia has demonstrated how the underlying philosophy is a direct legacy of colonial aerial surveillance and bombardment conducted during the 'pacification operations' of the interwar period ... Aerial bombardment carried out by Britain's Royal Air Force (RAF) in interwar Afghanistan attracted the vociferous criticism of Indian activists like Mahendra Pratap, a revolutionary Pan-Asianist who petitioned the League of Nations in 1933, calling on the international community to raise their 'pious voices against every barbaric trespass on the rights of Man'.[30]

Resistance

Of course there had always been efforts, often desperate, to fight back against colonial control. Those 228 conflicts noted by Heath did not come from nowhere; the Mahdist revolt that led to the Battle of Omdurman was not a one-off; and the destruction of Dublin in 1916 had its immediate cause in the revolutionary efforts made by a small group of Irish nationalists in the 'Easter Rising' of that year. In an earlier generation's revolt against the settler-colonials of what was to become the United States, the native Americans had quickly realized that pitched battles were certain to lead to 'catastrophic defeats', and so soon 'avoided directly engaging European armies and instead resorted to guerrilla warfare'.[31] Intelligent reactions by vulnerable peoples to colonial violence have a long history; hence the need for imperial power to come down hard on asymmetrical challenges to its monopoly of violence. Native resistance was damned if it took to open conflict and damned anyway (through reactionary terror) if it conducted its battles in what colonial power regarded as 'underhand' or 'sneaky' ways. Empire everywhere was steeped in blood shed for political ends, remembered differently depending on one's perspective. Conventional imperial history is full of campaigns successfully waged, battles heroically fought and the occasional defeat brutally revenged, with the natives everywhere requiring at all times to be controlled and, when they asserted themselves, unequivocally suppressed. As Caroline Elkins has sarcastically put it, '[t]he British Empire was not carved from *terra nullius* with a minimum degree of force and, over time, a maximum amount of cooperation from gratefully indebted local populations'.[32]

European nations had long needed to explain to themselves why the staggering levels of political violence to which they resorted, initially overtly and then (as we shall see) formalized into legal codes, were not obviously morally wrong; why it could somehow not be profoundly unethical for a Christian and (in the case of the United Kingdom throughout the period and that of increasing numbers of colonial polities over the years) *liberal* imperial power to engage in such acts. This is where the work of Nasser Hussain and other authors referred to at the start of this chapter comes back into play. The 'states of denial'[33] achieved through the cloak of law find their echo in contemporary justifications of anti-terrorism practices in foreign lands, as we shall see when we turn much later in this book to the 'war on terror'. This project of constructing imperial impunity went further than the law. Various ruses to distance the victims from humanity – their exotic savagery; their animal-like brio in the face of certain death – were routinely deployed. Justifying British aerial attacks on defenceless locals, which as we have seen took place as late as the 1920s, military officials explained that they 'regarded the north-western frontier region that separates Pakistan from Afghanistan as an unruly place full of barbaric cultural practices and "religious fanaticism"'.[34] Another device that was sustained into the late colonial period engaged a range of educational tropes casting natives in the role of children, needing a firm hand to guide them towards European-style maturity. Influential theories of imperial war-mongering ignored the victims altogether, stressing the value of terror-as-communication, the need to use arbitrary and disproportionate violence in order to make a point, to instil what was later to be described (by the most prominent successor to Europe's imperium, the United States) as 'shock and awe' in their opponents. When Brigadier General Reginald Dyer explained in his official report why he had ordered his men to open fire on some 15,000 or so unarmed civilians in Amritsar on 13 April 1919, killing 400 and injuring well over 1,000, he wrote of the need to 'produce the necessary moral and widespread effect' that 'it was [his] duty to produce'.[35] True he was condemned by some leading politicians, with Winston Churchill describing Amritsar as 'an extraordinary event, a monstrous event, an event which stands in singular and sinister isolation'.[36] But Dyer's orders were no aberration – he was lionized by the British public as the 'Saviour of the Punjab' and his actions were defended by military strategists for decades to come.

Justification for colonial violence flowed, too, from the reaction it provoked in those subjected to it. Resistance was a reason why the violence was necessary – even if it had been colonial violence that had led to the resistance in the first place. This trope was present from the start. As early as 1756, the alleged deaths of large numbers of British prisoners under Mughal control in the 'Black Hole of Calcutta' provided the rallying cry for reactive violence of great brutality, even though subsequent studies have shown the event to have been on a far smaller scale than was asserted at the time.[37] The bloody response to the Indian revolt of 1857 discussed above was explained by a series of lurid accounts of the extremist violence engaged in by the 'mutineers'. During Ireland's revolutionary period from 1916 to 1921, vast retaliatory violence in response to the smallest of subversive gains was once again the norm; it was the heinousness of their opponents that was uppermost in the mind of British opinion-formers. (The Irish had long been regarded in popular British culture and even in many informed political circles as an inferior race as compared with the 'mainland' British.) Nor were the liberal laws discussed at the start of this book, protecting foreign politically violent offenders, of any assistance to these colonial dissenters: 'the very notion of "political offences", while of central importance to British metropolitan and international law, was . . . wholly excluded from the prosecution of anti-colonial revolutionary activities in India, which the imperial government instead criminalized as apolitical terrorism'.[38] When in 1909 the radical nationalist Vinayak Damodar Savarkar published an article praising an assassination of a Raj official as an act of patriotism, he was arrested and detained in the UK; while being shipped back to India as a prisoner, he escaped at Marseilles but the British went and got him anyway. The matter came before the Hague tribunal, which upheld the British action.[39] The colonies didn't count.

By the mid-1920s, the impact of the calamitous First World War was making itself felt across all empires. The European powers had been greatly weakened by their vast and bloody civil war, with some losing their imperial dominions altogether, while those that inherited them (principally the UK and France) were much less able than they had been in the past to police their vast new demesnes. It was partly lack of money that fuelled the UK's aerial bombardment across present-day Iraq and Afghanistan – the country could no longer afford its usual military adventures (and so much of the world had now come under its control anyway, presenting an added challenge). Significantly, there was also clearer and more widely reported evidence of resistance across many strata of society. It was around this time, 'in India, West Africa, the Caribbean, Australia, and elsewhere, [that] colonized populations harnessed their agency in the face of an increasingly more sophisticated British imperial regime'.[40] Challenges to colonial power were infused with greater levels of intellectual energy than before, spreading more widely and with more ideas to back them up. An important driver here was the spread of nineteenth-century aspirations of nationhood – once exclusive to Europeans but now (not least as a result of the rhetoric accompanying the Versailles peace discussions and the League of Nations which followed) travelling further afield.

The 1914–18 war might have weakened the colonial project, but it did not destroy it. British and French global power persevered into the era of the League, seeing off small nations' rhetoric by making spurious concessions rooted not in conceding the freedom of a place but in designating colonized territories as 'Protectorates' of empire. Despite this successful obduracy, however, changes did have to be made. Colonial power judged that it had to exert itself in a different, more organized and less nakedly militaristic way. The clearest precedents for contemporary anti-terrorism law in the British empire are to be found in the first half of the twentieth century rather than during earlier phases of colonial aggrandisement. The changes involved the increased reconfiguration of imperial brute force into legal form, supplanting martial law and acts of state with statutory schemes of control. Here is Caroline Elkins again on what this 'increasingly . . . sophisticated . . . imperial regime' entailed so far as the key surviving empire, the British, was concerned: 'Initial acts of conquest gave way in the twentieth century to elaborate legal codes, the proliferation of police and security forces, free market and labour controls for the colonized, and administrative apparatuses that marginalised and oppressed entire populations while fuelling racial and ethnic divisions within and between them.'[41] This did not mean that the violence inherent in these new regimes of control was novel. As Heath puts it, '[l]ate colonial regimes simply *seem* to have become more repressive following the emergence of anti-colonial nationalist movements because they have been largely analysed in isolation from the structural and systematic violence that not only made colonial movements possible but that gave birth to such movements'.[42] Colonial violence did not suddenly arrive when opponents of the imperial forces began to operate in subtler, more indirect ways; it had been there from the start: this form of rule 'was at core absolutist and authoritarian'.[43]

Legalization

There had been early examples of colonial legislation aimed at the legalization of severe retribution towards those who challenged British rule: the Thuggee Act of 1836 in India, for example,[44] and (again in India) the Murderous Outrages Act of 1867. The late Victorian drive towards codification of the law in imperial lands and the deployment of a more assertive rule of law had rarely impeded deployment of the draconian powers judged necessary to fight subversion: as we saw Nasser Hussain observing earlier, the disjunction between law and executive/military necessity was an old one. But as the trend towards law gathered momentum, so the free zone marked 'military discretion' shrank. It was mainly as part of a post-First World War move to a more nuanced, law-based approach on the part of colonial power in answer to the ever-widening range of objections to its rule that we find the language of 'terrorism' and 'terrorists' beginning to creep into the codes and practices of counter-insurgency. The increasingly elaborate legal frameworks of administrative control that were gradually put in place from 1918 onwards marked the end of the discretion of the military commander on the spot and its replacement with frameworks of legally sanctioned authoritarianism. The regulatory initiatives taken within Britain during the First World War (the defence-of-the-realm legislation) may have had an influence here; certainly the Restoration of Order in Ireland Act 1920 (typical of this new genre of legalistic insurgency management) borrowed much from that war-based framework of emergency laws,[45] and more laws of this sort were to follow thick and fast across the empire, not least in India, where a Defence of India Act (modelled on the British wartime legislation) was passed.[46] The effect of war legislation enacted during the 1914–18 period was to accelerate this growing shift towards subtler forms of violence-legalization. Martial law found itself redundant, or (as in Ireland) not only constrained but on occasion downright rejected by courts determined to compel counter-insurgency practices to remain within the bounds of the (ordinary) law.[47] Whatever the reasons for the change, it strongly resembles the shift from arbitrariness to legalization that occurred in the years following the attacks of 11 September 2001.

A definite driver of the changes ushered in after the 1914–18 war was a deepening opposition in India to colonial control. At the start of the century, this had begun to manifest itself in covert acts of violence, part of the wider rejection of colonialism mentioned earlier. It was at this time that 'groups of predominantly middle-class urban youth, most notably in Bengal and Punjab, were emboldened to take more direct action against British rule', embracing 'acts of revolutionary terrorism which included targeted assassinations of British and Indian officials, including members of the police', a method of engagement which 'generated tremendous fear and paranoia among the British'.[48] The killing celebrated by Savarkar in 1909 was not a rare event: for decades either side of the turn of the century, assassination was the favoured 'new strategy of "propaganda by deed", through which revolutionaries and radicals disillusioned with the colonial order sought to undermine the sovereignty of the state by exposing the mortality of its representatives'.[49] The anarchists may have been leaders in such mechanisms of violent dissent, but the anti-colonials (principally the radical Irish and Indians) were not far behind.

All of this was intensely irritating to colonial power. Taking India as its focus, Joseph McQuade's study of the origins of the language of terrorism identifies a range of movements on the subcontinent during the nineteenth century which clearly anticipated modern-day labels but without being precisely so described: '[w]hether in the clandestine Kali-worship of the "thugs", the collective nature of dacoit gangs, the international nature of the pirate threat, or the unreasoning religiosity of Muslim "fanatics", colonial assumptions regarding indigenous criminality would heavily inflect the genealogy of terrorism in ways that are still evident to this day'.[50] Occasional uses of the language of terrorism can be found in the period before 1914, even if it was not yet mainstreamed into the law and practice of the imperial authorities. Gradually the term 'terror', having previously been applied to this or that anti-colonial 'sneaky' strike, became a way to describe the perpetrators themselves. The colonial insurgents were by no means exclusively described as terrorists at this time ('bandits', 'criminals', 'fanatics',[51] 'gangsters', 'thugs' and 'cut-throats' also rose to the linguistic occasion), but after the First World War the term became especially prominent among the labels used.

Set up to enquire into 'criminal conspiracies connected with the revolutionary movement in India',[52] the Rowlatt Committee, reporting in 1918, used the language of terrorism to describe the elusive rebels in India with whom the empire was then increasingly being confronted.[53] The Committee observed that 'the difficulties attending the enforcement of the criminal law' had been 'enhanced by other causes and chiefly by terrorism'; among its recommendations was to dispense with juries in the relevant criminal areas 'because of the terrorism to which they are liable'. As McQuade notes: 'The word "terrorism", alongside its physical personification in the figure of "the terrorist", appears so frequently in the colonial police records of 1930s India that a reader could easily be misled into assuming that this term was the natural definition through which revolutionary activities were always described.'[54] The Commissioner of Police in Calcutta for much of the 1920s, Sir Charles Tegart, spoke on the topic of 'Terrorism in India' at the Royal Empire Society on 1 November 1932,[55] and in 1937, H.W. Hale of the Indian police wrote *Terrorism in India, 1917–1936*, a book that was 'instructive of an evolving colonial prose of counterterrorism during this period. By the time that Hale composed his volume . . ., the term "terrorism" had definitively replaced older labels such as "sedition", "conspiracy", or "political crime" as the primary lens through which acts of anti-colonial revolutionary violence were understood.'[56] For Hale, terrorism 'as distinct from other revolutionary methods such as Communism . . . may be said to denote the commission of outrages of a comparatively "individual" nature'.[57] As early as at his trial for sedition in 1922, Gandhi had sought to turn the linguistic tables on the British, asserting that they had created a 'subtle but effective system of terrorism' in India.[58]

In India during this period of late imperial control, 'terrorism' had become a useful way of delegitimizing the tactics of revolutionaries while simultaneously justifying the creeping expansion of executive rule into the legal arena. The label was particularly useful to the colonial authorities, who were at this time ostensibly devolving a share of power to elected Indian legislatures.[59] It was a 'justification in advance of state sanctioned violence'.[60] The concerns expressed by the Rowlatt Committee about the way in which 'terrorism' was impeding the legal process produced the Anarchical and Revolutionary Crimes Act of 1919 (the 'Rowlatt Act').[61] Reflecting on a government proclamation of 1924 that made frequent references to the terrorist movement of the time, McQuade suggests that, so far as India was concerned, '[t]he emergence of "terrorism" as the defining category to be used in subsequent legal and political pronouncements on the Indian revolutionary movement should . . . be understood as a deliberate and calculated attempt on the part of colonial officials to make emergency measures more palatable both to the British Parliament back home and moderate opinion within India'.[62]

India was not alone as a platform for the emergence of this equation between anti-colonial forces and terror/terrorism. But its precedent value was undoubtedly very important: the significance of developments in Indian law on, among other things, counter-insurgency lies in the fact that these 'formed the basis for legislation not only in India but also in colonies such as Burma, Ceylon, Singapore, the Straits Settlement, Brunei, and Aden'.[63] Palestine, Malaya and Kenya – successive centres of violence in the British empire through the 1930s, '40s and '50s – were among the arenas of conflict in which the language of terrorism later found expression.[64] In 1938, at the height of the Arab Revolt in Palestine, the much admired (by the British) Captain Orde Wingate was remembered by a colleague as having called for the colonial forces 'to terrorize the terrorists . . . [to] catch them and just wipe them out'.[65] As it had in India, the terms 'terror' and 'terrorism' evolved to describe not an act as such but rather a kind of person whose inclination was towards such acts, in other words towards violent opposition to the state. A particularly serious atrocity in Batang Kali in the early years of the insurgency in Malaya was explained behind the scenes by Sir Alex Newboult, an official in the Colonial Office, as being the consequence of having 'a war of terrorism on our hands', a situation made altogether more complex by the fact that 'we are at the same time endeavouring to maintain the rule of law'.[66] The head of Malaya's Special Branch in the 1950s recalled fondly that 'a captured or surrendered terrorist' was 'quite reasonably treated, kindly treated'.[67] The imperial and imperious 'Tiger of Malaya' General

Sir Gerald Templer, driving force behind Malaya's counter-insurgency operations in the early 1950s, solved the problem of those opposed to him being communist by renaming them '"communist terrorists," or CTs for short'.[68]

Action by the colonial authorities in Kenya in the 1950s was likewise focused on what a carefully composed government explanation of a particularly difficult senior resignation at the time (1954–5) described in the language of terrorism. The Secretary of State for the Colonies Alan Lennox Boyd explained to the House of Commons that it was 'essential that the Administration, the police and the military should jointly concentrate all their efforts on bringing terrorism to an early end'.[69] The 'problem' the authorities were encountering was a particularly strong anti-colonial movement, the Mau Mau: '[w]ith around 12,000 insurgents, mostly Kikuyu, at its outset in 1952, the rebellion spread over the forested area of the central highlands, and involved attacks on settlers and (more commonly) Kikuyu loyalists'.[70] One historian has catalogued how 'Britain's colonial administration in central Kenya had been militarized in this conflict, imprisoning more than 80,000 people without trial, hanging over 1,000 convicted "terrorists", and subjecting the local people to surveillance and interrogation on a massive scale in the manner of a police state'.[71] The usual defensive tropes were deployed to justify the violence of the British reaction: the 'Mau Mau "terrorists" were regarded as certifiably insane, and one of the most common interpretations at the time was that the revolt was an outbreak of madness – a primordial, atavistic scream, as members of the Kikuyu struggled with modernity'.[72] In 1958, the Secretary of State for War Christopher Soames asserted, now with Cyprus in mind, that 'we must never forget that the role of the security forces . . . is to conquer terrorism, and that there are and will be many instances when the minimum of force necessary is quite a lot of force'.[73] It was clear, the minister said, that 'we cannot compromise with this terrorism'.[74] As the Director of Operations on the island explained, harsh security forces operations were designed '[t]o bring home to the ordinary people the hard fact that the results of terrorism include hardship to themselves and so to create conditions predisposing people in favour of a political settlement'.[75] And of course there was always that half-home within the home, Northern Ireland, from within which emanated regular efforts to force its British six counties into unity with Ireland: an Irish

Republican Army (IRA) campaign in the late 1930s targeted attacks in Britain, and in the late 1950s a resurgence of the same organization's activity led to stringent counter-measures, including the widespread deployment of detention without trial in Northern Ireland. Reference was regularly made to 'terrorist attempts' and 'terrorist outrages' when the violence was being discussed in Parliament.[76] One is reminded of 'Peter Fitzpatrick's focus on one particular purpose of the colonial world: to provide modern law with its constitutive negative – to posit law, nation, and civilization in contrast to custom, tribe, and savagery'.[77]

Nor was it just the British. In the late 1940s, facing an anti-colonial insurgency in the Dutch East Indies, many in authority followed 'the official line of anti-communist, colonial interpretation and saw the Komintern lurking behind the uprisings . . ., defaming the protestors as "communist terrorists"'.[78] The leader of the nationalist movement was not acknowledged, and his declaration of independence in August 1945 was condemned 'as an act of "terrorism" by Sukarno's "dictatorial republic"'.[79] '"It is hard to tell where nationalism stops and terrorism begins", the Catholic journal *De Tijd* lamented.'[80] The Dutch only gave in when threatened with the loss of Marshall funds, and transfer of sovereignty was effected in December 1949.[81] In Vietnam, the French found themselves facing a guerrilla force that enjoyed support among the people due, among other reasons (from the French perspective), to 'the terror it inspired'.[82] The Vietminh troops had an advantage over the French that could almost be said to have been derived from their bad sportsmanship: 'they can appear and disappear whenever they like into the mountains, hide themselves in the ditches, along the banks of the rice paddies. The men of the Vietminh can become civilians, again, peasants by day . . . and soldiers at night.'[83] Colonial records are full of such laments about insurgents not playing fair (and so guaranteeing their obliteration). The French were finally defeated in 1954.

Eventually of course things had to give for the British as well. The colonial enterprise could not hold the line against the resurgence of national sentiment in imperial territories that gathered pace in the 1950s and the first half of the 1960s. The collapse of British power after the Second World War made change inevitable. But '[a]s the Union Jack was lowered, and the flags of new nations were raised in ceremony after ceremony – in Cyprus (1960), Nigeria (1960), Sierra Leone (1961), Tanganyika (1961),

Uganda (1962), Jamaica (1962), Zanzibar (1963), Nyasaland (renamed Malawi) (1964), Northern Rhodesia (renamed Zambia) (1964), Malta (1964), and The Gambia (1965) – the consequences of colonial rule did not recede into the night'.[84] Why this was so requires us to move from colonial coercion to post-colonial authoritarianism, with the set of laws that had sought to control insurgency now being repurposed to stifle domestic dissent. The collapse of the French empire in Indochina in the 1950s is indicative here: the US was so concerned about the consequences of Vietnamese independence that it launched a rearguard action to preserve Western power in the country. It was not Vietnam that the US was particularly scared of, and nor was Vietnam the only example of the threat that was to shape our understanding of terrorism (and therefore of anti-terrorism law) both at the end of and after the colonial era. It was the Soviet-oriented evolution of anti-terrorism law, and the subject of my next chapter.

TWO

Cold War

Anarchist beginnings

I have already made passing reference to the role of the anarchist movement in the evolution of our anti-terrorism laws. Its proponents embraced subversive violence in Russia throughout its various nineteenth-century incarnations. Among its leading intellectuals were men like Mikhail Bakunin and Peter Kropotkin, whose reflections on how to maximize political opportunity through the use of violence-as-communication (for example, the former's well-known concept of the 'propaganda of the deed') have sustained the anarchists at the centre of many contemporary studies of the origins of terrorism. The assassination of Tsar Alexander II in 1881 by members of one leading anarchist group, the Narodnaya Volya (the 'People's Will'), did not, however, inflame the Russian peasantry into the state of revolutionary fervour that theory demanded; rather it produced a repressive backlash which reversed previous liberal gains and 'stimulated [a] consolidation of absolutism'.[1] This self-evident failure did not diminish subversive enthusiasm: the first decade of the twentieth century saw a particularly sharp rise in revolutionary violence or anarchist 'terrorism', a term that was used at the time. As we saw when discussing anti-colonial violence, it was in that decade that 'would-be revolutionaries around the world embraced the use of symbolic modes of assassination'.[2] Nowhere was this truer than in Russia where, in '1905–7, terrorism reached its peak in terms of incidents and casualties, which increased manyfold'.[3] In a way that echoed the 1880s, these actions provoked further repression from the state, together with deeper international cooperation, the latter being an important factor in the decline of anarchist activity that set in around this time.[4] So too was the 'more preventive and pre-emptive approach' that was being taken by the Russian authorities, 'with more attention to human intelligence and undercover work'[5] than in the past.

The experiences of anarchists in Russia during the Tsarist era introduce us to one of the recurring features of our history of anti-terrorism laws, and explain why there is a liberal democratic slant to much of what is dealt with here. The truth is that the kind of symbolic violence terrorism encapsulates does not generally fare well in authoritarian states, however well-intentioned those behind it are or however careful they may be in their choice of targets. The deed rarely (if ever) does revolutionary work on its own,[6] while the extreme anti-terrorism law that it can often bring about will not need to be explained in such places, merging easily as such laws do with other, pre-existing indicators of a police state. In despotic political environments, there is no liberal double standard that needs to be explained away, either to the people on whom such laws are imposed or (as with the colonial anti-insurgency laws discussed in the last chapter) the liberals back home. The resulting repression may be dismal, but it is hardly – from a legal point of view – interesting, being just one more way in which subject populations are controlled. This is why my focus is on the ways in which serious atrocities of a terrorist complexion can appear to demand responses from liberal (and later liberal democratic) states, and how these responses can be made to square with liberal values.

As we noted in discussing the *Castioni* case, a liberal line was usually taken where the threat was domestic, in the 'home-home' of the sovereign power (to use the language of Chapter 1). This was the case with anarchists challenging local power in the UK for example, where state responses operated within the confines of the criminal law. Indeed, the infamous anarchist-related siege of Sydney Street in London in 1911 was so scrupulously prosecuted that it did not produce a successful criminal conviction. This is not to say that domestic legal proceedings were without their double standards. There is some truth in James Martel's acute but possibly overly glum observation that, 'when we resort to a more spectacular theory like the theory of the exception (one that Schmitt and then Agamben have done so much to popularize), we risk losing sight of the way that the law in its normal operations is just as pernicious, just as "exceptional." In doing so, we actually give aid to the argument that ordinary law is fine, that it's just zones of exception like Guantánamo that are a problem.'[7] The reaction to the Chicago Haymarket riots of 1886 in the United States – following a bombing for which anarchists were held responsible – supports this thought, being unusually extreme for an 'ordinary' legal system; but so too was the violence of the occasion, in which many police and civilians were killed and injured. In response, Chicago briefly 'became a police state in all but name',[8] 'one in which constitutional rights were ignored; mail was seized and read; anarchist newspapers were closed down and their editors arrested; the meetings of trade unions were suspended; and the records of their organizations were seized'.[9]

Martel is certainly right that there were limits to the forbearance of even those polities that described themselves as adherents of constitutional propriety and the rule of law. These anarchist challenges were a foretaste of what the twentieth century was to bring. All liberal/democratic states face the challenge of what to do about politically motivated violence aimed at radical change within the domestic polity itself, rather than a colony or an entirely foreign place. This is the case whether such states are emerging, inherently fragile or well-settled. This book is concerned not with the violence as such but with the nature of the reactions to it, how corrosive (or not) those reactions are of liberal values, and how the state explains them to itself and its citizens. The anarchists were irritating but (even on the scale of Haymarket-style mayhem) hardly likely on their own to produce a successful revolution; hence, during the nineteenth century right through to the onset of the First World War, the ordinary criminal law was usually enough. The threat was simply not sufficiently substantial to warrant more.

Things become altogether more serious, however, if a group can express the same level of hostility to liberalism as was shown by the anarchists while also being able to draw inspiration and support from a foreign power, one that is committed to the same radical ideals as the aspirant revolutionaries and which (as a state in its own right) has not only the desire but the capacity to assist. If anti-terrorism law is the child of two parents, and the first is anti-colonial legislation, then the second is the law and practices designed to consolidate liberalism in the face of the communist threat. This is the subject of the present chapter: 'the enemy within' assisted by the 'enemy without'; an old Cold War anxiety that has been reignited and refuelled by our contemporary fear of terrorism and 'terrorist states'.

The Red Scare

The founding fathers of the Soviet Union knew all about anarchist futility and were single-minded in their pursuit of power. Lenin and Trotsky had also imbibed an important lesson from the failure of the direct effort at revolution made by the French Commune in 1871: that if they were to succeed they had to be 'organised and ruthless in the struggle to win and retain power', even if (as Trotsky recognized) this demanded 'a readiness to engage in "Red Terror" and the employment of all forms of violence'.[10] The Russian Revolution of 1917 was of course achieved by means of a seizure of power rather than a campaign of subversive violence, but the immediate commitment of its leaders to global subversion was naturally of immense concern to the established (liberal) powers in Europe and North America. Here was a set of industrialized countries emerging (whether as winners or losers) from the consequences of a terrible conflict, while at the same time trying to manage concessionary moves towards democratization – moves that were bound sooner or later to lead to a majority of voters being drawn from the working classes. The Russians had set a powerful example of what could be achieved by those impatient with the old capitalist order if they had enough determination and grit, and also in all likelihood (unlike in Tsarist Russia) the vote as well to assist them in the realization of their aims. Throughout its existence, the USSR consistently expressed support 'for foreign communist and other left-wing insurgencies, anti-colonial movements and other militant groups, including those who . . . combined guerrilla warfare with terrorism'.[11]

These post-1917 revolutionaries could from now on rely on Moscow's support, or at the very least its cheering on from the sidelines. This put a new complexion on the anarchist/socialist challenge. Even before Soviet success added this new and dangerous twist, the threat of radical constitutional change had sometimes seemed not entirely whimsical. Standing for president in 1912, the US socialist Eugene Debs had secured nearly a million votes. True, the UK's Labour Party was hardly revolutionary in intent, but it had gone from fledging new organization to government (in 1924) in the space of a couple of decades. Left radicalism carried a dangerous Soviet-insinuation after 1917. Following its catastrophic defeat in the First World War, post-war Germany found itself almost immediately in the throes of revolutionary turmoil, with clear links between Moscow and the political agitation on German streets.[12] The anarchist movement remained a violent presence in Europe and north America well into the post-1918 era, with its actions now carrying a whiff of the international. 'In the United States, for instance, the "Galleani" movement was linked to a wave of small-scale bomb attacks; and anarchists of this stripe were blamed for the 1920 car bombing of Wall Street which killed over thirty people.'[13] The reaction to such violence hardened. The bombing by anarchists of US Attorney-General A. Mitchell Palmer's home in 1919, among other targets, precipitated the 'Palmer raids' during which thousands of suspects were rounded up with hundreds of deportations following.[14] A new immigration law, designed to prevent revolutionaries from suspect European countries reaching the US, followed in 1924.[15] Fear of Soviet-infiltration was the driver of a range of legislative measures put in place across the emerging democracies at this time, in an attempt to control the potentially destabilizing effect of anarchist violence and the popular vote that might support its effort to stimulate radical change.[16]

Liberal vigilance continued long after the anarchist bombings and shootings had died away. The enemy was now potentially within the home-home of the domestic legal order as well as the home-away of the colonized territories. The principal targets of the state were alleged 'fourth columnists', radicals whose loyalty was said to lie with the Soviet Union rather than with their home nation. Increasingly after 1917, this came to mean members of the local Communist Party. In the period between the two world wars, and afterwards during the Cold War, Western democracies dealt with the threat to their domestic order posed by communism through deployment of a variety of repressive measures intended to strangle Left-inclined views at birth. While this book is not concerned with controls on radical speech during the period, the evidence is everywhere, and significant (albeit in a peripheral way) for the story this book is telling. There was the conviction for sedition in 1918 of former presidential candidate Eugene Debs, and many other similar and successful prosecutions in the United States, all surviving constitutional challenge despite the apparently unequivocal words of the first amendment of the US constitution.[17] A particularly revealing highlight was the successful insulation from constitutional challenge of the post-Second World War 'McCarthyite' hounding of Left-radicals in the US Supreme

Court decision *Dennis v United States* in 1951. This was a case in which, in a concurring opinion affirming the convictions of the Communist Party leaders, the noted civil libertarian Justice Felix Frankfurter felt compelled to write in alarming terms about the horrifying spectacle of the remaking of the US that would follow a leftist triumph, and how this pointed sharply in the direction of controls on communists, however unlikely was the achievement of any (much less all) of their aims.[18] A generation earlier, the British Home Secretary Sir William Joynson Hicks had defended himself against charges of partisanship following his celebration of the prosecution for sedition of members of the Communist Party by telling the House of Commons that they had been engaged in 'the wrong kind of speech'.[19] (The men were convicted.) In 1956, attempts by the German Communist Party to challenge its post-war ban in its home country on grounds of an infringement of the rights to freedom of expression and association – both rights embedded in the newly drafted European Convention on Human Rights and Fundamental Freedoms – were unsuccessful. There was, the European Commission on Human Rights asserted, an even more powerful article in the Convention, article 17, which was specifically designed to prevent liberal freedoms being used to destroy 'the free operation of democratic institutions'.[20]

There are many such examples, drawn from the various jurisdictions that were at this time trying to square democracy with the dangerous possibility of subversion from within by popular vote. It is necessary at this point to say – even if the remark might appear as startling as it is obvious – that none of these liberal democratic states engaged in the mass killing of those who opposed them at home. Quite the reverse. In the *Dennis* case, one of the factors guiding the Supreme Court to its conclusion was quite how gentle the action against the revolutionary communists had been: state surveillance leading to criminal prosecution was seen as hardly worth the dissipation of protective liberal energy.[21] Of course it was more serious than this assertion by Frankfurter J. might suggest – but never fatally so (unless one was sentenced to a capital crime for spying, as the Rosenbergs were in 1953). This was not the European colonies; the enemy was 'within' – disloyal, traitorous even, but not waging direct war on the state, and for all their faults they were members of the home team. There might be communist-inclined communities, but there were no villages scattered about the country from which military operatives might emerge to engage the enemy on behalf of a resistance that could be marked out as 'communist' and promptly razed to the ground with impunity. The criminal law (expanded sometimes it is true, and with vigorous discretionary power to harass opponents for sure) was still generally enough – even if you had to suffer the occasional defeat in court.

What these successive 'Red Scares' established – and here is their relevance to the story this book is telling – was an enduring basis for resistance to subversion *within* the state, an official hostility to dissent that is able plausibly to describe itself as compatible with rather than destructive of the liberal and democratic values that these states assert they hold dear, a plausibility that was from time to time underpinned by anarchist violence (as with the Palmer raids for example) or, more frequently, by the exposure of foreign agents among the citizenry.[22] This rationale survived into the 1970s, with radical offshoots of Left-inspired movements rediscovering a commitment to anarchist-style violence so as to challenge the integrity of Western European (and to an extent US) democracy. With the response to the Soviet threat and these later ideological spin-offs we see the double standard that had been evident in the management of insurgency in the 'home-away' of the colonies begin its journey home: the search for the 'enemy within' was well and truly on. By the time of the attacks of 11 September 2001, democratic states had entirely familiarized themselves with the idea that legal and administrative controls on dissent could not only co-exist with such governmental frameworks but might actually be necessary to their very survival – to invoke a notion that was to become popular in the 'war on terror', and was already implicit in Frankfurter J.'s judgment in *Dennis*, that the threat posed was 'existential'.

The rest of this chapter fleshes out these preliminary and somewhat abstract remarks by examining in more detail the direct impact that the Cold War had on the development of anti-terrorism law. It begins with developments both during and immediately after the colonial period. The language of the Left not only informed radical traditions within the democracies, provoking the retaliations we have been discussing; its critique of the coercive power of the imperial state (allied to a good socialist awareness of and emphasis on the costs of inequality) also found willing listeners among the colonized – in places where, as we have already seen, resistance on nationalist grounds was often already strong.

The Left analysis did not disappear when national freedom was achieved in such places: exploitation was not the exclusive preserve of the foreign oppressor (as the anarchists in Tsarist Russia, for example, already knew). The Marxist critique never reified the nationality of the oppressor. So, unlike in straightforward nationalist struggles, the battle did not end with the raising of a different state flag above government buildings; the new occupants of these buildings (invariably leaders who had risen to power as nationalists rather than anything more radical) knew this full well, even in those situations (often to be found) where Communist Party members had been their allies in the struggle just ended. Where the American side was chosen in the great Moscow versus Washington rivalry that emerged after the Second World War, it became necessary for these communists to be controlled, however valuable they had been in the past. In such circumstances, anti-terrorism laws inherited from the defeated colonial power were too good to waste.

Imperial legacies

There had always been various drivers pointing towards the survival into the independence era of colonial anti-insurgency/anti-terrorism laws which have existed quite independently of any international threat. To start with, the dead hand of the past should never be underestimated. In the immediate post-revolutionary situation, laws are needed to fill the inevitable vacuums across the legal system that follow such radical disruption, pending substantive change (which might of course never come). The obviously available laws are those already in place, on the statute book at the moment the revolution inherits power. United States jurisprudence is currently awash with efforts to understand eighteenth-century common law as a means to interpreting a US constitution that is now firmly judged to be rooted in its immediate historical moment. Both the Irish Free State constitution of 1923[23] and (to the extent that they had been unaffected in the Free State period) its successor document in 1937[24] carried forward all pre-existing British laws until such time as they were superseded (if they ever were), albeit without any presumption of constitutionality in their favour if they were challenged in court. Pakistan did not adopt a new constitution until eight years after it had established its independence, with pre-existing imperial law filling the vacuum in authority.[25] When Kenya secured independence, a British Order in Council ensured legal continuity in the same manner.[26] There are multiple similar examples.

Continued domestic conflict (or the fear of such disorder) made the retention of these laws more attractive, adding prudence to statis as a reason for their continuation. The older colonies that secured dominion status in the late Victorian/early Edwardian era (especially Canada [1867] and Australia [1901]) maintained pre-existing laws, including those that might prove useful in managing political resistance in the territories from anyone inclined to question the new authorities.[27] South Africa (1909) emerged out of violent conflict only to carry into its new dispensation models of the laws that the old establishment had once deployed with such force against what was now the new leadership.[28] Israel, born in violence, retained its old emergency laws from the time of the British Mandate while also promulgating immediately upon its foundation a prevention of terrorism ordinance[29] – decisions it was able later to exhibit to the UN in the post-2001 atmosphere as evidence of its good practice in the field of counter-terrorism.[30] Ireland is a particularly good illustration of how post-independence conflict can drive the retention of pre-existing anti-terrorism laws without any ideological threat from abroad. The compromise made by the Irish nationalist authorities to conclude their agreement with Britain, achieved in December 1921, led directly to a feud between the newly established Irish government and erstwhile colleagues which was so severe as to amount to what can plausibly be described as a civil war. In these circumstances, which lasted until May 1923, it was hardly surprising that the state authorities seized upon pre-existing frameworks of repression to deploy them against their one-time colleagues, now their implacable enemies. Even when the situation settled enough for fresh legislation to be enacted, there were 'clear parallels' between what now emerged and the British law which had governed the same space in colonial times.[31]

Even if there was no immediate civil conflict, it was not unusual to find states that had just achieved sovereignty needing to act immediately to stem further nationalist fragmentation and so turning to pre-existing anti-insurgency law as the most useful route to the assertion of control, as with Pakistan and its Balochistan region for example.[32] There needed to be no *global* aspect to such deliberate preservations of the status quo. For many countries that achieved statehood after the Second World War, the retention of strong police powers could also come to be independently justified (quite apart from any Soviet or domestic menace) on the basis of their necessity if the goals of 'progress' and 'development' were to be reached. Jeremy Harding's perceptive comments on Morocco under King Hassan have a general relevance here: 'Hassan's colonial predecessors had administered drastic punishment in the name of empire . . . Most colonial possessions, Morocco included, won independence in the thick of the Cold War. Whether they opted for a socialist model or a Western-style arrangement, they were able to spin disappearances, torture and maiming as regrettable features of state formation, much as the colonial powers had described them as instruments of progress.'[33] There will always be a tension between the dictates of development on the one hand and the protection of human rights on the other, with the former's utilitarian momentum appearing to justify the deployment of all state resources (including anti-terrorism law) to the job at hand.

Jeremy Harding's passing remark about the Cold War brings us back to the main thrust of this chapter. Even allowing for the various drivers towards retention just discussed, it is clear that the fear of radical, left-wing revolution played a very large part in the maintenance of anti-insurgency laws in the post-war, post-colonial states. We have already come across Sir Gerald Templer's description of his Malayan insurgents in the 1950s as 'communist terrorists'.[34] By the late 1940s and during the whole of the late colonial period, it was becoming increasingly clear that much of the opposition to colonial power was indeed being driven by communist radicals. The threat posed to many of these newly minted post-1945 sovereign authorities was of a different order to its predecessors, no longer exclusively local and nationalist in its horizons, but spreading itself ambitiously across the globe. In his recent study of the genealogy of anti-terrorism laws in India, Joseph McQuade has observed of the region of which India was such an important part that, '[w]hile the postcolonial states of South Asia finally returned sovereignty to the people of the subcontinent, many of the legal and bureaucratic structures that had provided a framework for colonial rule remained in place'.[35] We have already noted how Israel seized upon its old repressive laws to tackle Palestinian opposition to its existence (and immediate expansion). For the newly established states that chose the American side – many of them spread across the old imperial domains of France and the United Kingdom – the anticipated gateway to freedom that colonial resistance had seemed to offer speedily reconfigured itself as a route to new forms of authoritarianism, deployed in support of what were generally now US-oriented independent governments. The Americans were determined to fill the newly liberated colonies with (as one senior politician put it) 'military strongmen' to dominate on their behalf, and in particular 'as an offset to Communist Development of the Labour unions'.[36] In these places, unsurprisingly, communist-inspired domestic subversion was the main target.

The point can first be made by reference to formerly French-controlled territories in the Middle East. 'Lebanon and Syria were among the first Arab countries to criminalise terrorism',[37] with the newly independent (of French control) Lebanon defining the term (in 1943) as 'all acts [that] aim to create a state of panic and are committed by means such as explosives and inflammable materials, toxic or burning products, epidemiological or microbial factors that could cause a public danger'.[38] Syria chose the same definition in 1949.[39] With the colonial authorities finally departing the scene, it was clear that the spectre of communism lay behind this continued concern about violent subversion driving 'attempts to overthrow tyrannical regimes'.[40] Many similar stories could be told across South East Asia.[41] Having been under French and, later, British subjugation, Egypt is another good example. Under British occupation from 1882 through to 1952, the country was subject to martial law in 1914 and again in 1939, with its constitution of 1923 including (at British insistence) provisions for draconian measures where circumstances required their deployment.[42] 'In 1946, article 98(b) was added to the Egyptian Penal Code, condemning "whoever promotes in the Egyptian Republic in any way to change the fundamental principles of the constitution . . . or to overthrow the state's fundamental social or economic system . . . when the use of force or terror or any other illegal means is noticeable".'[43] Terror was 'not considered a crime by itself' but 'was linked to acts that aim[ed] to overthrow the government or change the system'.[44] And its remit was very broadly construed. As the scholar Fatemah Alzubairi comments, '[t]he early use of the term "terror" at the legal level was to protect the regime, not necessarily from violent acts, but from civil acts that included speech and meetings'.[45] The revolution in 1952 that ended the monarchy and brought British power in Egypt to a close saw no reduction in hostility towards members of the Communist Party.[46] Secret intelligence leading to pre-emptive action, backed by the courts and aimed at communists as such rather than their actions, became (as under British rule) the order of the day.[47] According to one scholarly study of the region, such 'practices have thwarted democratic progress and consolidated authoritarianism in post-independence Egypt'.[48]

Egypt's near neighbour Tunisia offers a further example. Under its first and long-serving president Habib Bourguiba, dissent came quickly to be equated with terrorism, with (as in Egypt) radical Islamist activity as well as Leftist engagements included. In 1979, article 123 of the Tunisian Penal and Procedures Military Code criminalized any Tunisian 'who puts himself during peacetime under the dominance of a terrorist organisation operating abroad'.[49] These aggressive legal interventions, clearly rooted in the pre-existing colonial laws, survived Bourguiba's departure from office in 1987. In her penetrating study, Fatemah Alzubairi observes that 'law and crime control in [Arab] countries and in the West are closely related, both because the colonialists left the roots of these strategies in the countries they had colonized, which have developed them further, and because colonialists also continue to use them in a similar way in their homelands'.[50] In these countries, 'counter-insurgency and counter-terrorism depend largely on colonial and wartime strategies to deal with mostly domestic peacetime crimes',[51] thereby serving 'the authoritarian ambitions of Arab rulers and dominant groups within the Arab world'.[52] Such states 'still cling to the colonial rationale as a "legal" way of securing their authoritarian regimes'.[53]

The willingness to embrace such counter-terrorism strategies was not always directly aimed at pleasing America. In many Arab states fear of Islamist radicalism played a part, as just noted in relation to Egypt and Tunisia. Even where non-alignment with either of the two great blocs was achieved, this did not necessarily mean that anti-insurgency laws were set to one side. Yugoslavia, for example, was under pressure of fragmentation from the start, and so coercion was built into its authoritarian structures from its inception.[54] In India, the Naxalites have been a thorn in the government's side since the mid-1960s:

An anti-government insurgent group active across a third of India's states. Formed in 1967 in Naxalbari in West Bengal, and committed to a Maoist ideology, they are seen as the most potent threat to India's internal stability. They largely represent native tribal communities, Adivasis, and lower castes concerning land rights, unemployment, and socio-economic exclusion. They have caused over 6,000 deaths since 2005, through widespread attacks against police stations, army camps, state infrastructure, businesses, and individuals, including bombings, bank robberies, kidnappings, and assassinations.[55]

For those who took the American side, a blank cheque to weed out 'terrorists' quickly became one of the perks of this dependency. A recent study of the role of the CIA in post-independence Africa shows quite how invasive US influence was on that continent in the 1960s.[56] South Africa persisted until the Cold War had neared its end as one of 'the last vestiges of imperialism and racial injustice'.[57] 'In 2008, in the final days of the Bush administration, it was discovered that Nelson Mandela – by that point arguably the most loved and revered person on the planet – was still on the US's "terror watchlist", in addition to other senior figures in the African National Congress (ANC)'.[58] They had been placed there in 1986, by a Reagan administration that had been busy currying the favour of the stoutly anti-communist apartheid regime of P.W. Botha. For their part, both the United Kingdom and Israel were acting sensibly in their own interests when they sought (as both frequently did as late as the 1980s, albeit with limited success) to cast their domestic opponents, the IRA and the PLO respectively, as communist rather than nationalist 'terrorists'.[59] Templer would have approved.

Strategies of provocation

Successful colonial resistance has a longer and broader history than that discussed in Chapter 1. To pick the most prominent example, Latin America had on the whole successfully fought its battles for freedom against weakening European empires well before the newer colonial powers like Britain and France had even properly begun: Argentina, Bolivia, Chile, Colombia, Ecuador, Paraguay, Peru, Uruguay and Venezuela gaining independence from Spanish rule in the opening decades of the nineteenth century, Brazil from Portuguese rule in 1822. Over the years an impressive momentum towards democracy was evident in many of these countries – but this was not matched by any march

47

towards equality. As the leading historians of the government of the region have remarked:

> By the early decades of the twentieth century, most of the major countries of Latin America had managed to establish at least 'oligarchical democracies', that is to say, regimes in which presidents and national assemblies derived from open, if not fully fair, political competition for the support of limited electorates, according to prescribed constitutional rules and which were largely comparable to the restricted representative regimes in Europe of the same period.[60]

By the late 1950s and early 1960s, the result of this trend towards oligarchy was all too evident in the deepening chasm that existed between the wealthy and the rest: colonial-style exploitation could occur even in countries free of colonial occupation.

The success of Fidel Castro in Cuba in 1959 appeared to presage a new means of taking on and overcoming entrenched *non-colonial* power within a state. Cuba had fought a series of wars against Spanish rule in the nineteenth century and after the third of these (with American assistance) independence had been secured in 1902. Liberation was not complete, however. The influence of the US in the first half-century or so of the Cuban republic was pervasive, leaving the country unable to develop any kind of independent diplomatic or domestic policies not agreeable to their much larger neighbour. There were high levels of unrest, but an effort at long-term change faltered in 1952 when the progressive constitution adopted in 1940 was suspended following a US-backed coup by the failed presidential candidate Fulgencio Batista. The already close connections between US commercial interests (particularly the sugar industry) and Cuban elites deepened further under the Batista regime, producing ever higher levels of American control over the country's assets and even greater – and annually increasing – inequality. The resistance of the 26th of July Movement (named after an early attack on Batista forces on that date in 1953) gradually gathered momentum in the field, eventually producing victory after a politico-military campaign of great effectiveness. A new Cuban Republic was duly established, coming into being at the start of 1959. Its first prime minister (and afterwards president) was the revolutionary leader Fidel Castro.

The military tactics deployed by Cuba's aspirant (and eventually successful) revolutionaries in the late 1950s have come to be known as those of the 'guerrilla' fighter. The term dates from the Peninsular War of 1808–14, in which Spanish and Portuguese irregular combatants helped the British forces under the Duke of Wellington to drive the French from their lands, the word echoing the Spanish for war, 'guerra'. In the Cuban context, guerrilla warfare involved the successful use of mobile paramilitary forces with the capacity to strike in a flexible way at their stronger military opponents, appearing from nowhere to fight, and melting back into the countryside after the attack on their chosen target was completed. Deployed intelligently, these forces also acted as focal points for domestic discontent, the idea being that by their very presence they would both reflect and stimulate popular anger at the oppressive nature of the governing regime. The Cuban guerrillas were successful on both these scores. But they never intended to do the whole work of revolution themselves. Borrowed from the military ideas of previously successful insurgents like Michael Collins in Ireland and Mao Zedong in China, the idea was that, operating largely in the countryside, they would gradually build up strength until the moment came when the enemy could be deposed by a combination of popular and more orthodox military resistance. This is indeed what happened. Cuban success in the use of these guerrilla tactics appeared to confirm that proto-revolutionaries did not need to wait for the people to join their side – they could jumpstart their desired revolution by a combination of vanguardist military prowess, inspirational example and clarity of political messaging (about the oppressive practices and corruption of their opponents and the imperative need for change).

Cuba's proximity (both geographic and cultural) to South America made its revolution an important, indeed exemplary, model to those in the various republics that had not made the progress towards the kind of social and economic equality that, elsewhere in the world, was still expected to flow from the achievement of national sovereignty. By the mid-twentieth century many of these states might have called themselves democratic, but whatever their notional political complexion, their common and often grotesque inequalities left many radicals in despair at the inability of conventional (non-violent) communist parties to achieve change. Reacting to the apparent futility of parliamentary opposition, the technique of terrorism (as it was coming to be known) became the method of choice for many on the radical Left in various of the South American states where colonization was little more than a distant memory (if it was even that), but where US influence was immense and often barely concealed. However, unlike Cuba, the subcontinent was increasingly becoming urbanized, at a rate not seen at this point in other parts of the post-colonial world.[61] This suggested that the cities were the places in which to concentrate revolutionary energy. And, as had been the case with Castro, the revolutionaries were inevitably bound to find themselves forced to confront American support for established power, this being one of the key 'geopolitical realities of the Cold War'.[62]

Uruguay stands as a good example of the developments in subversive violence – and government reactions thereto – in Latin America. By the early 1960s the country was organized on democratic grounds (with a constitution agreed in 1952) but, characteristically of South America as a whole, was deeply unequal in its distribution of wealth and (even by Latin American standards) highly urbanized.[63] Raúl Sendic, a young law student, attempted to organize the sugar-cane workers; when this was prevented by a combination of commercial and military force, he 'resolved to challenge the state through violence'.[64] His National Liberation Movement quickly came to be known as the Tupamaros 'in honour of the Incan leader Tupac Amaru II who had led a rebellion against the Spanish in the late eighteen century'.[65] It was immediately obvious that the Cuban precedent did not apply in Uruguay; the countryside there was not the place in which to fight battles or from which to mount military operations. It had to be the city: the concept of the 'urban guerrilla' was born. The strategic ambition was the same as had been adopted in Cuba – to light the spark of revolution among the people – but the tactics deployed were necessarily different. In its first phase of operation, the mid-to-late 1960s, the Tupamaros engaged in glamorous, almost romantic heists designed to illustrate to Uruguayans what a nice, compassionate government would look like.[66] At the turn of the new decade, however, the group embraced a more aggressive strategy of confrontation, one that had been 'espoused by Carlos Marighella, a Brazilian legislator turned communist revolutionary who was killed in a shootout with police in 1969'.[67]

The Francophone Afro-Caribbean philosopher Frantz Fanon and the charismatic fighter Che Guevara had both written about the place of violence in the remaking of the world,[68] but Marighella's words have a direct if (from the perspective of today) haunting eloquence. In his *Mini-Manual of the Urban Guerrilla*, he laid out a theory of urban subversion that was to prove disastrously influential among the revolutionaries of his generation. We have already seen, in the case of Cuba, the idea that in addition to working politically to persuade the people of the rightness of your cause, your active presence as a violent subversive/guerrilla could educate by its actions. It has long been the case that radicals of all sorts have turned to violence in impatient desperation at the slow process of ordinary political agitation – the Russian anarchist group Narodnaya Volya, for example, whose members 'got frustrated with the "outreach to the people"' required by traditional socialist advocacy.[69] Marighella had been an active member of the Brazilian Communist Party before founding his own party of the Left, which under his leadership took a violent turn in its engagement with the authorities in Brazil (then, unlike Uruguay, under military rule). In his writings on urban violence, Marighella added into the mix a new, fully thought out 'strategy of provocation'. Of course, as with the idea of the guerrilla as the spark that ignites resistance, the insight that the subversive can provoke the authorities into actions that will reveal their true repressive colours (and in doing so turn the people into allies of the rebels) has a long history: one of the 'declared goals' of the Russian anarchists was 'to provoke disproportionately harsh counter-reaction by the state',[70] while in the late 1950s and early 1960s the Algerian liberation movement (the FLN) had been 'in many ways no match for French military power, but it effectively used terrorist tactics in order to draw out (according to Leninist-Marxist thinking) the brutality of the colonial regime'.[71] But in his *Mini-Manual*, Marighella placed this insight at the centre of his approach to violence as a means of achieving change.[72]

There can have been few more catastrophic misjudgements in the history of our subject than the belief that provoking a government into intensified repression is bound to produce increased support for the subversive provocateur. It entirely disregards the alienating impact of the violence: letters covered in blood tend to be noticed for everything except what they have to say. All that the strategy of provocation achieved in

South America was to turn the urban guerrilla/terrorist into an ally of the state so far as draconian 'anti-terrorism' laws were concerned. Under the stress of events, Uruguay quickly degenerated into an authentic military state.[73] It was the same elsewhere on the subcontinent, with urban guerrilla activity turning into a midwife for dictatorship rather than egalitarian revolution. In Colombia the conflict generated from the early 1960s onwards by two radical groups (the National Liberation Army [ELN] and the better known Revolutionary Armed Forces of Colombia [FARC-EP]) provoked the by now predictable military response, with 'death squads [being] legalised through Decree 3398 (1965) and subsequently Law 48 (1968), setting the precedent for the terrorist activities of the paramilitaries in the closing decades of the century'.[74] In Peru, the Communist Party of Peru-Sendero Luminoso (PCP-SL) 'rose up in arms not to fight a repressive military dictatorship . . . but to boycott an emerging democracy'.[75] Intending by their attacks 'to elicit a level of repression that would justify branding the state as "fascist"',[76] all they precipitated was a return to military control, a dirty war in which thousands of innocent people were killed by the military and their paramilitary supporters, and eventually a reactionary coup in 1992 that introduced even wider anti-terrorism powers. Making due allowance for some exaggeration, Randall Law is surely right to suggest (in his history of terrorism) that '[t]he most common errors of those who follow Carlos Marighella's *Mini-Manual* . . . are that they overestimate the revolutionary potential of the masses and underestimate the repressive power of the state'.[77]

The urban guerrilla comes to Europe

The late 1960s and early 1970s saw a serious escalation in Left-inspired political violence in democratic Europe. Many states were affected – Belgium, the United Kingdom, France, the Netherlands among them – but the most serious incidents occurred in West Germany and Italy. The driving force behind these subversives was similar to that of their South American equivalents: a belief in the rottenness of their countries' political structures allied to an impatience with the lack of revolutionary energy shown by others on the Left, and a determination, Marighella-like, to lift the lid on so-called European freedom, exposing the repression that (they asserted) lay just below the surface. The movement also reached the United States, where the Weather Underground and to a lesser extent the Symbionese Liberation Army sought to challenge established authority with violence: '[i]n the era of the American-Soviet confrontation, they frequently championed the anti-imperialist politics of the Third World' with 'Lenin and Stalin . . . supplanted by Frantz Fanon and Che Guevara'.[78] My concern here is of course to some extent with what these groups did, but more directly with how democratic states reacted to the political and public pressure that their violence induced. Here was an enemy within that sought to destroy the state not through the ballot box or by means of an abrasive discursive engagement but via the 'propaganda of the deed', a reworking of anarchist tropes for the modern age. The states under attack were more stable democracies than those in South America, with stronger social democratic traditions and much lower levels of inequality. But the threat felt more dramatic than that posed by the communists of past generations. How did these liberal democratic states respond to the challenge?

If one had to summarize it in three words, the answer would be: 'not too badly'. West Germany is the most important exhibit in our assessment of the state response.[79] The Baader-Meinhof gang and, later, the Red Army Faction (RAF), 'declared war on the Federal Republic of Germany (FRG) for its failure to rid itself of the vestiges of fascism, for its hierarchical-authoritarian structure, and for the abuses of western consumer society'.[80] The anti-imperial struggle was certainly a model: '[i]nspired by national liberation movements in the formerly colonized world, the groups aimed both to raise revolutionary consciousness among the West German population and to demonstrate the state's vulnerability through illegal action'.[81] Support from the Soviet bloc was always available, including sanctuary when apprehension in the West threatened.[82] But Marighella's South American disciples were another model: the 'RAF, in particular, stressed the importance of violence as a simultaneous act of emancipation and defense – the latter understood as counterviolence necessitated by state-initiated violence. The repeated violation of norms would, its members argued, undermine Germans' traditional "habit of obedience" and, at the same time, force the state to reveal openly its fascism.'[83] The violence began in 1968, but it was a series of bomb attacks in May 1972 that led to the arrests in June of the RAF group's leaders.

The 'following year the RAF prisoners embarked on what would be the first of ten collective hunger strikes between 1973 and 1989'.[84] A second surge of violence, remembered as the 'German Autumn', was initiated on 5 September 1977, when RAF members kidnapped the president of the Employers' Federation, Hanns Martin Schleyer, from his car, leaving his three bodyguards and chauffeur dead at the scene.

The response of the German authorities to the threat posed by this violence was undoubtedly robust, more so after Schleyer's kidnap, but it was a robustness that remained located within the realm of criminal law. The legislation on the interception of communication that was authorized against RAF members and suspected sympathizers survived scrutiny in the European Court of Human Rights.[85] There were no 'death squads', nor were arbitrary emergency powers invested in the police and/or the military. The state's reaction was more reminiscent of the UK's engagement with the domestic anarchist challenge before the First World War than it was of that power's treatment of its colonial insurgents. This restrained approach was not inevitable. The then main political opposition the CDU/CSU were consistent advocates for going much further than the social democratic (SPD) administrations of first Willy Brandt and afterwards Helmut Schmidt judged necessary. After the murder of a Berlin judge, Günter von Drenkmann, in 1974, 'the CDU/CSU had four proposed laws rejected out-of-hand by the SPD, which argued that legislation made in the heat of the moment tended towards overreaction and endangered democracy as much as or more than the terrorists did'.[86] Instead, the authorities focused on the modernization of the police, and in particular the relocation of relevant responsibility away from the *Länder* (states) and towards the federal government, with consequent improvements in technological and (general) professional prowess.

With the successful criminal prosecutions that resulted from these changes came an intense focus on RAF prisoners, the conditions in which they were held, and their capacity (through the use of sympathetic intermediaries) to direct their membership from within their prison cells. As we will see also happened following a less persuasive move towards criminalization in Ireland in the 1980s,[87] hunger strikes became a means of challenging the state from within prison. After Schleyer's kidnap a new law (*Kontaktsperregesetz*), giving ministers the right to suppress prisoners' contact with one another and the outside world if there was a strong possibility they posed a 'present danger to life, limb, or liberty', was rushed through the Bundestag (German parliament), afterwards surviving constitutional challenge before the *Bundesverfassungsgericht* (the German Constitutional Court).[88] When in October 1977 the Popular Front for the Liberation of Palestine (PFLP: more on this group in Chapter 4) hijacked a German airliner to show their support for the RAF, the government overcame its scruples about militarizing their response to terrorism enough to deploy special forces (GSG-9) to secure the plane while it refuelled in Mogadishu, Somalia. The operation was a complete success, with all passengers and surviving crew rescued. (The captain had already been killed by the hijackers.) When they returned in triumph, the special forces operatives projected 'the image of the non-militaristic military Social Democrats had set out to create in 1972. Dressed in blue jeans and black leather jackets, the men of the GSG-9 did not evoke comparisons with Prussian or, worse, Nazi soldiers. Instead, accounts of modest heroism and technical efficiency abounded in descriptions of these "rocker-cops" with "honed 007 skills that made the use of weapons redundant".'[89] The undeclared state of exception initiated by Chancellor Schmidt during the 'German Autumn' involved the executive ruling without parliamentary engagement, but this was brought to an end after some six weeks.[90] The underlying message was that 'a German state could indeed manifest strength without fear of being authoritarian'.[91]

Alongside this criminalization strategy, the German authorities engaged from very early on in 'a program of "political education" (what they referred to as a "positive" policy of constitutional protection) [that] went beyond their immediate target – terrorism – to take aim at the democratization of state and society'.[92] Here is an early example of a strategy of official communication to counter the propaganda of a state's violent domestic opponents, a foreshadowing of the 'crack down' on 'terrorist Godfathers' that was to be seen around the world from the mid-2000s onwards and which has been a feature of UK counter-terrorism since the emergence of the Prevent programme in 2003. Overseen by a Federal Centre for Political Education (the BPB), the twin goals of the German programme were 'the prevention of violent radicalism and the enlistment of the population in government efforts to contain it'.[93] The BPB engaged in the publication of documents which drew public attention to the innocent victims of terrorism, while also highlighting the connections the RAF had with both 'international terrorism' (which PFLP 'solidarity' of course made easier) and ordinary crime, all the time emphasizing that the government was fully up to meeting the challenge with which it was confronted.

There was also a muscular side to this. On 28 January 1972, the federal government and leaders of the various *Länder* had instituted the so-called *Radikalenerlass* (Anti-Radical Decree) under which people who were considered to be members of or aligned with extremist groups were banned from working as civil servants (which in Germany included teaching posts). The popular description of this controversial policy was *Berufsverbot* ('jobs-ban') and it continued long after the threat from the radical Left had dissipated, surviving challenge before the European Court of Human Rights when it mattered,[94] and falling foul of that same tribunal some twenty-three years later when it didn't.[95] Of course the breadth of the ban did have some damaging impact on free speech, particularly in the way it encompassed those aligned with the RAF as well as the organization's proven members. But it is hard to see how that inclusion could have been avoided if the policy was to have any bite. And its rigorous focus on support for an organization rather than for the ideas of that group meant that the risk of seepage into the wider world of political activism was reduced. In this way the ban differed from, for example, the British 'media ban' on the IRA and supporters of its ideas imposed by the British government in 1988.

Germany was not alone. In Italy the Red Brigades had grandly declared that '[o]ur ideological mould is communist. Our reference points are Marxist-Leninism, the Chinese Cultural Revolution, and the ongoing experiences of metropolitan guerrilla movements'.[96] The state reaction was to deploy the criminal process in innovative ways in order to break the strength of the group, including the use of informers (*pentiti*) to emasculate their organizational coherence. In the UK, the Angry Brigade was responsible for a series of politically motivated subversive actions before going the same way as the Red Brigades, albeit without having done nearly as much damage.[97] The trial of the 'Stoke Newington Eight' that ran at the Old Bailey in London from May to December 1972 was at the time the longest criminal court case of its type in British legal history. British commitment to due process did not extend to preventing jury vetting, designed to make sure that no juror was unduly sympathetic to those in the dock, 'a leniency overseen by Mr Justice James'.[98] In the Netherlands, Maoist urban guerrilla groups in the late 1960s 'initiated several violent episodes, causing major material damage but no deaths'.[99] But even when the pressure of outside events (not least the Olympic attack of September 1972 in neighbouring Germany) made some action inevitable, prime minister Barend Biesheuvel assured Dutch parliamentarians and the general public that 'counterterrorism will not be shaped in a way that will harm the open nature of our society', an 'attitude of reserve'[100] that persisted so far as radical-Left violence was concerned, albeit not so much in the case of the quasi-colonial South Moluccans whose penchant for train hijackings was productive of high drama. In its death throes, Dutch ideological subversion was seen off in the way that had worked for earlier generations: 'A last wave of left-wing, non-lethal, political violent activism resurfaced around 1985, but again, no new laws were deployed and the movement (named RaRa, Revolutionary Anti-Racist Action) was "neutralised" by means of the intelligence services'.[101]

Conclusion

By the end of the story told in this chapter, we can see that 'terrorism' remained a problem, with various specific and singular manifestations around the world warranting particular national solutions. Its proponents hankered after the coercive power that came with military force, clothing themselves in the vocabulary of organized violence ('army', 'brigade') that fitted their ambitions if not their capacity. The 'terrorists' discussed in this chapter were all driven by despair at the inequality they saw around them, allied to an intense determination to do something (anything) about it. In the democratic states exposed to this violence, a major additional factor was impatience with the slow pace of ordinary political activism. All those involved – whether in authoritarian or democratic environments – believed that the public would be persuaded by their violent actions to embrace their cause. As was proved time after time, this assumption was hopelessly misguided. Again and again the public – whether in an authoritarian state or a democratic one – were not persuaded that the (often random) killing of civilians or implausibly guilty parties, or the widespread destruction of property, were the way to respond to injustice. The message was invariably swallowed by its means of communication. With nothing other than symbolic violence to offer, the various armies and brigades were soon seen off by the forces of the state against whom they had hoped through their violence to galvanize the people. Their actions were quixotic, and always bound to be hopeless. Their radical ambition either destroyed or badly damaged the South American democracies with whom they came into contact, and seriously challenged even the more stable European polities that faced their random wrath.

The counter-terrorism of the authorities facing these groups in Europe worked hard to remain within the traditional criminal model, one that emphasized the need for proof of individual guilt before condemnation, and sought to deploy ordinary police procedures and evidential rules as far as possible. Of course, this was not always possible: administrative actions like the *Berufsverbot* in Germany, and tricky manipulations of the criminal process (*pentiti* in Italy; jury vetting in the UK), could on occasion prove irresistible. But the tweaks to power and process never went so far as to call into question the fundamental integrity of the process: the vetted jury in the trial of the Stoke Newington Eight acquitted the defendants of the main charges, just as their predecessors had done in the anarchist trial arising out of the Siege of Sydney Street in 1911. This assimilation of the politically subversive to the ranks of the ordinary criminal will usually be a major victory for the state, a sure sign of the imminent defeat of radical elements when it is successfully achieved. The key point here is balance: the criminal process may need to be altered, but it must never become a sham. The German subversives bitterly resented their classification as ordinary prisoners – and the clampdowns that affected their treatment when incarcerated – but in the end could do little about it.

In contrast, Irish republican prisoners in Northern Ireland in 1981 were prepared to die over their classification as criminals, and were widely supported and admired by large sections of the relevant national publics for taking this stand. As we shall see in the next chapter, this was partly because the British deployment of the criminal process in 1970s Northern Ireland had come close to (and perhaps crossed the line into) transparent manipulation, reducing the law to a front in what was in truth a military campaign against terrorism. But it was also, perhaps mainly, because the campaign by the Irish Republican Army in Ireland was of a different order of magnitude than the desultory violence of the radical leftists taking place across Europe (including the UK) at the same time. These Irish subversives were similar to those in Spain, France, Canada and elsewhere who sought to achieve liberation for their bit of their state from the authority of a centre whose sovereign jurisdiction they denied. Nationalism has always proved superior to communism in terms of garnering local support – Mazzini is invariably a better bet than Marx. It is to the contribution of these quasi-colonial struggles to the development of anti-terrorism law that we now turn – the ambiguous homelands that we discussed in Chapter 1. None of this can yet be plausibly described as part of 'a global war' requiring a global response. But the stage for this escalation was being prepared.

THREE

Uncertain Homelands

Liberation

The last chapter ended with a slightly glib allusion to Mazzini and Marx.[1] The first of these may be less well-known than the second. The Italian politician, journalist and activist Giuseppe Mazzini was one of the early drivers for Italian unification during the mid-nineteenth century. It is easy to forget quite how powerful was the resurgence of national sentiment across Europe during that period. Not only Italy but Germany and (earlier) the Netherlands, Belgium and Greece owe their existence to the fragmentation of Europe into separate national entities in the aftermath of the Congress of Vienna, a meeting that had sought a definitive reconstitution of Europe after the Napoleonic period.[2] Even Luxembourg got involved, escaping control by the Belgians in 1839, just as Belgium itself had seceded from the Netherlands a few years before. These liberation stories were driven by a strong sense of national identity (cultural, historical, linguistic, religious) and accompanied by various levels of disorder that covered the gamut of disruption, from street protests through irregular combat into proper war waged by organized armies, often (in the last of these cases) topped off by a grand treaty made by the established European powers, usually (at that time) the United Kingdom and France.[3] This ferment of revolt produced such success, and involved such a variety of politico-military tactics, that it has rarely attracted the direct attention of those tracking the history of terrorism. Nor (and as a direct result of this omission) have the efforts of resistance to these changes made by established power secured a place in the lexicons of anti-terrorism law, or influenced the development of that law in the twentieth century. From the perspective of this book, and however odd it may seem to the reader coming at the subject without preconceptions as to what terrorism is, these national revolutions are a non-story.

What they did leave, however, were loose ends. We saw in Chapter 1 how nationalist ideas gradually filtered into the colonized world. The sentiments behind the drive for independence within continental Europe at this time were felt not only where they succeeded but within the established European powers as well, whether these were the rising liberal democracies (like the UK and France) or waning empires (like Austria-Hungary, Spain and the Ottoman). Some among this latter group of imperial powers had already lost territory in the immediate post-Napoleonic period, and fragmentary forces continued to lurk within most of them: communities of residents/citizens/subjects who did not feel they fully belonged, and who – looking at the new European states being formed around them – thought 'why not us too?' This sense of unfinished national business has persisted into the modern era. In earlier chapters I have noted how liberal states usually reacted differently to subversive violence depending on where it occurred, the 'home-home' of the domestic political environment being treated more carefully, more benignly (even if often, admittedly, harshly), than the 'home-away' of the colonies. This was the case even where, as we saw in Chapter 2, those states encountered an 'enemy within' that rejected domestic authority for non-nationalist, ideological reasons, on occasion even going so far as to embrace the support of a foreign power. But the liberal contradiction (destroying freedom while celebrating it at the same time) was nevertheless inevitably more starkly exposed by the crushing of *domestic* rebellion, particularly when that state violence was being deployed to destroy nationalist dreams similar to those on which the state itself had been erected and in the celebration of which its people regularly indulged.

The dilemma that concerns us in this chapter can be usefully encapsulated in a question: what happens when the instinct of the nationalist insurgent finds expression *within* rather than *outside* the parameters of the liberal, colonial state? Here is a test for such places (either already liberal democratic or on the way to becoming so) that puts enormous stress on the assumption that the 'ordinary' criminal law can with a few small modifications do the work of 'counter-terrorism' (or 'counter-insurgency', or whatever it is called) for domestic opponents. We are not concerned here with territories recently liberated from colonial rule that are then dogged by new secessionist waves seeking to emulate the achievements of the broader national movement. Nor do domestic, ideologically based rebels interest us at this point. Rather our focus is on secessionist pressures within settled states, usually colonial/formerly colonial powers or places. The problem has produced the greatest range of anti-terrorism crises in the post-1945 period, and as a result we find it doing important additional work in making plausible the idea of a global terrorist crisis that first appeared in the mid-1970s and would explode onto the world stage after the attacks of 11 September 2001. There were the post-Franco Basques in Spain (and France to a limited degree), the Corsicans in France, the Canadian secessionists in Quebec, the South Tyrolese in Austria, and even the Puerto Ricans within the wider American hegemony. We turn to these various places later, not only for assessment of the political violence that occurred there but also (indeed mainly) so as to consider the nature of the various anti-terrorism responses that violence stimulated, and how far these states drifted away from the liberal democratic model to which all of them (including Spain after Franco) declared their commitment. Pre-eminent among these nationalist stories, though – as perhaps the most intractable 'terrorism' problem in the liberal democratic canon – is Ireland, part of a British home that nevertheless has always felt different to the rest of its co-national occupants. British responses to Irish separatist violence in the twentieth century cover the whole spectrum of the possible so far as anti-terrorism laws and policies are concerned; they are both a warning of what not to do and also (in their later configurations) examples of how to get counter-terrorism right. If Palestine (the subject of the next chapter) is one of the two central milieus from which modern anti-terrorism law emerged, then Ireland is the other. Here was the primary empire of the twentieth century doing battle with what it insisted on calling its own people. It is to that country – and Britain's relationship with it – that we now turn.

Home or away?

England's efforts to control Ireland began during the twelfth century and continued in an aggressive but not wholly successful way during the following four centuries. Castles were built, lands were distributed, loyal subjects were introduced in places previously the domain of the 'native' Irish, and administrative structures were created further to embed control. None of these actions ever managed to draw Ireland into England, in the way that, for example, Wales was being absorbed at around this time. A fairly narrow strip of land in the east of Ireland, closest to England and centred on Dublin, gave common currency to a newish term in the English language: it was 'the Pale' beyond which no English settler or administrator could (it was thought) safely go. The wider Anglo-Irish aristocracy irritated their English masters by invariably embracing native habits, becoming, as it was widely said, 'more Irish than the Irish themselves'.[4] Laws were required to limit the separatist impulses of Ireland's Dublin-based parliament (despite it being itself a creature of English control).[5] Henry VIII had himself declared king of Ireland in 1541, but this was more wishful thinking than a reflection of territorial reality. There were revolts and counter-insurgency campaigns aplenty, mainly military in character and so outside the central interest of this book.

The exigencies of foreign policy eventually caused an increasingly powerful England to exert its grip. Fears that Spain might ally with their Roman Catholic co-religionists in Ireland as a means of attacking England proved real enough in the late sixteenth century, when native leaders operating with Madrid's support were only defeated after an intense nine-year war that culminated in a comprehensive defeat for the native Irish in 1601. Extensive land confiscation followed, a process that was greatly expanded in the century of religious wars that was to follow.[6] A relatively benign eighteenth century, during which a now more centrally controlled Ireland was permitted to develop its settler institutions in more autonomous directions, came to an end in the late 1790s when fear of foreign incursion (in the shape on this occasion of revolutionary France and a very early Napoleon) once more stimulated London's defensive attention. In 1800 the independent parliament of Ireland long-established in Dublin voted itself out of existence by join- ing its Westminster equivalent, already a parliament of Great Britain after a similar dissolution of Scotland's elected assembly in 1707. With effect from 1 January 1801, a new country came into being: the United Kingdom of Great Britain and Ireland. At the start of the century of European liberation, Ireland found itself travelling in the opposite direc- tion, into rather than away from her larger neighbour's embrace.

The welcome Ireland was given on its arrival in its new British home was, however, anything but warm. To start with, and this problem has persisted to this day, the description 'Great Britain' does not include Ireland – it refers only to the island containing England, Scotland and Wales. Until 1800 Great Britain could accurately be regarded as coterminous with a United Kingdom of England, Scotland and Wales, but this was not the case after 1801. A home which from the start refuses to include you in the routine description of itself might be considered not to be promisingly hospitable. There was also the matter of religion. Participatory rights in the newly established UK parliament were denied those of the Catholic faith, to which the overwhelming majority of Ireland's population belonged. This was despite promises given at the time of the passage of the Union legislation; the failure to persuade the king and his cabinet to follow through on their undertaking on this matter precipitated the resignation of the then prime minister, William Pitt. Ireland never reconciled itself to its new status to the point of taking it for granted, as Scotland and Wales had come to do (at least until very recently). The Catholic Relief Act ('Catholic emancipation') was eventually enacted in 1829, after which Irish resistance to the Union continued, finding expression across the spectrum of political possibility, from a failed insurrection in 1848 through the 'terrorism' of the Fenian 'outrages' and the land wars of the 1860s, to the astute political operations of the constitutionalist parliamentarian Charles Stewart Parnell and his disciplined Irish Parliamentary Party in the 1880s. The British state's anti-insurgency policies ran through a similar spectrum, oscillating (one might almost say wildly) between the deployment of military force to crush dissent, the use of expanded criminal processes to hinder subversive actors while maintaining notional adherence to the rule of law, and (from time to time) desultory efforts at conciliation – 'killing home rule with kindness', as the turn-of-the century effort to challenge pressure for Irish devolution came to be called.

Firmly embedded in the range of tactics available to Union-rejectionists was what we would today instantly see as terrorism. Irish insurgents' use of opportunistic violence in urban environments in order to communicate their message of estrangement was a consistent feature of mid-to-late nineteenth-century Britain, and it caused real concern to the authorities. As Martyn Frampton has noted in his recent survey of the wider history of the subject, in the early 1880s 'it was those acting in the name of Irish self-determination who succeeded in conducting the first sustained campaign of terrorist violence, using explosive devices, aimed at symbolic targets'.[7] This was when the Fenians (as the Irish insurgents were known at this time) were using dynamite to conduct 'the first urban bombing campaign in history'.[8] As with the anarchists of the same period, high-profile assassination was also on the dissidents' menu. The 'Phoenix Park murders' of two leading figures in Britain's administration in Dublin in 1882 caused especial outrage, and is an early example of a radical offshoot (in this case the 'Irish National Invincibles') of the wider subversive movement doing sensitive work in uneasy tandem with a more mainstream (and therefore less unacceptable) national campaign. The Invincibles did not live up to their name: those involved were quickly apprehended, prosecuted and either hanged or sentenced to long prison terms. True, the determination of the authorities to secure successful outcomes led to retrials when juries were not initially convinced, and in one case even to a third trial before a jury could finally be found to convict. But there was always a jury, as well as recognizable mainstream offences with which the accused persons before the court were charged, and by the standards of the day plausibly fair procedures by which their trials were conducted.

It had been the same with the deaths of innocent civilians in a notorious failed effort by the Fenians to spring colleagues from a London prison in 1867: prosecutions had quickly followed, producing a successful conviction – but also a number of acquittals. Ireland may have been chaotically resentful of British rule, with some of its more extremist defenders determined to embrace high levels of violence, but this was, after a fashion, 'home-home' rather than the 'home-away' of the colonies. Retaliatory action focused on the culpable individuals and associations to which they belonged rather than the wider communities from which they came. The treatment meted out was closer to that accorded local anarchists than to that of imperial opponents operating far from home. As Fearghal McGarry notes, '[a]rguably the most significant consequence of the bombing campaign was its impact on the British political and security establishment', in the form of the establishment of Special Branch and the Secret Service.[9] As with the German response to its radical opponents in the 1970s, discussed in Chapter 2, the state reaction was to strengthen its capacity to respond successfully to such lawlessness *within* rather than *outside* the ordinary criminal law of the day. Systems and procedures were made fit for purpose, not set to one side. True, surveillance powers were increased and allegations of a 'police state' became less easy to rebut. But, like the German Federal republic decades later, what was the state supposed to do?

The Victorian response was made easier by the comparatively low level of Fenian violence in Britain and Ireland at the time. The 'outrages' were therefore occasional rather than routine. The return by Irish republican activists to old-school insurrection in 1916 (taking major public buildings in Dublin and proclaiming the establishment of an Irish republic once safely ensconced within them) forced a reversion to more primitive tactics on the part of the British authorities, whose power in Ireland these self-appointed revolutionaries had so brazenly challenged. The conflict sparked off by the Easter Rising of 1916 (engineered by a maverick group within a group within the wider nationalist movement) was to continue, on and off, for some six years before an uneasy peace was achieved with the signing of a treaty between the British and the rebel Irish leaders in December 1921. In the first phase, in the midst of a huge continental war it is true, old-style colonial militarism came to Dublin, in a rare display of overseas practices in this (ambiguous) part of the homeland. An immediate state of martial law was declared first in Dublin city and county and then throughout Ireland. General Sir John Maxwell was 'given plenary powers under martial law', with the Irish executive having 'placed themselves at his disposal to carry out his instructions'.[10] The army promptly reoccupied the city at great cost, laying waste to large parts of it. In an action more reminiscent of colonial Africa or the Indian subcontinent, the gunship the *Helga* bombarded targets from Dublin's River Liffey. However, apart from the performative power inherent in its very description, martial law added little to what was already available to the authorities under more general wartime legislation, the consolidated Defence of the Realm Act 1914. It was under this emergency code of laws (rather than via military order) that news blackouts were imposed, internment deployed against Irish republican suspects, and jury trial suspended. Both general and field general courts martial were introduced under its authority, the last of these empowering officers on the ground to make judicial decisions about the guilt of those brought before them, meting out harsh penalties (including the death penalty) if required. Here we have a dramatic example of what was discussed in Chapter 1: the shift in twentieth-century counter-insurgency away from the exercise of raw military power *simpliciter* and towards deployment of substantively the same powers albeit henceforth lightly cooked in a suitable legal sauce. The shift to law did let in some level of judicial oversight, but, in the few cases that came before them in these early counter-revolutionary days, the courts were largely sympathetic to the pressures under which the authorities were acting, while the 'ruins in Dublin were still hot cinders'.[11] The proclamation of martial law simply fell away, never being formally revoked.

The primacy of legislation was confirmed in the government's approach to the wider insurgency that came two years after the 1916 rebellion.[12] This was sparked by an ill-judged attempt to impose wartime conscription on Ireland (hitherto protected from such compulsion), and was also due in no small part to simmering resentment – and eventual revulsion – at the treatment accorded the leaders of the Dublin uprising in its immediate aftermath, particularly the peremptory execution of the senior leadership. Special military areas designed to control the movement of peoples were imposed under the wartime regulations and an old Victorian law (the Crimes Act 1887) was dredged up to prevent local juries delivering verdicts on crimes outside the remit of offences under the Defence of the Realm Regulations (where juries could of course be safely dispensed with). Since that same law also empowered the authorities to ban organizations deemed to be dangerous, on 3 July 1918 five such groups – all nationalist (including Sinn Féin, by now the most prominent radical nationalist group) – were duly prohibited. Despite this ongoing governmental repression, the Irish revolt nevertheless took a more serious turn in early 1919, when active violence from insurgents combined with the establishment of shadow institutions (a Dáil or parliamentary assembly; special Dáil courts; a rebel executive) in a way that increasingly threatened British power. The crisis became acute when this separatist campaign was embraced by an Irish electorate given the chance to back it through the crafty hijacking by the rebels of the process of elections to the Westminster Parliament. Here was a device of self-legitimation available to the Irish that was never open to the home-away of the colonies, and the Sinn Féin leadership was not slow to exploit it. By-elections to the Westminster Parliament were fought and won; the post-First World War election of 1918 produced further dazzling success. Internees and other rebels were duly elected to a Westminster Parliament that they had no intention of attending, instead setting up their own legislative assembly of 'duly elected' members in Dublin for those at liberty (in a very real sense) to attend.

Despite the growing military crisis, the British initially held fast to the legal route that wartime legislation had opened up in the immediate aftermath of the 1916 revolt, replacing the Defence of the Realm Act powers with a purpose-built Restoration of Order in Ireland Act in 1920. Though being deployed at home (albeit of course a part of home even more than ever unreconciled to its family environs), the measure was to become an important mediator in the shift from the military to the legal across the empire as a whole. The swingeing powers available under continuing wartime legislation, and afterwards the 1920 Act, allowed the authorities to wage a counter-insurgency war in Ireland that they could assure themselves was rooted in law and so present as part of their liberal polity rather than a contradiction of it. Their efforts were made more difficult on account of the embracing by the rebels of the tactics of the guerrilla in their resistance to British rule: no more hanging around in large public buildings waiting to be shelled. There were curfews, extensive deployment of stop and search powers, and a return to the internment of suspects which almost inevitably led (as it was to do once again in the 1980s) to deployment by internees of the weapon of the hunger strike. By the start of May 1920 there were 'nearly 300 such protests under way in Wormwood Scrubs and Mountjoy prison'.[13] After the 1920 Act came into force there was increased use of courts-martial in place of increasingly undependable juries against which the 1887 Act had failed to provide full protection. The 'rule of law' was being attenuated to breaking point.

When none of this stemmed the vibrancy of the nationalist revolt, and in particular did not halt the rising fatalities among Crown forces, a counter-insurgency weapon redolent of the old times in Ireland and colonial regimes across the empire once again forced itself back onto centre-stage. On 10 December 1920, the Lord Lieutenant of Ireland Field-Marshall Viscount French of Ypres declared martial law across four of Ireland's south-western counties. In their study of civil liberties in the United Kingdom, Ewing and Gearty describe the event and what happened next:

The phrases ringing through the proclamation seemed to come from a different age; there existed 'certain evilly disposed persons and associations' whose intent was 'to subvert the supremacy of the Crown in Ireland', and who had 'committed divers acts of violence' to achieve that end. Specific reference was made to [an] ambush on 28 November, a 'massacre and mutilation with axes of sixteen Cadets of the Auxiliary Division, all of whom had served in the late war, by a large body of men who were wearing trench helmets, and were disguised in the uniform of British soldiers, and who are still at large.'

Two days after Lord French's proclamation, the . . . commander-in-chief of the Crown forces, Sir Nevil Macready, issued his first martial law proclamation. This made into capital offences (after conviction by a military court) the unauthorized 'possession of arms, ammunition, or explosives'; the unauthorized wearing of military appareil; and the harbouring or assisting of any rebels who were 'levying war against His Majesty the King'. As with French's document, the tone was gloriously colonial and old fashioned: 'Irishmen! Understand this: Great Britain has no quarrel with Irishmen: her sole quarrel is with crime, outrage and disorder; her sole object in declaring Martial Law is to restore peace to a distracted and unhappy country.'[14]

Here we have all the usual justifications to underpin colonial violence that we encountered in Chapter 1, albeit played out on the home stage. The savages with their axes and their mutilations were not deserving of being treated as ordinary human beings. The territory subject to military rule was an unhappy one, in need of being rescued by the benign forces of the occupying power. But the times had moved on from the days when such rhetoric could be relied upon to be persuasive, even to the authorities themselves. The policy of official reprisals that took its dubious legal basis from this effort to revive martial law was abandoned after five months by a regime embarrassed by the bad publicity it generated. It's true that there were more capital offences as a result of these military proclamations, but the 1920 Act continued to operate even in those areas subject to martial law, as did – to add further confusion – the ordinary courts. In its operation, martial law resembled (to adapt a cliché) an imperial elephant in a tea shop full of delicate legal china carefully constructed for the home market. The times had almost passed for martial law abroad, much less at home.

The judiciary were inevitably drawn in, especially where martial law produced a death penalty that would have been impossible without it, as in *R v Allen*.[15] The bench was sympathetic to the state on that occasion, regarding itself as under a duty 'not to interfere with the officers of the Crown in taking such steps as they deem necessary to quell the insurrection, and to restore peace and order and the authority of the law'.[16] But even victories like this one annoyed General Macready, who saw his hands being tied by legal red tape whatever the outcome might be in the end. At one point he went so far as to unilaterally suspend the jurisdiction of the ordinary courts over military matters in martial law areas.[17] This half-baked effort at a kind of de facto military coup was then dramatically challenged by a finding by one of Ireland's senior judges, the Master of the Rolls Charles O'Connor, sitting alone in a later case, *Egan v Macready*.[18] O'Connor declared the whole edifice of martial law to be unlawful, an exercise of the ancient Royal prerogative to keep order which had however been fettered (in its entirety so far as Ireland was concerned) by enactment of the Restoration of Order in Ireland Act. It was the 1920 statute or the 'ordinary' law – or nothing. Macready and his military colleagues refused to obey the order of habeas corpus requiring release of the litigant that O'Connor MR had made, and defied also the writs of attachment which followed. The crisis was only resolved when the government released the men without Macready's knowledge: there were larger issues at stake here related to negotiations to deliver a truce that were ongoing at the time the case was being heard, and came to a successful conclusion shortly afterwards. The martial law card had been played, but had failed to pacify Ireland: politics rose to the challenge, even though it involved talking to the leadership that had sent these crazy rebels and traitorous axe-murderers into the field.

Recurring patterns of state reaction: Northern Ireland 1968–98

The ceasefire agreed in the summer of 1921 created the space for negotiation of a draft agreement between the UK authorities and the Irish rebels that culminated in what was to become known as the Anglo-Irish Treaty, signed in London in December 1921. The deal gave the Irish nationalists much of what they wanted, but not all. There was to be an Irish Free State: not a republic exactly but an entity that was to enjoy a broadly analogous status to that enjoyed by Canada and other self-governing states within the 'Community of Nations known as the British Empire'.[19] Diluting this considerable nationalist achievement, however, the north-east corner of the island (comprising six of the nine ancient counties of Ulster) was given the opportunity to opt-out, promptly exercised by its leadership through a decision of a local assembly, already in place in 'Northern Ireland' as a result of an earlier effort by the British authorities to bring hostilities to a close.[20] The partition of the island reflected the fact that for various historical and cultural reasons the most fervent defenders of the union with Great Britain were to be found in those six counties, albeit with a large Catholic/nationalist minority also present. This sub-state of Northern Ireland, embedded with its own devolved government and enjoying relative institutional freedom within the newly named United Kingdom of Great Britain and Northern Ireland, took this radically different path to the rest of Ireland to its south and west, where the Free State was finally superseded by the status of a republic in 1949. That newly independent state promptly made its presence felt by being an early seceder from the British commonwealth; at the time, London was seeking to reconfigure the empire in light of the growing strength of the anti-colonial movement. The departure from its already attenuated orbit of ('southern') Ireland was not easy for the UK government, a fact attested to by a peculiar provision in the relevant Westminster legislation, grumpily declaring (in the teeth of all the evidence) that 'the Republic of Ireland is not a foreign country'.[21] The parent was insistent that the child had not left the family home to strike out on their own.

The agreement of 1921 achieved a peace of sorts but it was always uneasy and contingent. The authorities in the Irish Free State immediately found themselves enmeshed in what was to all intents and purposes a bloody civil war against a substantial proportion of those of their fellow nationalists (included amongst whom were members of the senior leadership) who regarded the treaty just concluded as a sell-out.[22] We have already touched on this point in general terms in Chapter 2: how civil conflict has often necessitated the preservation of anti-insurgency laws in the aftermath of successful detachment from colonial dependence. So it was in Ireland. These anti-subversive laws might have been necessary in the Free State's early, conflict-riven years. The gradual acceptance of the legitimacy of the state's institutions by the vast majority of its citizens did not, however, act as a spur to their removal. Familiarity bred content so far as successive governments were concerned, with those who had been hounded by the repressive reach of these laws happy to deploy them against their own political opponents now that they had accessed the levers of power. Nor did Ireland's constitutional guarantee of rights make any difference. Judicial challenges to repressive legislation were either unsuccessful or seen off by the government, as was the case in 1940 when the elected leader of the day (and one-time republican who had been jailed by the British) simply re-enacted provisions of the Offences Against the State Act that had been judicially condemned and dared the courts to do their worst. (They didn't.)[23]

The survival of the state provided a powerful explanation for an ongoing emphasis on security in Ireland that might otherwise have been seen as hypocritical in a supposedly democratic state that respected human rights.[24] This was especially the case with the resurgence of violence north of the Irish border from the late 1960s onwards. Liam Cosgrave, the mid-1970s Irish Taoiseach (prime minister), was a resolute defender of the demands of national security; his own father had occupied the same position of leadership at the very lowest point of the post-treaty conflict of 1922–3 (taking over from the charismatic Michael Collins on his murder by opponents of the treaty). Liberalization in the field of anti-security law was well-nigh impossible to contemplate in Ireland throughout its history, from Free State to Republic. And with the return of violence in the North from 1968 onwards, even if the stars were to happen to align so as to make such change possible, there was always the risk of what one of Ireland's finest intellectuals was to call 'the politics of the last atrocity'[25] taking hold, as occurred in 1972 when a proposed reform of Dublin's Offences Against the State legislation unexpectedly failed in the immediate aftermath of a series of bombing incidents in Dublin that caused three fatalities (for which British special agents have long been suspected of responsibility).[26]

The same elements of convenience allied to reaction to (or the fear of) atrocity worked to an even greater extent in Northern Ireland: there anti-subversive legislation was (if it were possible) even more entrenched. A Special Powers Act (SPA) had been enacted early in the new sub-state's life to protect it from a perceived risk of obliteration by a combination of the irredentist elements within the territory and its hostile neighbour to the south. In contrast to the unionist minority in the Free State/ Republic (admittedly always very small), the large nationalist minority in Northern Ireland was never reconciled to its retention within the British homeland. Campaigns of political violence were a recurring feature across Northern Ireland's first fifty years, particularly in the 1930s and again in the late 1950s/early 1960s. Once enacted the SPA could not be removed: '[o]riginally designed to lapse after one year, [it] was kept in force first by an annual vote, and then in 1928 for a further five-year period without the need for annual parliamentary renewal'.[27] The legislation was to survive for over fifty years, persisting through times of conflict but also of (relative) peace. Northern Ireland's experience with anti-subversive laws was to become a familiar one in all liberal jurisdictions facing colonial-style insurgencies: if there is violence it goes without saying that the law is necessary, but if there is not then (as Northern Ireland's Attorney General put it when defending the SPA in 1927), '[h]aving succeeded in restoring law and order, what the Government [was] now [being] asked to do [was] to throw away the weapon with which law and order was restored'.[28] The circularity of this logic did more than perhaps anything else to entrench anti-terrorism laws across democratic society in the decades before the 9/11 attacks.

What eventually did for the SPA (at least in its original form) was a dramatic increase, already briefly alluded to, in cross-community violence in Northern Ireland in the late 1960s and early 1970s. Nationalist unease with the sub-state had gradually matured into a politically motivated anger which during 1967–8 expressed itself through a lively (and peaceful) civil rights movement. Brutal repression from Northern Ireland's militarized police forces (mainstream and the reserve 'B-Specials') followed and – in the absence of any intervention from Westminster (whose political establishment had long before opted out of any involvement in the Province's 'internal affairs') – sectarian conflict escalated to the point where an already partisan home affairs ministry was unable to impose any kind of order on the streets. The very earliest months of this new phase of Northern Ireland's perennially repetitive conflict saw high levels of street disorder and mob violence rather than politically motivated subversive violence by organized groups. The prospect of extensive 'ethnic cleansing' (as it would be called today) of Catholic nationalists from their home areas eventually precipitated London's reluctant intervention, with troops being deployed on the streets as an emergency measure in the summer of 1969. Bizarrely, these newly deployed forces remained under the control of a devolved administration that somehow or other (another sign of British passivity) had survived despite its combination of partisan-ship and incapacity having been a major cause of the problems which the troops were now being sent in to manage. Just as the idea of a threat of 'global terrorism' was gaining currency, this ancient conflict revived itself to deadly effect.

These early years of state management of subversive violence in Northern Ireland took their lead from twentieth-century British engage-ments as an imperial power. Encouraged by their local unionist masters and drawing on their responses to rebellion in Palestine, Malaya, Kenya and Cyprus, the army leadership viewed the problems they encountered through the lens of their recent colonial experiences. Here were loyalist settlers whose commitment to the Crown was beyond question, while over there were the natives being roiled up into insurrection by their leaders, driven to reject a Crown that had their own interests at heart. There was some truth to this caricatured perception: with the arrival of Crown forces on the streets, the separatist tradition rooted in mili-tant Irish nationalism that had already begun slowly to reassert itself as the defender of urban nationalist enclaves developed into a rejuvenated Irish Republican Army ('IRA'). Now reorganized on a provisional basis (as the 'Provisional' IRA or 'Provos'), and with the long history and culture of Irish separatism to draw upon, the organization set aside the socialist direction in which it had been heading and, embracing history, reimagined itself as a vanguard for an undoing of partition and the final achievement of a united Ireland, the 'fourth green field' of Ulster/ Northern Ireland joining the three provinces to the South. Inevitably the British army saw the IRA as another Mau Mau or bunch of 'communist-terrorists', as the 'Tiger of Malaya' Sir Gerald Templer had called his opponents in the 1950s.[29]

Prompt military action was judged to be required, and was forthcom-ing. If this was not martial law then that was only because the (at this point) still-functioning SPA gave the authorities all that they needed, just as the Defence of the Realm legislation had immediately after the 1916 rising. Curfews were imposed, suspects arrested and held on a near-arbitrary basis, and multiple house searches of nationalist areas became routine. Eventually, egged on by the local administration – which had enjoyed some success with it as a tool of anti-terrorism in the late 1950s – the executive power of indefinite detention ('internment') was exercised in the summer of 1971.[30] Hundreds of supposed terrorists (all Catholic nationalists) were rounded up. A selection of them were subjected to interrogation-in-depth during which techniques of sensory deprivation that had been well-honed in the colonial context were used to extract information from these supposedly high-value detainees. When protest against this and other actions to 'restore order' predictably escalated, and the simple expedient of banning all public demonstrations failed, the temptation to behave in a way normalized by decades of colonial rule proved impossible to resist: on 30 January 1972, members of the army's Parachute Regiment opened fire on civil rights demonstrators in a Catholic area of Northern Ireland's second city Derry (Londonderry), killing thirteen civilians and injuring many more ('Bloody Sunday').

But Ireland was not Kenya, Palestine or Cyprus, and Derry was not Amritsar. Northern Ireland was, for good or ill, part of the United Kingdom. Here was a British state which had long taken pride in its commitment to civil liberties and the rule of law, and which (more recently) had even persuaded itself that decolonization had been a managed process in which territories had been 'given' their independence in gratitude for which they had remained within Britain's world as part of an expanded Commonwealth of nations. Colonial repression needed to be hidden and, if at all possible, forgotten. Northern Ireland made that impossible. If it was not a faraway colony, nor was it 1920. Developments in communication made anti-insurgency violence much harder to hide than in the past; the Colonel Dyers of Bloody Sunday saw their actions broadcast in real time around the world. Within days of the killings in Derry, a crowd of angry protestors had burned to the ground the British embassy in Dublin. In vain did the British authorities deploy the usual legalistic device of a judicial inquiry – the report into Bloody Sunday by the serving Lord Chief Justice John Widgery was widely derided as a 'Widgery whitewash'. Later judicial inquiries into the abuse of internees acknowledged ill-treatment but refused to condemn what had happened.[31] Reports by the *Sunday Times* on the ill-treatment of internees had a greater impact, with an infuriated Republic of Ireland (now effectively acting as proxy guardians of Northern Ireland's nationalist community) launching proceedings against the United Kingdom before the European Commission on Human Rights, alleging the deliberate torture of the suspects. (The case concluded in 1978 with a finding against the UK of the infliction of inhuman and degrading treatment on the detainees.[32])

Something had to give. During this phase of full colonial-style militarization, the London administration inevitably found itself secretly engaging with their nationalist opponents about how best to manage their secessionist demands. If the IRA were indeed the Mau Mau, then their Kenyatta needed to be identified and given his chance. But Northern Ireland was not only just a few miles of water away from Great Britain, its peoples (loyalist and nationalist) had migrated in vast numbers to British cities. So had the Irish from the South of course, enjoying the free travel that flowed from not being a 'foreign' country. There was no guarantee that the departure of the British from the island would not precipitate a conflict so severe that it would quickly spread to cities like Glasgow, Liverpool and London. The British decided to stay and in doing so turned to another technique of anti-insurgency: a combination of, on the one hand, the energetic pursuit of politics with 'moderates' so as to identify and support a 'middle ground' upon which institution-building could take place and, on the other, the deployment of the full force of the law to castigate as criminals those engaged in violent subversion against the state. The first of these is a fascinating story of great political import but of secondary interest to this book: however carefully contrived (and in Northern Ireland it took the shape of an ingenuously constructed Sunningdale Agreement, achieved in December 1973), appeals to the centre ground in such circumstances simply could not (and in Northern Ireland did not) survive the malevolent attention of hostile militants on the margins. The Sunningdale power-sharing initiative was destroyed within six months by the contempt in which it was held by the IRA and (more directly) by a politically motivated strike by the loyalist-inspired Ulster Workers' Council. Two decades of searching in vain for a sustainable middle ground were to follow before it eventually dawned on the British authorities in the early 1990s that the militants did indeed need to be brought into the story if progress was to be made. The momentum generated by that insight led eventually to the Good Friday Agreement in 1998.

What of the use made of the criminal law as a device for tackling the extremists on the edges while these years of futile politics were going on? A comparison with West Germany, also much preoccupied with terrorist violence during the 1970s, is instructive. We saw in Chapter 2 how the German authorities went down the rule of law route, eschewing any kind of direct contact with the militants, treating them instead as an extreme sort of criminal who needed to be pursued with the full force of the law, and who (just as importantly) needed always to be seen in this light – as a particularly nasty brand of criminal – by the general public. As we also saw then, this approach could be said, broadly speaking, to have worked. The legal tools used to hound the radicals into oblivion in Germany never departed far (and often not at all) from the mainstream criminal process. The state's efforts to curb their opponents by use of the ordinary law against them were always plausible. Stuck in prison and asserting a political status that convinced no one, it was little surprise that the hunger strike became in Germany a (generally unsuccessful) weapon in the pursuit of minor gains, a way of performing when the stage had shrunk to the four walls of a cell and the audience had in the main long departed.[33]

Such a careful holding of one's nerve was never going to be enough in Northern Ireland. The civil disorder in the Province was far greater, its roots in the community much deeper. While it's true that the German radicals had support from outside the state in the shape of a sympathetic East Germany and the Soviet bloc generally, the IRA had multiple fans in the Republic of Ireland (some occupying high offices of state in the early 1970s and prominent political positions thereafter) and a strong following among Irish-American communities as well. A history of a colonial-style manipulation of the law lay within the living memory of nationalists, and beyond too, into the distant past. That said, the authorities could certainly have been more careful than they were. Facilitated by a report in 1972 by a senior Law Lord with a long history of an association with the security apparatus of the British state,[34] the switch to law was erected on uncertain foundations from the start. True, the hated SPA was finally dispensed with, and much was made of the primacy of the legal process going forward. The effectiveness of the code of law that replaced the SPA was, however, judged to require a wholesale disposal of the principles upon which the British criminal process was said to depend: a switching of the burden of proof to defendants in many cases; an end to jury trial for 'terrorist' cases; and (in later years) a multiplicity of new and vague offences, and an expansion of the inchoate nature of many offences.

77

During the very violent early 1970s, the reality on the ground was that the securing of successful convictions was facilitated by the ill-treatment of suspects when in police custody, and by the tactical use of informants to underpin the pursuit of suspects in single trials that involved masses of prisoners crowded in the dock. At the back of nationalist minds was an awareness that even during this period of the supposed primacy of law, the state was being regularly tempted into extra-legal actions – not just stop, search and arrest as forms of unlawful harassment, but a secret 'intelligence war' as well.[35] State killings were facilitated by a ruling in favour of self-defence where a soldier had shot dead a person running from them, a judgment handed down by the very same judge whose report had precipitated the switch from the military to the legal in 1972.[36] Various 'shoot to kill' controversies, complete with sometimes desperate state action to cover them up, remained a feature of 'the Troubles' through to their end, as did the miscarriages of justice that did so much to destabilize the British judicial system at the end of the 1980s.[37] It was little wonder that, embedded in their militarized courtrooms, Northern Ireland judges should have become prime IRA targets, just as lawyers representing suspected IRA prisoners became targets of murderous loyalist gangs that (as we now know) were often working in tandem with the security state.[38]

This was not the rule of law. It had no credible connection with the virtues supposedly secured by deployment of the term. The British use of law in Northern Ireland in the 1970s and 1980s had more in common with its colonial antecedents than with the ordinary criminal law in the (often irritatingly described) mainland (of Great Britain): it was transparently a means of waging war through, rather than subject to, law.[39] Despite being targets themselves, Northern Ireland's judges did their best with the cards they were dealt, but the appellate courts in London were always on hand to curb any liberal excess.[40] This was Ireland, after all; British perhaps, but not British in a truly British sense. When protests at their criminal status led IRA prisoners into a series of hunger strikes, culminating in the death of thirteen inmates in the harrowing spring and summer of 1981, the nationalist community – northern Irish, Irish and further afield – saw a sacrifice that they could understand, not criminals intent on suicide by proxy. The hunger strikes generated vast support for the republican cause, with (as in 1918) nationalist opinion making use of Westminster elections to make their point: the lead hunger striker Bobby

Sands was elected an MP shortly before his death, with the by-election that followed being won by his election agent. In what would have been a bitter irony to Sands and his cohort of sacrificial absolutists, their very success generated a mass following that was soon to find political expression in a party (Sinn Féin) that gradually accommodated itself to the reality of a partitioned island and, having done so, worked tirelessly and eventually successfully to achieve political power within it.

How was the 'terrorist' political violence of Northern Ireland brought to an end? The key initiative, involving the extremists in solution planning, has already been referred to. It is clear that neither the military nor the implausible criminal approaches of the British state had any kind of significant role to play, and of course the option of total obliteration by military force was never on the table, not even in 1920 and certainly not by the 1970s. It was the administration of prime minister John Major in the early and mid-1990s that eventually gave up on the failed search for a solution involving only non-violent political actors, seeking behind the scenes and with great patience to draw Sinn Féin into talks with the intention of securing a cessation of violence so as to allow negotiations to take place without fear of atrocity.[41] Major was, however, unable to deliver on his policy; his Conservative Party had too many imperial memories within its DNA to contemplate such a 'betrayal' of the 'loyalist' community in the North – true Brits rather than colonial expats. It was left to the radical reformer, Labour's Tony Blair, to deliver the outcome for which Major had yearned: a reliable cessation of violence, followed by talks involving all the political parties (and not just those who could be depended upon to condemn 'terrorist atrocities'), culminating in a nuanced agreement seeking (and brilliantly succeeding) in balancing all interests in a final document (deliberately illegible at the edges) with which all parties could live. The lever of law had a role to play but it was now a consciously benign one from the nationalist perspective: wholesale reform of Northern Ireland's police; a guarantee of human rights for all; the release of paramilitary prisoners from jail – far, in other words, from the usual staple of anti-terrorism excess. There was also the promise of a legal guarantee of a referendum on a united Ireland if the province looked as though it was inclining in that direction. Accompanying these liberal reforms, and playing at least as significant a part, were the external guarantors of the agreement in the shape of a supportive European

Union and an American administration alive to the domestic political value for it of delivering peace in Ireland. Vital too was the courage of the Blair administration, and the prime minister personally, in resisting over-reaction to atrocities designed by rejectionists on the margins (as in 1973) to make first the talks and then the agreement politically impossible to sustain.[42] When the 'politics of the last atrocity' lost their force, everything became possible. Once symbolic violence loses its power to symbolize anything other than the user's own weakness and directionless cruelty, the coast is clear for compromise.

The failure of the colonial analogy

For all its strength, soft civil support and rootedness in history, IRA violence did not achieve its goal of a united Ireland. After a brief wobble in the early 1970s, the United Kingdom proved to be too resiliently embedded as a state of various nations to allow the dismemberment of its remaining Irish limb. Nor did the story the IRA and its supporters told carry sufficient power to divert attention from the killing and the destruction deployed to get that narrative before its desired audiences: there were always nationalist alternatives to the bombs and the bullets. British violence played its part too, or rather (to be counter-intuitive) the lack of violence: for all their dirty tricks, their assassinations and their twisting of the law, the occasional atrocity aside, the extreme brutality of the colonial responses to insurgency was not seen in Ireland, certainly not after 1972. It is significant in a positive way that the greatest reach achieved by the IRA campaign was through the self-destruction of Bobby Sands and his fellow hunger strikers rather than through indiscriminate state violence (though internment and Bloody Sunday in 1972 came close). There was, simply put, not enough in the message to cut through to deliver the IRA goal in the absence of massively misguided retaliation from the British forces, and, despite the inevitable military hotheads calling for the arm behind the soldier's back to be 'untied' so as to 'finish the job', it was a retaliation that never came.

The same fate awaited other rebellious forces seeking to carve their own state out of a settled democratic entity with a past as a colonial power. The closest analogy to Northern Ireland is the Basque region of Spain, an ancient territory sprawling into France and with a long separatist identity: its mainstream nationalist party (the PNV) was founded in 1895. The Basque Euskadi ta Askatasuna ('Basque Country and Freedom' or ETA) split from the PNV in 1959 and developed a radical perspective inspired by 'Africa's and Asia's successful anti-colonialist movements against powerful empires and their colonial rule'.[43] Just as was the case in Northern Ireland, the violence started in 1968, targeting police and others deemed complicit in the oppression of the Basque people. These targets included, most famously, Admiral Luis Carrero Blanco, heir apparent to long-time fascist leader General Franco, killed in a huge explosion while travelling by car to Mass in Madrid in December 1973. In a familiar trajectory for such subversive groups, such accuracy could not be sustained. The bombing in Madrid in September 1974 of a café used from time to time by the security police – which injured eighty and killed thirteen, all but one of the casualties being civilians – 'triggered a slow, gradual change in the public perception of ETA'.[44] The achievement of a democratic system of government after Franco's death in 1975 did not end ETA resistance, but complicated further its effort to explain itself as a mass movement engaged in justified military action against an oppressor 'colonial' state. Continued violence involving non-culpable civilians made the picture even grimmer.

Newly democratic Spain faced similar challenges to those of the British in Ireland.[45] Efforts to build 'Sunningdale'-type agreements involving only moderates foundered on ETA's determination to refuse anything short of Basque independence: 'To them, the game was not between dictatorship and democracy in the form of Basque regional autonomy, but rather between Spanish colonisation and Basque independence.'[46] Arbitrary police violence continued through the late 1970s and into the 1980s with government complicity in deliberate killings by a police unit (Grupos Antiterroristas de Liberación – GAL) being exposed many years later. As Mees notes, again echoing counterproductive British tactics in Ireland, '[t]here is no doubt that these illegal practices in the fight against ETA terrorism provoked the opposite of their intended effect'.[47] In 1978 the Herri Batasuna (HB, Popular Unity) party was founded as a political outrider to ETA's more military face, and over time the same pattern of secret talks, sporadic ceasefires and inclusive negotiations as occurred in Ireland appeared to be cumulatively persuasive as to the counterproductivity of the militants' campaign. This is where the Irish analogy ends: ETA persisted in their military strategy past expected moments of reconciliation, duly provoking intense police reaction and the banning of HB, a decision upheld by the European Court of Human Rights in Strasbourg.[48] The organization never quite pulled off the connection with politics that the IRA had achieved, and its diasporic community was neither as large nor as well-disposed to the armed struggle as were those many who traced their origins back to Ireland. When in the mid-2000s yet another laboriously contrived ceasefire broke down, the pointlessness of the return to violence was by now unmissable, even to its erstwhile supporters. Further secret interactions between governments and militants followed, inspired by the example of the Good Friday Agreement and supported by declarations of commitment to an effective peace process by external backers. The habit of militancy gradually foundered on its own contradictions. ETA finally disappeared in May 2018, signing off with one last piece of self-regarding rhetoric: 'ETA was born from the people, and now it dissolves into the people.'[49]

One Irish constitutionalist nationalist politician memorably described the Good Friday Agreement as 'Sunningdale for slow learners'.[50] The negotiations that eventually took ETA out of its militant groove in 2018 could likewise be described as 'the Good Friday Agreement for even slower learners'. The combination of secret diplomacy and international backing, combined with governmental patience and self-control, eventually secured a political dividend in the shape of lasting peace. As with Northern Ireland, illegal practices by state actors were hard to avoid and indeed were occasionally condoned as useful tactics in the long war, but they were invariably counter-productive in strategic terms, never remaining covert for long, breeding estrangement in the militants' target market, and so generally setting back the chances of a final settlement. The Catalonian independence movement of recent years appears not to have developed any kind of coherent military side – an indication perhaps of an awareness, rooted in the ETA example, of the ineffectiveness of such violence. It has been the same with the recent movement towards independence in Scotland, and insofar as there ever was a serious drive for Wales's independence it was embarrassed rather than energized by the sporadic burning of English-owned homes in the Principality that was its brief signature-tune. Irish nationalism now also expresses itself in primarily constitutional terms.

Other efforts to detach from old colonial powers have barely regis-
tered. The National Liberation Front of Corsica seeking freedom from
France has been one example, the South Tyrolean independence movement pushing for unification with Austria or even (on some accounts)
a free state is another. Eccentric efforts by Puerto Rican nationalists to
liberate their territory from American control, productive of a series
of self-defeating violent actions within the US in the 1970s and early
1980s, was another. The determination of South Moluccans from the
isle of Amboa to reject Indonesia and declare their own republic led to a
curious, violent cameo in the Netherlands in the late 1960s–70s, ending
in 1978 after a series of highly publicized events incurred the wrath
of their own community.[51] Among the older erstwhile colonies whose
long-standing freedom and relative prosperity resemble the condition of
the former colonial states, only Canada has had to deal with a secessionist movement backed by violence serious enough to challenge (briefly)
the integrity of state institutions. This was the Front de Liberation du
Québec (FLQ), whose sporadically high-profile violence included the
kidnapping in October 1970 of the politician Pierre Laporte (who was
murdered by his captors) and a British diplomat James Cross (released
after sixty days). The actions of the organization precipitated deployment
of emergency 'wartime' measures and the use of a variety of illegal activities by the security service which upon their discovery led eventually to
radical reform of the Canadian security agencies.[52]

Conclusion

The homeland within a settled liberal democratic state that is only
ambiguously committed to its parent sovereignty is a perennial problem
in the management of political power in many countries. Every now
and again the estrangement is such as to produce a violent reaction from
sufficient numbers of the sub-state entity so as to challenge the security
of the state's institutions. This chapter is about those examples, and
though few in number such violent dissidents have been productive (the
IRA and ETA in particular) of meaning in the field of anti-terrorism
law and practice. We saw in Chapter 1 how the language of terrorism
was used to describe anti-colonial insurgency across Europe's declining
twentieth-century empires, and indeed was expressly deployed to explain

and justify nationwide prevention of violence legislation aimed at the IRA and enacted by the UK Parliament in 1939.[53] It was also the case with similar legislation enacted in 1974 to counter the IRA's renewed campaign on the British 'mainland', now explicitly named as 'prevention of terrorism' legislation.[54] The other examples mentioned in this chapter increasingly took on the character of 'terrorist' events as that language embedded itself more and more from the early 1970s onwards.

Yet if this language of 'terrorism' seems to suggest a problem of violence with shared characteristics wherever it occurred, then the stories told here undermine that assumption. They are all specific to their circumstances: even the IRA and ETA (the closest comparators) needed to be addressed in different ways and, perhaps it goes without saying, very little (if anything) bonded the Puerto Ricans with the South Moluccans, the Corsicans with the FLQ of Quebec, and so on. This was understood to be true at the time, just as it was with the ideological subversives discussed in Chapter 2. True, the political capital to be gained by making spurious linkages was on occasion not resisted, and of course the groups themselves were also tempted to present themselves as larger (more international) than their provincial selves, 'to big themselves up' on a global stage where they were in reality small-time actors. But the problems they created could only be successfully resolved if their particularity was taken fully into account, if the global were set aside and the local put front and centre. Swirling around all the conflicts in the late 1960s and 1970s that we have discussed in this and the preceding chapter was, however, a new language of global terror, one with great energy behind it and a determination to generate an understanding of the subject of terrorism as one that was without borders, without nuance, without any strand of justificatory meaning. It is to the epicentre of the language of terrorism (and therefore of anti-terrorism) that we now must turn, the place where the idea of 'global terror' was successfully forged: the Middle East.

FOUR

Terrorism Goes Global: The Case of Palestine

Introduction

We ended the last chapter on a deliberately local note. The campaigns by the IRA and ETA, and by the other groups we touched on, were all driven by geography and provincial ambition. A bit of land was sought by groups claiming to represent the people who lived on it. Foreign support was gratefully accepted but not a *sine qua non* of operational effectiveness. The violence wrought was either focused on the territory under dispute or deliberately deployed in the heartland of the 'enemy' – Madrid for example (where General Blanco was killed), Montreal (the site of the FLQ's most notorious actions) or London and other British cities (the focus of various IRA attacks over the years). Targets abroad were occasional and centred on their opponents' military forces (albeit – inevitably – mistakes were made: the IRA killed a major-general in Germany in 1990 but a week before had killed two Australian tourists in the Netherlands, mistaking them for British soldiers). None of these various actions amounted to anything grander than what they appeared to be – efforts to secure via the technique of communicative violence an outcome to a conflict which none of the groups was strong enough to deliver by way of orthodox military action. It was the same for the organizations discussed in earlier chapters: the radical leftists behind the ideological violence of the late 1960s and early 1970s may have hankered after global solidarity in pursuit of their idealistic, anti-capitalist ends, but the reality was altogether more prosaic – a small group of embattled individuals fighting a losing battle in their effort to ignite local populations in their support; a different kind of provincialism to that of the IRAs and ETAs of this world, but provincial nonetheless. There was no hint in any of this of anything that crossed borders into a global sphere, with a threat transcending the local.

Palestine changed this assumption about the localism of this kind of political violence, both in terms of what the equivalent sub-state groups in the region were prepared to do and how the state most threatened by them (Israel) reacted to their actions. The 'terrorism' crisis in the region came to the fore in the late 1960s and early 1970s but had of course a longer history. The Israeli–Palestinian conflict was a complex problem of land possession, growing out of a (British) imperial past but with two local communities jostling for the decolonized prize of, as one side saw it, a unified free Palestine, or as the other put it, a viable independent state in which Jewish people could finally locate in a place they could call home. The first of these communities, the Palestinians, claimed the land as of right by virtue of long possession; the second on account of their religious commitment to an ancient homeland, supported by the Zionist ideas developed by Theodor Herzl and others in the last decades of the nineteenth century. Directly after the Second World War, empowered by the tragedy of the Holocaust, the latter group's Zionism came to be articulated as a commitment to a new state of Israel. It is to the bitter battle for space launched by the UN's failed attempt at the partition of Palestine in 1948[1] that our contemporary understanding of terrorism owes its origins; without it we would not have had the language to understand the attacks of 11 September 2001 as demanding a 'global war on terror'. The roots of today's anti-terrorism laws may indeed be found in the colonial and Cold War pasts discussed in earlier chapters, but it is via Israel's answer to the Palestinian question that our subject comes of age.

Rival sovereignties

We have already noted how during the inter-war period the British authorities had to manage the rejection by the local people in Palestine (or at least large sections of them) of colonial rule. The high point of this was the 'Arab Revolt' of 1936–9, in which the traditional anti-imperialist engagement of the insurgents was even then complicated by the presence on the scene of a third party – a Jewish community whose numbers had grown over the previous twenty years and whose landholdings had also increased, to the point where they could credibly lay claim to a stake in the future of the region. In 1937, a British commission chaired by Lord Robert Peel[2] floated partition as a possible solution: 'while neither race can justly rule all Palestine, we see no reason why, if it were practicable, each race should not rule part of it'.[3] The partition was finally agreed by the United Nations in 1947 and took effect the following year. It was, however, immediately submerged in a bitter and violent struggle. In the years since the Arab Revolt, there had been a sharp escalation in Zionist-related political violence, in particular from two organizations on the fringes of the wider Zionist resistance (represented by the Haganah), the Stern Gang and Irgun Zvai Leumi. The first of these outriders included future Israeli prime minister Yitzhak Shamir among their number and was responsible for various acts of isolated subversive violence, most notoriously the assassination in 1944 of Lord Moyne, the British minister of state in the Middle East. The second, the Irgun Zvai Leumi, was run by another future Israeli premier, Menachem Begin, and is most remembered for the 1946 bombing of the King David hotel in Jerusalem, in one of the wings of which the British administration had based itself. Of the ninety-one people killed in that attack, twenty-one were senior government officials, thirteen were soldiers and three were police officers: the remaining fifty-four were a miscellany of civilians caught in the wrong place at the wrong time.[4]

It was into this atmosphere of violence that the UN plan was expected to insert itself, but those responsible for it had no capacity to exert any kind of controlling grip on the rival expectations of the populations. In particular, the Zionist view of the agreed partition not as a settled fact but as a staging post en route to a greater Israel drove the speedy imposition of new facts on the ground. This was resisted by neighbouring Arab states for many of whose leaders the very fact of a new Israeli entity in the region was anathema, UN or no UN. The rigorous, part defensive (but also part ambitiously expansionist) instincts of the new Israeli state soon saw the forced flight of tens of thousands of Palestinians. Atrocities added to the general terror and (in the minds of Palestinians) the imperative of escape; for example, in April 1948 Irgun and the Stern Gang attacked a small Arab settlement (Deir Yassin) awkwardly placed between Jerusalem and Tel Aviv, killing two-thirds of its inhabitants. When the dust settled early in 1949, Zionist control of Palestine had increased from their allocated 57 per cent to 77 per cent of the country, with hundreds of thousands of Arab inhabitants displaced. The proposed Palestinian state never got off the ground, with the fragments left over after Israeli expansion coming under the control of Jordan (to the east) and Egypt (to the west). When in the autumn of 1948 the UN mediator Count Folke Bernadotte expressed concern about the way the Arabs were being treated, the Stern Gang shot him dead.

What followed were twenty years of violence and counter-violence, with the occasional Palestinian atrocity being met by a dependably overwhelming Israeli response. In 1953, the killing of a Jewish mother and her two children in a grenade attack by Palestinian militants who had infiltrated into Israel from Jordan provoked the destruction of the entire West Bank village of Qibya (close to where the killers were said to have come from). Some seventy of Qibya's inhabitants died. The operation was carried out by special army forces, led by yet another future prime minister, Ariel Sharon, and the denial of official complicity by the Israeli government was widely disbelieved. There were no doubts as to army involvement in the killing three years later – in the Arab village of Kafr Qasem, close to the border between Israel and Jordan's West Bank – of some forty-eight local inhabitants following the declaration of a curfew of which the villagers were largely unaware (not enough notice having been given of its existence). The soldiers involved were subsequently prosecuted and given long prison sentences, only to be released within a year. As we can see from this, while in theory the rule of law operated to control the counter-insurgency instincts (and indeed raw criminality) of the Israeli defence forces, a combination of deniability and executive solidarity with wrongdoers meant that in practice it had little or no meaning.

The killings at Kafr Qasem took place on the eve of a second Arab–Israeli war, one in which the old imperial powers France and the United Kingdom were also involved, and which was initiated by an invasion, in late October 1956, of Egypt by Israeli forces. The *casus belli* was the nationalization by Egypt's leader General Nasser of his country's strategically vital Suez Canal; in the crisis that followed, the intentions of the three invading parties were foiled by universal condemnation, led (crucially) by the United States. Though short lived, this 1956 war was a reminder that, in the context of the Middle East, old-fashioned 'terrorism' and 'counter-terrorism' have always shared the stage with conventional war. It was to this traditional form of violence that Israel turned once again in 1967 when it responded to aggressive naval manoeuvres orchestrated by President Nasser with a series of devastating moves both in the air and on the ground that destroyed Egypt's air force and debilitated its ground forces. With Syria and Jordan also caught up in the fighting, the result came after only six days and was definitive: an overwhelming victory for Israel over its neighbours. The spoils of war were vast: the Gaza Strip and Sinai from Egypt, the Golan Heights from Syria and the entire West Bank from Jordan. A United Nations Security Council resolution, adopted unanimously in November 1967, noted the 'inadmissibility of the acquisition of territory by war', and committed all parties to negotiation leading to an end of Israel's occupation of the lands it had secured.[5] By now the Palestine of 1948 had receded further into the realms of the imaginary, and after 1967 it was without even the notionally sympathetic host states that had provided homes after the post-partition losses of that war. From then on it was the undoing of the 1967 rather than the 1948–9 land acquisitions that became the new reasonable option for those resisting Israeli expansion.

Terror

What were the Palestinians to do? The Palestine Liberation Organization (PLO) had been established in 1964 as an umbrella group for dissident Palestinian groups. At the same time, and linked to the PLO, a movement emerged which captured the mood of desolation felt by many Palestinian people, Harakah al-Tahrir al-Falastini, or (to give it its better-known name) Fatah. The small group of fedayeen ('the men who sacrificed themselves') who gathered around the Fatah leader Yasser Arafat preached the violent destruction of Israel and a securing by force of the whole of what they were convinced was their exclusive homeland. In those very early days there were occasional incursions into Israel but nothing consistent or particularly troubling from Israel's point of view. After the West Bank came under Israeli control, Arafat and his fighters promptly sought to emulate the success of insurgents in other colonial-style situations. He and his fighters attempted the tactics of the guerrilla: hiding, engaging the enemy forces in combat, and then melting back into what they anticipated would be a sympathetic environment. But the West Bank did not yield to the then prevailing guerrilla paradigm. After a series of defeats, Arafat and the PLO that he now controlled were forced out of the territory. By 1968, Palestine stood alone, fully gone from all maps, disowned or increasingly disliked by the defeated Arab states around them. The drift towards symbolic, communicative violence gathered pace; 'the tragedies of their own people now inoculated them against the hurt they began to impose on others'.[6]

At the start the focus was on domestic targets, with little if any regard paid to whether these were military or civilian. In March 1968 an Israeli school bus in the Negev desert hit a mine, killing two and injuring some twenty-eight children, an action that provoked an Israeli retaliation against Jordan and non-state 'marauders' which in turn led to unanimous condemnation of Israel at the UN Security Council.[7] In November that year a bomb was detonated in a crowded marketplace in Jerusalem, killing twelve (ten of them Jewish) and injuring fifty-five; the explosive had been concealed in a parked car. Three months later, also in Jerusalem, two young people were killed when a bomb was placed in a crowded supermarket where Jewish shoppers were buying provisions in large numbers in anticipation of the approaching Sabbath. The following year there were attacks on the Hebrew University of Jerusalem and the central bus station in Tel Aviv. Violent incidents in the occupied territories were also occurring at this time, more frequently, and often equally fatal. The Israeli defence forces continued their policy of disproportionate retaliation involving punishments that were not always focused on those specifically responsible: the number of house demolitions was disputed, but that they were on a large scale during this period was undeniable. Nor were their actions restricted to their own jurisdiction. Palestinian bases in both Lebanon and Jordan were always vulnerable to raids from the Israeli air forces, whose effortless aerial supremacy (confirmed after the Six-Day War) meant that such retribution came with little or no immediate cost to the military personnel involved. As with the house demolitions, such rigorous Israeli action inevitably affected many who were not in any way (directly or indirectly) involved in Palestine's Arafat-led quarrel with Israel. In December 1968, an Israeli raid on Beirut airport involving eight helicopters and the deployment on the ground of military commandos led to the destruction of thirteen planes owned by Arab airlines. An Israeli air strike killed eighteen civilians in a town north of Amman in Jordan in March 1969 and led to a strong Security Council resolution censuring Israel; however, the United States and the United Kingdom abstained (together with Colombia and Paraguay).[8]

The Beirut airport raid was explicitly stated to be in response to an expansion by the PLO and affiliated groups of the range of their potential targets. There had long been a temptation to spread the message of Palestinian oppression directly into the homelands of a seemingly indifferent European audience,[9] but in these early days the targets remained Israeli-related (albeit not governmental). In the summer of 1968, an explosion in the London offices of an Israeli shipping company injured two people. In the following months the Brussels office of the Israeli airline El Al was bombed and (in an unusual direct attack on the state) grenades were thrown at the Israeli embassies in the Hague and Bonn. In November the same year, an attack on El Al offices in Athens wounded fourteen and killed a two-year-old boy. A new group, the Palestine Popular Struggle Front, claimed responsibility for the last of these attacks. Around this time, air traffic began proving to be an increasingly tempting target. Fast-moving developments in flight technology were making such travel increasingly accessible to a wider public and without (yet) much security regulating its use. There was also another factor driving the turn to the air now made by Palestinian groups: the mainstream television news media were enjoying both much larger audiences (due to the increased availability of televisions) and a vastly improved capacity (due to improved technology) to report on events as they happened.[10] The temptation to lay on subversive mini-dramas for political communication purposes was impossible to resist. As early as July 1968, another of the violent groups on the fringes of the PLO, Dr George Habash's Popular Front for the Liberation of Palestine (PFLP), had hijacked an Israeli commercial airliner en route to Tel Aviv from Rome. Negotiations involving the Red Cross and the Italian and Algerian governments led to a promise from Israel to release sixteen convicted Arab infiltrators captured prior to the Six-Day War, and so crew and passengers were released unharmed. Here was a tactic that seemed to be capable of securing not only publicity for the cause but also tactical wins like this release of prisoners, all without loss of life.

As the Athens attack showed, however, a benign scenario along these lines was always going to be unlikely so far as the avoidance of casualties was concerned. On 26 December 1968, a further attack in Athens (by PFLP operatives), on an Israeli airliner at the airport, led to the death of a passenger; two months later, yet another El Al flight, this time in Zurich, was targeted with guns and grenades, leading to the death of the pilot and one of the assailants, and causing injury to a number of civilians caught up in the cross-fire. The Israeli Beirut aerial attack in late December 1968, mentioned above, came just two days after the Athens action, and was specifically linked to it (and other similar assaults) by the Israeli authorities. Undeterred, the Palestinian attacks continued. Early in 1970, in Munich, grenades thrown in an airport departure lounge, and at an airport bus crowded with passengers being taken to an El Al flight, killed one and injured eleven. And why stop at El Al, especially as the flagship Israeli carrier was (hardly surprisingly) speedily improving its security and so reducing its exposure to attack? In a move that we have already seen in earlier chapters of this book – and by now would be right to think of as dispiritingly predictable – the reaction to improved protection from attack was simply to spread the range of the culpable. There had already been clear indications of this new approach when a passenger airliner operated by the US-based company TWA was hijacked over southern Italy in August 1969; the PFLP operatives took the plane to Damascus where, in a deal brokered by Syria, all the hostages were freed in return for the release of thirteen of its nationals from Israeli jails.

In September 1970, the tactic of air-hijacking in pursuit of the Palestinian cause grabbed more global attention than even its most optimistic protagonists might have desired. In an action that was in some ways anticipatory of 9/11 some three decades later, members of the PFLP managed on the same day to take simultaneous control of three jet airliners bound for New York from Europe, securing no fewer than (in total) 475 hostages. (A fourth hijack effort was unsuccessful.) One of the planes was flown to Cairo, emptied of all passengers and airline staff and blown up. The remaining two were landed at Dawson's Field, a deserted airstrip in Jordan, where they were soon joined by a further flight, a British VC-10 containing over a hundred passengers and crew. There followed several days of tense negotiations overseen by the Red Cross, all played out on the television screens of (among others) American and European viewers aghast at the thought that this could easily have been them. Several Palestinian-supporting detainees were released from prisons in West Germany, Switzerland and the United Kingdom; in return, all hostages were released unharmed. As a final coup-de-théâtre, the hijackers blew up all three stranded airliners before making their escape.

What kind of legal response to such violence was appropriate? The nightmare for European states was the unwanted consequences that flowed from the successful prosecutions of captured Palestinians for the obvious breaches of criminal law that were inevitably committed by them in the course of their subversive actions: as we have seen with the demands made in many of the events detailed so far, the imprisonment of such people merely incentivized further action against their reluctant jailers. The Dawson's Field actions secured the release from a British jail of the unsuccessful hijacker of the fourth flight, Leila Khaled, an executive decision that was directly ordered by the UK prime minister despite strong objections from the US administration. When a Swiss airliner was blown up in February 1970 (with forty-seven fatalities), it was widely believed to have been an act of revenge for the imprisonment of Palestinians following the February 1969 Zurich attack. Despite an official enquiry reportedly identifying the PLO as responsible, no action was taken, and suggestions have recently been made of a secret deal between the Swiss government and the PLO to ensure no further such attacks.[11] The legal position adopted by the Israelis with regard to their strategy of responding with aerial attacks into neighbouring countries was squarely based on a principle of retaliation that, as we have seen, had framed their reaction to Palestinian-inspired violence since the foundation of the state. With its indiscriminate approach to the damage it did, and the casual attitude it took to the status of its victims, the 'principle' (if that is what it was) could not be easily grounded in international law. The orthodox view was that such reactive engagements were entirely prohibited by the UN Charter and could only with great difficulty be conjured out of customary international law, and even then in a way that did not fit with Israeli practice in the region.[12] King Hussein of Jordan took an even more radical line than the Israelis, initiating a large-scale military effort against the militant Palestinian presence in his country even before the Dawson's Field episode had concluded. After over a year of bitter fighting, approximating at times the level of a civil war, the PLO and its affiliate organizations found themselves driven out of Jordan.

The result of Hussein's action was that by the autumn of 1971 the PLO were without a regional base in Jordan while being also largely shunned by their other immediate neighbours. Yet more loosely connected groups bubbled to the surface of its porous organizational structures, each more violent than the last. One such, Black September, announced itself with the November 1971 assassination of a primary architect of the PLO defeat in Jordan, Wasfi al-Tal, the Jordanian prime minister. In the two years that followed, Black September joined with the PFLP and other affiliates (including the exotically named but terrifying-to-encounter Japanese Red Army) greatly to escalate the random killing of civilians at airports across Europe and (when the chance presented itself) in Israel (such as the killing of some twenty-six people at Lod airport in Tel Aviv in May 1972). A bloody high point – but not the culmination – of this crescendo of violence was Black September's taking of nine Israeli athletes as hostages, an operation achieved with cruel daring during the 1972 Olympic Games in Munich in which their victims were participating (two further members of the team had been killed at the start of the action). The by now usual demand for the release of prisoners followed: on this occasion, over 200 detainees in Israeli prisons. The Israelis refused to engage and after a tense negotiation the German authorities appeared to come to an agreement involving the offer of a safe passage to Cairo. This was a trap, but one that in its execution was imperfectly sprung – in a gun battle at Munich airport all the hostages, five of the Palestinians and a German police officer were killed. (The surviving Palestinians were shortly afterwards released by the German authorities following the hijacking of a Lufthansa jet and the threat to blow up its crew and passengers.)

The violence continued through the early to mid-1970s, spiralling beyond Arafat's control and now greatly affecting his emerging desire to put the destruction to one side and engage on the diplomatic (as well as) military front. By this point, however, there were more than enough Palestinian splinter groups to maintain the bloody momentum without any need to rely on Arafat's PLO; indeed, many of these saw themselves as dedicated to exposing what they saw as the traitorous turn to peace represented by Arafat's recourse to diplomacy.[13] During the 1970s and into the early 1980s the extent of renegade Palestinian violence appeared unrelenting. This was the case both in Israel – with the 1974 Passover massacre at Kiryat Shimona in which eighteen Israelis (including eight children) died and the Ma'alot massacre the same year in which twenty-five Israeli hostages were eventually killed (twenty-two of them children) – and around the world, where hijackings and other performative acts of violence continued. Not for the first time in the history of subversive violence – and not for the last – the spiral of such violence proved impossible to contain by those who had initiated its first rounds. Efforts by the PLO and Yasser Arafat to disassociate themselves proved largely unavailing: the genie of violence was now well and truly out of the bottle, and through the mid-1970s it found itself increasingly being described in a new and (for the PLO) very damaging way.

The arrival of 'international terrorism'

When Israel justified itself to the United Nations Security Council after the Beirut airport raid in December 1968, it accused Lebanon 'of assisting and abetting acts of warfare, violence, and terror by irregular forces and organisations'[14] – 'terror' was still a thing enemy ('irregular') groups did. This was what was to change in the early 1970s. In a persuasive treatment of the field, *Disciplining Terror*, Lisa Stampnitzky has tracked how (as her subtitle puts it) 'Experts Invented "Terrorism"'.[15] During the 1960s, the descriptive word of choice for politically motivated violent subversion in colonial contexts had come to be 'insurgency'. Emerging out of the anti-imperial milieu – where, as we saw in Chapter 1, 'terrorism' had undoubtedly played a role as an abusive label to be affixed to a state's anti-colonial antagonists – this more modern discourse of insurgency now evolved in a way that was able to free itself of the dead hand of imperial self-interest. 'Insurgent' was a less value-laden term than 'terrorist' or 'bandit', or any of the other terms with which colonial power had sought to cloak their colonial opponents. This more neutral idea of insurgency came to the fore because imperialism was in its death throes at this point; the political weather was being made by the United States, a country that (regardless of its true power globally) had long positioned itself as anti-imperialist. US hegemony was duly reflected in a more benign approach to anti-colonial movements (as long as, of course, these aspirant liberators were content to remain within America's embrace).

In marked contrast to old-style colonial anti-terrorism laws, the counter-insurgency discourse of the 1960s was 'primarily conceived as a tactical and strategic opposition, and not generally a moral one'.[16] Those engaged in seeking to control insurgency expressed respect for their opponents and many acknowledged that their struggles emerged out of conditions of injustice and deprivation; for example, at a conference in 1962 organized by Rand (a leading US think-tank), the participants had no difficulty in acknowledging 'problems such as unemployment, inequality and colonialism' as potential drivers of revolt.[17] To the extent that terror showed up in these discussions, it was as a tactic of violence, and one moreover that was available to state and sub-state actor alike.

This moral neutrality did not last. As Stampnitzky puts it, such 'equivalence [between state and rebels] would begin to slip away as the discourse of terrorism took hold'.[18] And take hold it did, dramatically and at high speed. 'A survey of major newspapers and periodical indexes found that neither the *New York Times* index nor the London *Times* index included "terrorism" as a significant category before 1972.'[19] By the end of that decade however, 'authors [had] spilled almost as much ink as the actors of terrorism [had] spilled blood'.[20] 'Within the space of a few years terrorism was transformed from a problem with almost nothing written on it to a topic around which entire institutes, journals, and conferences were organised.'[21] The new journals included: *Terrorism*; *Conflict*; and *the Terrorism, Violence, Insurgency Journal* (*TVI*). Stampnitzky gives details of no fewer than twelve 'important conferences on terrorism' held between 1972 and 1978.[22] One terrorism expert based at SUNY Oneonta, Yonah Alexander, created an Institute for Studies in International Terrorism at his home institution, and between 1976 and 1979 this single professor 'organised at least six conferences' on the topic.[23] The political scientist Paul Wilkinson, later to become the doyen of terrorism studies in the United Kingdom, established a terrorism research centre at the University of St Andrews. Gone was neutral description and sensitivity to place; in was the need to study this assuredly immoral practice and the threat it posed to basic values of decency and democratic freedom around the world. 'Freedom fighters' and even 'guerrillas' were out; 'terrorists' were in.

How did this transformation come about? Looking back, we can see that Munich was a turning point. The world's reaction to it anticipated the response to the (admittedly much larger) Al-Qaeda attacks on the United States on 11 September 2001. The Israeli premier Golda Meir condemned the actions of Black September as 'insane terror' and the US Democratic presidential nominee George McGovern professed himself 'horrified . . . by this senseless act of terrorism'. At this stage, 'terrorism' remained only one word used among many to capture the perceived depravity of the act – 'insane assault' according to the British prime minister Edward Heath; an 'abhorrent crime' which was 'the work of sick minds who do not belong to humanity' (King Hussein of Jordan); 'outlaws who will stop at nothing to accomplish goals' (US President Richard Nixon).[24] Here we can see 'terrorist' mixing it with other (but now diminishing) tropes from the colonial era. One word that did not figure as a descriptive label for those behind the Munich attack was 'insurgents'. In the contemporary equivalent of a suicide video, the Black Septembrists involved had left a 'will', published in Damascus, in which they wrote of their desire for the world to know of the existence of a people 'whose land has been occupied for twenty-four years, whose honour has been trodden underfoot. It will do the world's youth no harm to reflect on the tragedy of this people for a few hours.'[25] But not for the first time in the history of this sort of violence, an appalled public saw only the carnage, not the message it was supposed to convey.

On 18 December 1972, the United Nations General Assembly issued its first resolution on the subject of terrorism. The unwieldy wording of its title reveals both the arrival of this new language, and also its roots in an old-school approach that still saw potential justification in conflict: 'Measures to prevent international terrorism which endangers or takes innocent human lives or jeopardizes fundamental freedoms, and study of the underlying causes of those forms of terrorism and acts of violence which lie in misery, frustration, grievance and despair and which cause some people to sacrifice human lives, including their own, in an attempt to effect radical changes.'[26] The UN was to be dogged by just this tension between action and cause in its many efforts to address the challenge of terrorism over subsequent decades. History was also to show that the kind of ad hoc committee envisaged and established by this resolution (tasking its thirty-five members 'to report with recommendations for possible co-operation for the speedy elimination of the problem'[27]) merely relocated rather than resolved the question of what the right reaction to 'terrorism' should be.

The United States was less squeamish. It 'played a key role in fostering the early growth of terrorism expertise: sponsoring and funding research, organising conferences, and bringing experts and policy makers together'.[28] Shortly after Munich, President Nixon established 'the first official US body charged with focusing on the terrorism problem, the

Cabinet Committee to Combat Terrorism'.[29] From this spun off a variety of official and semi-official (e.g. Rand) engagements with 'terrorism', more particularly 'international terrorism'. At the same time, the experts had by now pretty well entirely forsaken the more neutral language of 'insurgency' and were increasingly loading the new 'terrorism' descriptor with moral content: at one of the Department of State conferences on the subject, this one in 1976, 'the question of whether terrorists could ever be "freedom fighters" was hotly debated, with (according to the official report), the majority of presenters arguing that the categories were mutually exclusive'.[30] In other words, as Stampnitzky puts it, '"terrorism" was in the process of being redefined as a category with *a moral evaluation intrinsically built into it*'.[31] By the late 1970s, apart from occasional sustenance of the idea within the UN, the thought that grievances needed to be discussed had fallen away almost completely, with discussion having now moved on to arenas (such as terrorism as psychopathology, a big theme of the late 1970s) that accepted as foundational its moral obloquy.[32]

While the language of 'international terrorism' was embedding itself more and more in the realm of global public policy, the term was also increasingly coming to be treated as coterminous with Palestinian-inspired global violence. And in a further move, responsibility for that violence was increasingly being affixed not to this or that group but rather to the Palestinian people as such, as well as 'Arabs' in general. Stampnitzky has recovered fascinating exchanges between late Nixon administration officials and congressional representatives, the latter insisting on the 'barbaric' nature of these acts which should be regarded as 'an unspeakable policy in a civilized setting'. Indeed, said the same congressman, 'it has become respectable in some Arab circles to boast of the murder of innocent children', and 'only an unbalanced mind could conceive of acts of terrorism as an acceptable element of any kind of struggle'.[33] It is clear that some kind of elision between 'international terrorism' and Palestine was understandable, inevitable even. There had been the PLO's own violence in the late 1960s and early 1970s, culminating in the Munich operation conducted by its Black September affiliates. And as we have already noted, attacks launched by renegade Palestinian factions were by now coming thick and fast, often reaching new heights of performative engagement: the taking hostage of almost the entire OPEC (Organization of the Petroleum Exporting Countries) leadership in Vienna in 1975; the hijacking of an Air France jet in 1976, producing a dramatic Israeli rescue at Entebbe airport in Uganda; a similarly extraordinary rescue in 1977 (this time by German special forces) of a German passenger aircraft being held in Mogadishu, Somalia;[34] and much else.

These spectacular dramas hogged the news headlines with their stories of civilian terror, 'crazy terrorists' and heroic security responses. They secured vast amounts of airtime not only because of their intrinsic (horrifying) newsworthiness but also because they coincided with a period of relative calm in a post-Vietnam US and in a Western Europe where the only competitors for the same sort of attention were the indigenous violent groups we have discussed in earlier chapters – the Red Army Faction and Red Brigades, the IRA and ETA, and so on. These radical groups, moreover, were often supported by Palestinian militants: in 1972 the Munich hostage-takers had demanded not only the release of many Palestinians from Israeli jails but also freedom for the founders of the original Red Army Faction, Ulrike Meinhof and Andreas Baader. As late as 1977, the Mogadishu hijackers said they wanted Red Army Faction members released from jail. Directly after the operation was conclusively foiled, a number of the Faction's leadership died in prison, apparently in a joint suicide pact (though this explanation has not been universally accepted).

If there was this open goal lying in the field of international diplomacy – that of equating international terrorism with the whole Palestinian (and Arab) world – then it is hardly surprising that it was in the Israeli interest to score, and score they did. The way to get the world to stop talking about Palestinian grievances and their ill-treatment in the occupied territories and so on was to get the world talking instead about a contagion of crazy Palestinian violence across the globe – the madder, the more 'psychopathic', the more incomprehensible the better. It was the tactic of the British empire all over again: the opponent was a rebel without a cause, unhinged, untrustworthy, beyond the realm of human understanding. Those who resisted such irrationality were benign, well-intentioned, playing by civilized rules, replete with democratic and human rights values. Like the colonial authorities in earlier decades (not least in Palestine itself), the Israeli state and its supporters did not have it all their own way, but what made their deployment of the new terrorism discourse especially valuable was the way it inevitably challenged the

PLO's mid-1970s turn to diplomacy – to which we made brief allusion above but on which it is now time to say more. Successes here made embedding the new discourse of terrorism in international affairs and law all the more essential from the Israeli point of view.

Having grabbed the world's attention through the deployment of political violence, from about early 1974 Yasser Arafat pushed ahead with his diplomatic turn, seeking to replace the PLO's violent outbursts with an image of pained victimhood demanding of a just solution. At meetings in February and June that year, under Arafat's guidance, the mainstream Palestinian movement effectively came to terms with the existence of a state of Israel, moving to the margins its determination to destroy entirely its long-term enemy and focusing instead on demands for the creation of a new Palestine. After these major internal breakthroughs, the argument from the Palestinian perspective was ideally thenceforth to be about borders, not existence.[35] The strategy bore immediate fruit. On 14 October 1974, drawing on its embedded anti-colonial narrative rather than the newly re-emerging language of terrorism, the UN General Assembly recognized the PLO as the representative of the Palestinian people, with only eight countries voting against the resolution (the United States, Israel, Chile, Costa Rica, Iceland, Nicaragua and Bolivia).[36] The following week, the French foreign minister, Jean Sauvagnargues, became the most senior European politician to engage with Yasser Arafat, in what was described by a commentator for a Jewish yearbook as a warm meeting after the two had met in Beirut.[37] At the summit conference of the Arab League held in Rabat at the end of October, the PLO's erstwhile bitter opponent King Hussein of Jordan accepted a crucial resolution recognizing the right of the PLO to represent the interests of the Palestinian people in the occupied territories. Then, on 13 November, came the high point of this diplomatic offensive: Arafat was accorded head of state status on his visit to the UN, and from the podium of the General Assembly made his famous claim that he came before the representatives 'bearing an olive branch and a freedom-fighter's gun', going on dramatically to call upon his audience not to 'let the olive branch fall from [his] hand'.[38]

Even if laced through with threats, this moderation sat well in a world in which all nations – rich or poor; formerly imperial or subjugated – were increasingly turning their back on colonial models of governance. But it was bound to be concerning to an Israeli state that had grown well beyond its original, UN-sanctioned size on not one but two occasions, and had done so at a cost to a people who from afar (and possibly also up close) looked very much as subjugated as the colonial subjects of old. The best way to resist Arafat's shrewd diplomatic turn was to declare it to be spurious, and the route to this lay in successfully persuading the world of the double elision earlier referred to: that Palestinian terrorism, rather than being restricted to fanatics on the margins, was a general problem implicating Arafat and his PLO, and that such violence was of a piece with the despised terrorism of the European radicals. Of course, the renegade Palestinian groups were performing exactly as Israel hoped: they kept the pot of violence constantly simmering long after Arafat had wanted it removed altogether from the table, and they kept demanding the release of European extremists jailed for attacks unrelated to the Palestinian cause. A further boost to Israel came with the connection the United States chose to make from the late 1970s onwards (but especially during the Reagan presidency) between Soviet power and 'international terrorism'. Clare Sterling's 1981 book *The Terror Network*, making this exact point, had a significant impact, as did Senate hearings of the Subcommittee on Security and Terrorism between 1981 and 1986, the latter discussed at length by Stampnitzky.[39] The idea here was to subsume the problem of international terror within the Cold War, casting the Soviet Union as the evil driver of chaos through its patronage of terror groups around the world. The direct connection between the wider Palestinian movement and terror via this evil communist Godfather – which was, undeniably, its chief patron on the world stage – was not hard to make, and the Reagan administration made it relentlessly.

The academic juggernaut of 'international terrorism' studies underpinned with apparent scholarly rigour this elision of the Palestinian cause with terrorism and the connection of both with the Soviet Union. Many books in the spirit of Sterling's work appeared. The same, fairly narrow band of experts popped up time and again at the conferences they organized, on tours to promote the books they wrote, and on the many news programmes that sought their views – the mainstream media organizations inviting them on as neutral analysts of (to quote one editor) this 'new barbarism [conducted] not to win territory or even to cause destruction but to command attention, to instil fear, and to terrorize in the hope of forcing the world to listen and to right an alleged wrong'.[40]

Key experts included Yonah Alexander and Benjamin Netanyahu. I have already made a passing reference to the former. On top of his regional work, Alexander also edited *Terrorism: An International Journal* and wrote prolifically on the legal challenge of terrorism around the world, including on legal responses to terrorism in the UK, where he and his co-editor on this work noted how 'various Middle-East factions have carried their quarrels to Britain'.[41] Two critical commentators have identified in his writings 'a close spiritual affinity with the official Israeli and Reagan-era US doctrine' on matters related to terrorism.[42] Alexander was to the fore in pushing what one of the titles of his books aptly summarizes as *Terrorism: The PLO Connection*, in which it was argued (in 1989) that the PLO was 'the leading international terror group' of the past twenty-five years.[43] His *Terrorists or Freedom Fighters?*, co-authored with Eli Tavin,[44] was published in cooperation with the World Zionist Organization, while another, *Terrorism: The Soviet Connection*, 'was distributed freely by the State Department in response to public requests for information on the subject of terrorism'.[45] In his individual contribution, titled 'International Network of Terrorism', to his own co-edited (with Charles K. Ebinger) volume, *Political Terrorism and Energy: The Threat and Response*, Alexander asserted that '[t]he Palestinian movement has provided substantial assistance to various revolutionary organizations such as leftist terrorist cells in Iran, the Eritrean Liberation Front, and the Japanese Red Army. Other recipients include underground groups in Chad, Ireland, Panama, the Philippines, Sardinia and Corsica, and Thailand, to name a few.'[46]

Benjamin Netanyahu is yet another actor in this story who was to go on to become Israeli prime minister, a position which at the time of writing he still holds. Before formally entering politics, Netanyahu was a frequent and highly articulate presenter of the thesis that terrorism was an existential challenge to 'the West', one that had to be seen off if the civilized world was to continue to prosper. A particularly significant volume, edited by Netanyahu, consisted of papers drawn from the proceedings of a conference held in 1979 in Jerusalem, under the aegis of the Jonathan Institute (named in honour of Netanyahu's brother, who had been killed in the course of Israel's otherwise successful raid on Entebbe).[47] This was a key conference in terms of putting the 'problem' of 'international terrorism' on the map. The book covered the range of terrorism problems with which European states were then confronted, but its focus on the Israel–Palestine conflict was clear: among the many Israeli-based contributors was the then prime minister (and former Irgun leader) Menachem Begin, writing on the theme of 'freedom fighters and terrorists'.[48] Among the entries under 'PLO' in the index were the following sub-headings: 'destruction of Israel as goal of'; 'as catalyst for an overall Arab attack on Israel'; 'Soviet support of'; 'PLO's central role in international terrorism'; 'support of African terrorists by'; 'Italian terrorist groups and'; 'Latin American terrorists and'; and much else in a similar vein. Here was a grouping of experts and policy makers who made no distinction between the PLO and the dissident Palestinian groups still involved in terrorism. In his book *Terrorism: How the West Can Win*, published in 1984, Netanyahu, now the Permanent Representative of Israel to the United Nations, asserted that 'terrorism, under whatever guise or pretext, is an inexcusable evil . . . that the West, in short, must resist . . . and ultimately defeat'.[49] The connection between Soviet support for the Palestinian cause was a given, and therefore Soviet support for international terrorism was forcibly asserted and reasserted through the 1980s.

The emergence of anti-terrorism law

When in 1939 the British state had secured extensive executive powers to deal with an IRA that was then active on 'mainland' Britain, it had titled the necessary legislation the Prevention of Violence (Temporary Provisions) Act. The same persistent group found its renewed campaign of violence in Britain during 1972–4 – which culminated in an horrific set of bombings in England's second city Birmingham in November 1974 – stimulating a similar law, but this time entitled the Prevention of Terrorism (Temporary Provisions) Act 1974. The measure was an emergency one, rushed in at a time of great concern about the extreme nature of IRA violence, and empowering the state in various draconian ways to meet the threat it faced. The language of terrorism seemed by late 1974 largely to be taken for granted as the right way to describe such atrocities as those perpetrated by the IRA.

In explaining the bill to Parliament, the Home Secretary Roy Jenkins assured the House of Commons that his government, 'in common with their predecessors, have given the highest priority to measures to combat and to overcome terrorism'.[50] To Lord Harris, introducing the bill in the Lords, the country was embarking 'on what may well be a long struggle to eradicate terrorism from our land'.[51] One MP was 'profoundly troubled by the problem of world terrorism',[52] another thought it a 'worldwide factor in our lives today',[53] while a third considered that in 'a war on terrorism all our people must defend themselves because all are in danger'.[54] In the Lords, the son of a former, long-serving prime minister of Northern Ireland showed that he knew his terrorism history: 'in the world of terrorism we also have a book of the same sort, written by Carlos Marighella. He says, and all terrorists appear to follow him, that the first duty of the terrorist is to provoke repression, thereby creating support and also creating alarm and despondency in the community. They then hope to make life unbearable.'[55]

The criticisms expressed by the shadow Home Secretary Sir Keith Joseph anticipated the future trajectory of the law, initially limited as it was in 1974 to Northern Ireland-based violence:

> We recognise the importance of what the right hon. Gentleman calls the clear and present danger of the IRA as the predominant guide in this legislation, but we ask the Home Secretary to consider whether it may be possible, in this age of terrorism, that other bodies without connection with Northern Ireland may, under cover of apparent Northern Irish outrages, contribute their own terrorism to the national scene. If that be so, the powers of the Bill are sharply limited, and the protection of the public may require that the Government should consider whether to extend their powers to proscribe bodies that carry out terrorism even if they cannot be connected immediately with Northern Ireland.[56]

Whether or not 'under cover' of Northern Ireland this is exactly what happened, with first 'international'[57] and then all domestic as well as international 'terrorism'[58] being embraced within UK terrorism laws. As one Conservative MP was to assert with prophetic accuracy in the original 1974 debates: 'I am perfectly certain that the vast majority of the people of this country are only too ready to suffer some personal inconvenience if it means ridding our society of the cancer of terrorism.'[59]

The same process of embedment occurred across the legal systems of the liberal democracies. In Sweden, a new anti-terrorism law was enacted in 1973, with 254 votes in favour and only twenty-three against.[60] A bomb in Sydney during a regional meeting of Commonwealth heads of government in 1978 killed three, and was routinely described at the time as an act of terrorism, with the legislation that followed shortly afterwards defining the term as 'acts of violence for the purpose of achieving a political objective in Australia or in a foreign country'.[61] Canada had dealt with its FLQ threat (discussed in Chapter 3) through war powers legislation, and the emergency measure that replaced these laws in 1988 stayed clear of the language of terrorism, hinging its provisions more directly on various types of emergencies (public welfare, public order, international, war) than a generalized threat of terrorism. But prosecutions for explicit terrorist-related offences took place nonetheless, even if within traditional legal parameters that left them less effective in securing convictions than (it was suggested) they might otherwise have been.[62] In the United States, the Reagan presidency's emphasis on the problem of global terrorism led to enactment of the Act to Combat International Terrorism in 1984 and the Omnibus Anti-Terrorism Act two years later. Both of these initiatives had international wrongdoing in mind. The World Trade Center bombings in 1993, followed by the destruction of the Alfred P. Murrah federal building in Oklahoma City in 1995, may have had diametrically opposite origins (radical Islam and far-right domestic radicalism, respectively), but each was seen as a subset of a more general 'terrorist' threat, precipitating enactment under the Clinton administration of the 1996 Anti-Terrorism and Effective Death Penalty Act. It was in this decade before the 9/11 attacks that radical Islam fully inserted itself into the 'international terrorist' mix, with Iran replacing the now defunct Soviet Union as terrorist Godfather in chief. This is the subject of our next and final chapter in this part, on the roots of the global war on terror – roots without which the explosive reaction to the 11 September attacks would not have had the reach or durability that it has gone on to enjoy.

FIVE

Fear of the Other: The Rise of Jihadism

Prelude

The last chapter ended with the strong and often explicitly described anti-terrorism laws that were enacted in many countries in the 1970s and into the mid-1990s. During those years, Israel's main diplomatic concern had less to do with managing dissent within its borders (including the occupied territories) than with explaining its frequent extra-territorial actions to what was still, at this time, an often-sceptical global community. Such military incursions in response to Palestinian aggression had, as we have seen, long been a feature of Israel's counter-terrorism strategy, striking against the Palestinian Liberation Organization and other targets in neighbouring countries so as both to disrupt the organization itself and to disincentivize host governments from tolerating Arafat and his associates. The legal basis for such aggressive acts had, however, never been easy plausibly to assert: we have seen how 'retaliation' as a principle of international law had failed to embed itself when deployed to justify Israeli trespass into neighbouring air space in the late 1960s and early 1970s. The Munich Olympics action by Black September had produced an immediate series of aerial assaults on Palestinian targets in Syria and Lebanon, killing unknown numbers of innocent civilians. Over the longer term, Israel launched a covert campaign of assassination ('Operation Wrath of God') of those judged responsible for the Olympic attack; in time, this programme grew into a policy of ongoing elimination of the state's enemies.[1] Retaliation continued to be the underlying rationale for such actions, with the fact that the Wrath of God operation was conducted in secret surely being evidence of (so far as its authors were concerned) its insecure legal foundations.[2]

In 1978, and again in 1982, this supposed Israeli imperative of responding violently to terrorist atrocity took on an entirely new, all-encompassing dimension. Israeli's counter-terrorism policy had never been about an 'eye for an eye', but during this period it was to reach fresh heights of disproportionality, drifting well beyond the reach of any plausible international law explanation. The change in approach began in May 1977, with the election of a new government in Israel. The Likud Party – headed by Menachem Begin, the former leader of the 1940s subversive Jewish group Irgun – secured (by the country's complex electoral standards) a landslide victory. A new, more robust response to Palestinian violence was immediately in the air, particularly that emanating from Israel's northern neighbour Lebanon, the base to which Arafat and his PLO associates had retreated after their effective expulsion from Jordan in 1971 (mentioned in the last chapter). The opportunity – borne out of tragedy – did not take long to arrive: a particularly vicious Fatah attack in early March 1978, on the coast, twenty miles south of Haifa. This botched operation had involved hijacking, hostage-taking and random shooting; in the end, some thirty-eight Israeli civilians were killed (including thirteen children) and over seventy were injured. (Nine of the eleven attackers were also killed.) Four days after the raid, having promised retribution at a press conference immediately following the attack, prime minister Begin ordered 20,000 troops into Lebanon. This large force immediately occupied a swathe of southern Lebanon, some 425 square miles as far north as the Litani River, about one-third of the way to Beirut.

Here was counter-terrorism on a truly grand scale, anticipating the sorts of actions that were to be seen again in Lebanon in 1982 and in Gaza in 2023. Following the usual explanation of the day, the invasion was presented as retribution for the Palestinian attack, but it was also explicitly designed to secure northern Israel against infiltration from the north: 'to clear this infested area once and for all', as the Israeli defence minister Ezer Weizman put it.[3] If retaliation was not available as a legal justification, then it was also hard to root in any plausible set of facts Begin's assertion that the invasion was 'an act of legitimate self-defence'.[4] United Nations' condemnation was eventually followed by an Israeli withdrawal,[5] but not before a proxy army under Sa'ad Haddad had been embedded within Lebanon (in a new Israeli 'security zone') to police the border on Israel's behalf. Haddad's South Lebanon Army (SLA) was later to engage in assaults on UN forces in the region, leading to a number of fatalities among UN personnel and further international condemnation.[6]

As the terminology of state-sponsored terrorism bedded down in the 1980s, Haddad and his army were often described by critics of Israel in exactly these terms.

Four years after this first invasion, and amid further upheavals in the region precipitated by revolution in Iran and the Soviet invasion of Afghanistan, the same Israeli prime minister saw a chance to take the fight against the Palestinians more deeply into Lebanon.[7] Once again terrorism – in this case 'international terrorism' – provided the *casus belli*. A period of violence initiated by the 1978 invasion had culminated in an aerial bombardment of Beirut by Israeli forces which had killed some 300 (with many more injured); the attack was followed by a ceasefire between both sides orchestrated by the United States. Almost from its start, in late July 1981, supposed breaches of that agreement became a running sore, with Israel interpreting the ceasefire as involving a worldwide as well as regional cessation of political violence, something not apparent in the terms in which it was initially announced and also not accepted by the Palestinians.[8] During the first five months of 1982, Israeli language became increasingly bellicose and its threats of 'counter-terrorist' action more and more explicit. When on 3 June the Israeli ambassador to the UK was shot and seriously injured in London (an attack for which the renegade Palestinian faction the Abu Nidhal group was responsible), the Israelis promptly launched 'Operation Peace in Galilee', a now fully-fledged invasion of their northern neighbour. The similarities between this military engagement and the invasion of Gaza forty-one years later are striking.

> On June 6 the massive attack-invasion into Lebanon began and within a week it was estimated that 10,000 people were killed or wounded. The majority of the victims were Palestinian and Lebanese civilians. Some refugee camps were completely destroyed, and a number of towns and cities were reduced in large measure to rubble. There were PLO offices, ammunition dumps or other facilities in some of the population centers . . . but there was no attempt to limit the attack to military objectives as required by the humanitarian law applicable in armed conflict.[9]

Having pushed north in a speedy but brutal fashion, on 10 June the Israeli army laid siege to Beirut. Here was to be found the leadership of the PLO, embedded amid the thousands of Palestinian refugees who were gathered in enormous and inhospitable refugee camps. The Israeli intention was to root out once and for all the Palestinian leadership's presence in the city, with the architect of the operation, defence minister (and yet another future prime minister) Ariel Sharon, determined 'to eradicate PLO resistance'.[10] Sharon's forces did their best to realize his ambition, laying waste to the city in the course of a two-month siege (involving encircling military forces and an effective naval blockade). When hostilities finally ceased in August 1982, the PLO leader being given safe passage from the city with his followers so as to prevent further destruction, the Israelis immediately breached the undertakings they had given to secure Arafat's departure, entering the mainly (and now defence-less) Palestinian west Beirut. Israeli forces then stood by while their Christian Lebanese allies (following the assassination of their leader, and newly elected president, Bashir Gemayel) unleashed a mass killing spree in two of the Palestinian refugee camps in that part of the city, Sabra and Chatila. (It is said that Haddad's SLA were also involved.) The death toll from the whole operation will never be fully known, but is certainly in the thousands.[11]

The legal basis for such extravagant military action was – to put it at its mildest – highly doubtful. The concept of a legally sanctioned act of retali-ation remained as dubious as it had ever been, a point accepted even by scholars who were generally not unsympathetic to the state of Israel.[12] The almost desultory invocation of legitimate self-defence that had been used in 1978 was repeated in 1982, with the idea of 'anticipatory self-defence' now being deployed by Israel's Permanent Representative to the UN Yehuda Blum, albeit this was generally regarded at the time as 'a highly unusual and exceptional doctrine which may only be employed when the evidence shows a threat of imminent armed attack and the necessity to act is overwhelming'.[13] Undeterred, Blum assured the Security Council on the day of the invasion that it was 'imperative for the Government of Israel to exercise its legitimate right of self-defence to protect the lives of its citizens and to ensure their safety'.[14] The main difficulty lay with establishing the necessary proportionality where the action being defended as necessitated by self-defence was required to be judged by the future rather than past conduct of one's adversaries. Only on the longest of long views – one seeing the conflict as ongoing for decades and with past violence backing up chilling predictions of future action – could such an argument be credibly made;[15] but even then it was not obvious that Palestinian violence, however severe, warranted the scorched earth response of a full-scale military invasion with the vast destruction it had entailed in this specific context.[16] The Israeli government remained altogether more at home deploying the language of civilizational struggle – of the war against 'international terrorism' that, as we have seen, had become such a feature of the defence of its actions over the 1970s – than it was in explaining why the invasions of Lebanon did not run counter to one of their self-proclaimed civilizational principles, the rule of law. By the early 1980s, new developments in the region had made Israel's appeal to Western values all the more compelling.

The 'new' terrorism

Prior to the revolution of 1979, Iran had long been a creature of the West, in the shape first of its former imperial master the United Kingdom and afterwards that of the United States. The Pahlavi dynasty that ruled the country for fifty-eight years had started with a coup against the established order in 1921; the individual who had secured power in that operation, Reza Khan, found himself removed from office some twenty years later (after proving himself difficult over allowing Allied supplies through to the Soviet front following Hitler's invasion of the USSR in 1941). Khan was replaced by his son Mohammad Reza Khan, whose sympathies for the British, and afterwards the Americans, proved invaluable to Western power in the decades after the Second World War, particularly as the true extent of the country's gigantic oil reserves became apparent. A radical prime minister, Mohammed Mosaddeq, was forced from power by US and British hostility two years after his nationalization (over the opposition of Khan) of the entire Iranian oil industry in 1951. This successor 'Shah of Iran', as he was titled, remained dependent on Western power for the rest of his reign: by 1976 Iran was the largest single buyer of US arms in the world. For the Americans, only Israel rivalled the Shah's administration in terms of its strategic importance in the region.[17]

When the regime's end came in early 1979, it was sudden, dramatic and complete. Led by the charismatic and long-term campaigner against the Shah, the Ayatollah Ruhollah Khomeini, the newly styled Islamic

Republic of Iran quickly found itself immediately caught up in a religious fervour that combined an intense revival of Islamic Shi'ite orthodoxy inspired by Khomeini with a virulent anti-Western sentiment shared by much of the country's population. In November 1979, the US embassy in Tehran was seized by radical students, with all the US personnel found there being taken hostage. In total, fifty-two Americans were held for a total of 444 days; the crisis dominated politics in the US during the election year that followed and seemed to demonstrate for all to see the collapse of American power. A failed rescue effort in April 1980 only compounded this sense of global humiliation. The 'loss of Iran' was a huge strategic blow to the United States, which not even Iran's brutal eight-year war with the US-supported Iraq of Saddam Hussein could undo. Saddam's opportunistic invasion of Iran in September 1980 produced a vast death toll, but despite strong US support failed to realize its ambition of decapitating the Khomeini regime.

While the Iranian Revolution was unfolding during the early months of 1979, another drama that was to have vast geopolitical consequences was being played out. This was in Afghanistan, where the Soviet-supporting local administration was coming under severe pressure from Mujahideen rebels – a group of disparate organizations united by a devotion to Islam combined with a virulent anti-communism. A series of military interventions in December 1979 led to the Soviets taking control of the country, after which followed ten years of conflict between the central Soviet-backed administration and the Mujahideen in the field. The United States strongly backed the latter, supplying a number of their favoured factions with armaments capable of doing immense damage to government forces. When the Soviets eventually withdrew completely in February 1989, the country promptly fell into a state of de facto civil war as a vicious power struggle played out between rival guerrilla forces, before a particular group, the 'Taliban', emerged victorious in 1996. The Islamic beliefs of the new Afghan leadership were not the same as those of Khomeini-controlled Iran, so no bond of fellow-feeling developed between the two. But both Islamic states were united in their distaste for the Americans and for the global liberal hegemony in general.

It will be obvious from this short foray into recent Iranian and Afghan history that the political violence in the region that was now spreading from Israel in the West across to the Afghan/Pakistan border in the

East had developed an intensely politicized character. The United States could not help but be drawn in, its long-term support for Israel now supplemented by its hostility to the new regime in Iran and its desire to influence events to the disadvantage of the Soviets in Afghanistan. Discussion of 'terrorism' and the 'terrorist threat' became a focal point of diplomatic engagement. Welcoming home the US Iranian hostages on 27 January 1981, just one week after taking office, the US president Ronald Reagan said 'Let terrorists beware that when the rules of international behaviour are violated, our policy will be one of swift and effective retribution.'[18] In the months that followed that speech, attempted assassinations of Reagan himself and of Pope John Paul II, together with the brutal killing of US ally President Anwar Sadat of Egypt in October (at the hands of the radical Egyptian Islamic Jihad group), added to the sense of crisis. Then came a decisive moment in the evolving history of terrorism. Its stage was Lebanon.

Following the massacres at Sabra and Chatila in 1982, a multinational force of American, French and Italian troops had been deployed to Beirut, primarily to protect the remaining Palestinians and the local Lebanese Muslims from further violence. The Lebanese constitution of 1943 had long frozen the country into a confessional political structure, with the high offices of state shared between Christians and Muslims, and the inherent sectarianism of this arrangement (compounded by population shifts in favour of the relatively disempowered Muslim population) produced its own set of tensions. These were then further complicated by the presence of first Israeli and Palestinian and then also various UN and international armed forces in the country. The multinational force in particular soon found itself embroiled in an incendiary local conflict in which, despite the initial purpose of their deployment, they were widely and increasingly seen as being on the side of the Christians (key allies of Israel in the conflict just ended). On 23 October 1983, suicide bomb attacks were launched on the headquarters of the US and French battalions in Beirut, with lorries packed with explosives being deployed in frontal attacks. Occurring early on a Sunday morning and within seconds of each other, in the first incident there were 241 fatalities, in the second fifty-nine. The death toll for the Americans was worse than they had experienced in a single incident throughout their time in Vietnam; the French for their part had hardly lost a soldier in combat since the Algerian war.

The actor responsible for the assaults was Hezbollah, an organization supported and supplied by the Islamic Republic of Iran, whose Revolutionary Guards had entered Lebanon under cover of the chaos of the 1982 invasion.[19] This 'Party of God' (as Hezbollah means in English) was avowedly Islamic in its intentions, as was a second similar group to emerge at the time, Islamic Amal. This latter group was a breakaway from the more conventional Lebanese Amal group that had emerged in southern Lebanon to defend the local Shia in the mid-to-late 1970s, but the religious energies of its leader, the lawyer Nabih Berri, were now judged not sufficiently fervent for the revolutionary times. Islamic Amal was led by a former teacher, Husayn al-Musawi, while Hezbollah had a spiritual leader, Mohammad Hussein Fadlallah, the title of whose book *Islam and the Logic of Force* gives an indication of the direction of travel of both groups. The unorthodox war against the American/European presence that followed may have been conducted by an apparently non-state operation but it was one with the strong backing of a properly sovereign national power: an Islamic Iran determined to take the fight to its opponents. It was around this time that the idea of 'state-sponsored' terrorism emerged to describe this dangerous subset of subversive political violence. As a result of its external backing, Hezbollah was stronger than the usual isolated terrorist group, invariably (as we have seen) relatively friendless in the pursuit of what were often quixotic goals. Reflecting this relative strength, its violence was not merely performative in the usual way but had a more conventional military aspect as well – the attacks of 23 October 1983 weakened the multinational force in tangible ways that went well beyond the communicative. Iran may not have taken explicit responsibility for its client's actions in Lebanon, much less supplanted them with conventional aerial and military attack, but this can hardly have been surprising – why play by rules of war created by your enemies under which you are certain to be defeated, when unorthodoxy can self-evidently yield better outcomes? The Western powers were as cross as the European settlers had been generations earlier, when native Americans forsook open battle for guerrilla sniping, making them inconveniently harder to kill.[20]

The strategy certainly worked in early 1980s Lebanon: within six months, the multinational force was gone, 'the final evacuation . . . marked by a bombardment of the Lebanese coast by the huge, forty-year-old battleship

New Jersey. The shells from its 16-inch guns created craters 5 feet deep and up to 15 feet across. Each round was as heavy as a small car and casualties must have been suffered in the vulnerable villages along the coast.'[21] This could hardly be described as a counter-terrorism offensive; it was more like an angry outburst by a departing imperial force, determined to camouflage its feeling of humiliation. The French launched aerial assaults on the barracks in Baalbek in which it was believed the suicide bombers had been prepared for their action, and later a car bomb close to Sheikh Fadlallah's office in the suburbs of Beirut killed eighty but missed what was assumed to be the main target. Newspaper reports were later to claim that the CIA had been behind this second attack.

War of civilizations

As already suggested, from the mid-1980s onwards the impetus for defining international relations in terms of 'us' and 'them' gathered pace, with the language of 'terror' and 'terrorism' being the chosen vehicle for the expression of what would once have been seen as solely diplomatic positions. This now went further than its adoption as a propaganda tool in the Cold War – the identification of Soviet support for the Palestinian cause that was discussed in the last chapter. It also embraced the sort of 'state-sponsored terrorism' that was being deployed by Iran. In the short period of overlap between post-revolutionary Iran and the (albeit decaying) Soviet empire, the spectre of the 'new terrorism' of 'jihadism' jostled with the older secular violence of Soviet-supported groups for attention in the public mind. As briefly noted previously, US legislation in 1984[22] and 1986[23] had mandated a federal response to 'international terrorism', and this gave an immediate lift to law's involvement in the field. In February 1986, Vice-President George H. Bush's Task Force on Combating Terrorism issued an official report, one key proposal of which was 'to launch a public awareness effort to better inform the American people about the nature of terrorism and the threat it represents to our national security interests and to the freedoms we so deeply cherish'.[24]

In January 1989, the State Department duly published *Terrorist Group Profiles*, a booklet purporting to provide information on groups not only in the Middle East but also encompassing 'West European', 'Latin American' and 'Asian' terrorist organizations. 'Hizballah' (as it was spelt) duly made an appearance as (of course) did Fatah and various of the Palestinian groups that had broken away from the mainstream Palestinian resistance. State-sponsored groups included Hizballah (Iran) and Sa'iqa (Syria), but not (of course) Haddad's SLA. The Middle East's 'most notorious practitioner of terrorism' was not this or that Palestinian renegade, but was now rather 'the Libyan military dictator Muammar Gaddafi'.[25] The one entry under 'African Terrorism' was the African National Congress, Soviet-backed and responsible (it was said) for indiscriminate attacks from 1983 which had resulted 'in both black and white civilian casualties'.[26] Just as was the case with Israel's SLA, US support for anti-Soviet groups in Afghanistan or for the opposition to the Nicaraguan Sandinista government did not figure in the report. As the vice-president said in his prefatory remarks: 'The difference between terrorists and freedom fighters is sometimes clouded. Some would say one man's freedom fighter is another man's terrorist. I reject this notion. The philosophical differences are stark and fundamental. It should be clear to all those who read this book that terrorists are criminals who attack our cherished institutions and profane our values.'[27]

It was during the late Reagan and first Bush presidencies (1988–92) that the description of a group as 'terrorist' escaped its regional/Middle East constraints and took on a truly global character, catching a fresh *zeitgeist* which saw the world engaged in a new battle for civilization. Israel's characterization of the civilized world as at war with terrorism finally became the common sense of the moment, at least among Western powers and their global allies. Samuel Huntington's influential *Foreign Affairs* essay 'The Clash of Civilizations', published in 1993, argued that 'conflict between civilizations will be the latest phase in the evolution of conflict in the modern world'.[28] Inevitably attracting criticism from those who saw the message as reductivist and perhaps even inflammatory,[29] the theory expounded by Huntington was to gain traction in the late 1990s. It was midway through the Reagan presidency – the mid-1980s – that Israel moved to consolidate its own position in a decisive fashion, making a new and more durable case for the legality of its military actions against its neighbours. To do this effectively it needed to exchange the blunderbuss of invasion for the aerial and military precision strikes of earlier counter-terrorism times, but this time ranging far beyond their home base and with a new, more tailored (and plausible) legal explanation than had ever been attempted before. In doing so, and setting a precedent that the United States was to follow, Israel was to fundamentally change the way in which violent counter-terrorism would be understood and legitimized, particularly after the attacks of 11 September 2001.

The arrival of article 51[30]

On 1 October 1985, the Israeli air force carried out an attack on the PLO's headquarters in Tunis, its most distant operation since the raid on Entebbe in 1976. It was to this relatively remote country that Arafat and his colleagues had retreated following their forced removal from Lebanon in 1982. As with the raid on Beirut airport in 1968, this 1985 Israeli attack was in response to a previous militant action, on this occasion the killing of three Israeli tourists sailing off Cyprus (itself ostensibly a riposte for earlier arrests of Palestinian militants by Israeli naval forces in the Mediterranean). When the Cypriot authorities rejected requests for extradition of the perpetrators (whom they had apprehended), instead pressing criminal charges against them, the Israelis – not for the first time, as we have seen – took matters into their own hands. The raid, conducted by Israeli military aircraft, flattened the PLO's base, killing scores of PLO members and many Tunisian nationals. The international reaction was very hostile, with even the Reagan administration in Washington back-pedalling on early statements of understanding. On 4 October 1985, the UN Security Council condemned the Israeli operation as an 'act of aggression' which was 'in flagrant violation of the Charter of the United Nations, international law and norms of conduct', and declaring that Tunisia 'had the right to appropriate reparations'.[31] The vote was 14 to 0, with the US abstaining rather than deploying the veto it enjoyed as a permanent member of the Council.

The attack was initially seen as part of Israel's long-standing policy of retaliation, the strategy that had driven earlier counter-terrorist actions, laced now with the references to global struggle that had become *de rigueur*. In his capacity as Israel's ambassador to the UN, Benjamin Netanyahu struck his familiar note, observing that '[o]ur operation against the PLO headquarters should be viewed for what it is, one action in our larger, continuing struggle against international terrorism and its core – the PLO'.[32] The problem remained, however, that there was no plausible way in which to insert retaliation into the international legal order, and Israel needed to be seen to be playing by the international rule-book if it was to continue to be persuasive in its role as defender of Western values against the Arab threat. Just three days after the raid, the Israeli prime minister Shimon Peres remarked at a Foreign Press Association news conference that '[i]t was not Israel who violated international law' but rather that the country had 'acted out of self-defence'.[33] Israel's claim was that Tunisia had knowingly harboured the PLO and allowed it to use the country as a base for its attacks on their country. As Kimberly Trapp has observed, 'Israel's argument before the Security Council [was] interesting in that it invoke[d] a right of self-defence directly against non-State actors, and justifie[d] the violation of Tunisia's sovereignty and territorial integrity based on the fact that Tunisia did not show an inkling of a desire or an intention to prevent the PLO from planning and initiating terrorist activities from its soil.'[34] The position was from the start altogether more nuanced than the casual references to 'legitimate self-defence' of the past.

The UN Charter does allow for self-defence in certain limited circumstances, set out in article 51. Requiring an 'armed attack' against a member state as a necessary (but not sufficient) precondition for its operation, the article seemed at the time a far-fetched basis for a legal defence of the Israeli action, and was largely treated as such. Of course, article 51 had been deployed (both explicitly and implicitly) before, on over 200 occasions since the foundation of the UN, according to one careful study,[35] but these uses of the provision had invariably been presented as responses to supposed wrongdoing by states, not sub-state entities, and in any event rarely engaged article 51 directly. One effort made by Israel in November 1966 to claim legitimacy for an attack on Palestinian targets in Jordan by talking in general terms about national security (but without invoking article 51[36]) had led to a rare near unanimous condemnation by the Security Council (with only one dissent, New Zealand).[37] The condemnatory resolution passed on that occasion made clear that the Security Council was sure it was dealing with 'actions of military reprisal' in 'violation of the UN Charter'.[38] Later explanations of Israeli action against various 'terrorist' incarnations of Palestinian aggression invariably coupled these stateless people with their host countries, first Jordan and then Lebanon, but did so in a way that never drew upon any potential justification rooted in a right of self-defence. The recourse to article 51 in 1985 was rightly seen at the time, therefore, to be a 'novel legal argument',[39] with many contemporaneous scholars arguing 'that the right of self-defence could only be invoked in response to an armed attack by a State, and acquiescence in terrorist activities was evidently rejected as a basis for attribution'.[40] But the novelty of the Israeli approach was soon to secure a huge new jolt of supposed legal support.

Within a year of the Tunis attacks, the US had exploited the same provision to launch a series of attacks on Tunisia's neighbour Libya, and in particular the cities of Tripoli and Benghazi. This was presented as a response to that country's alleged involvement in 'international terrorism' in general and, more specifically, its culpability for the bombing of a night club in Berlin some ten days before the US attacks. Article 51 had arrived. So too had an altogether more militarily assertive US response to global terror. Why had the Americans acted in this way? Just a year before, the US had pulled back from full-scale support for Israel's Tunis attacks, but now it was seeming to be emulating them. True, here was a state alleged to be directly culpable rather than merely a host of terrorist miscreants, as Tunisia was claimed to have been. But the baldness of the action seemed breathtaking at the time.[41] Libya was just one indicator among many of a change in the shape of the global struggle against international terrorism that had occurred in the early 1980s, with its leader (as we have seen) presented as the most notorious terrorist of all in State Department analyses in the late 1980s. The driver of this expansive approach was now no longer just the Palestinians or even the Soviets. The new enemy was radical Islam.

The rise of Al-Qaeda

The State Department's *Terrorist Group Profiles* released in January 1989 did not mention a group that had come together just a year earlier, but even if the writers had been aware of it they would have left it out. The founders of Al-Qaeda were among those resisting the Soviets in Afghanistan and so, in American eyes, were at this time freedom fighters rather than terrorists. Hamas was not mentioned either, but for the more prosaic reason that it had yet to emerge: this radical Islamic group became prominent in the years after the 1993 Oslo peace accords had finally brought Arafat's PLO in from the diplomatic cold. 'In Palestine, the "normalisation" of Fatah . . . from an armed movement to a political party, combined with the decline of the leftist parties with the end of the Cold War, created a vacuum for Palestinian armed resistance that was increasingly filled by Hamas, Islamic Jihad and, across the border in Lebanon, Hezbollah.[42] Hamas's military wing, the Qassam Brigades, carried out its first suicide bombing in the Israeli town of Afula in April 1994 and another a week later in Hadera's central bus station. In October the same year a suicide bombing attack in Tel Aviv killed twenty-one Israelis and one Dutch national. In all there were some fifteen suicide attacks carried out by either the Brigades or their main rival Islamic Jihad between 1994 and 1999.[43]

While this embracing of Islamist radicalism by the Palestinian movement was new,[44] there had long been an Islamic-based challenge to the West's influence in its religious heartlands. In the 1940s, 'Islamic violence, carried out particularly by the Moslem Brotherhood, [had] emerged'[45] as a source of opposition to British rule in Egypt. This entailed bombings, multiple attacks on British troops, and in particular the 'constant assassinations of Egyptian officials'.[46] Independence brought no conclusion to this low-intensity warfare: the powerful second president of the new Egyptian Republic, Gamal Abdel Nasser, 'was clear in his war against the Brotherhood and other Islamist groups',[47] and deployed various special measures and court processes that drew explicitly on the British colonial legacy. This was also the case in newly independent Tunisia where, under its first and long-serving President Habib Bourguiba, 'Islamist identity was fought against as part of ensuring a secular state'.[48] These were newly independent countries who fought not only communist influence but radical Muslim ideas as well. The Afghan War of the 1980s was a '"watershed" moment' for the many militant Muslims who 'were among the thousands of volunteers from the Muslim world who fought together against the Soviet army over a prolonged period of time, in the process building up close ties with each other that were evident in subsequent decades'.[49] Global links nurtured in adversity in the 1980s were deepened in the years that followed.

Amongst these groups was Indonesia's Jemaah Islamiyah, 'established in 1993 in an area of Indonesia known for high levels of poverty and poor government'[50] but whose origins can be found 'in the programme of groups like Darul Islam (DI) during the late anti-colonial period and earlier era of independence in the 1940s'.[51] By the end of the 1990s, Jemaah Islamiyah 'had established a regional alliance called the Rabitatul Mujahidin (the International Mujahideen Association) that provided a framework for cooperation among like-minded groups, especially those in Malaysia and Southern Thailand. It also set up cells, operational bases and sanctuaries in Singapore, Thailand and the southern Philippines.'[52] As Dayyab Gillani has observed, it is also 'not possible to discuss geo-political dynamics and not talk about the complicity of the Pakistani state'.[53] That state's identity had been tied up with the Islamic faith from its inception, its first constitution in 1956 adopting the phrase 'Islamic Republic' to describe itself being 'testament to this verity'.[54] During the 1970s, with 'the USA's support, Pakistan [had] infamously trained and equipped the Afghan mujahideen that later turned against their former patrons and posed one of the most notorious of all terrorist threats in recent times'.[55]

Al-Qaeda's pitch was always global. Its founder, Osama bin Laden, 'fostered this perception from the outset by calling his Islamist umbrella organization, of which Al-Qaeda was only one part, the International (World) Islamic Front for the Jihad against Jews and Crusaders'.[56] The organization had been founded in August 1988 by Bin Laden and fourteen associates 'in a series of long meetings at a rented house in a western suburb of the noisy, dusty Pakistani frontier city of Peshawar'.[57] The instinct for the spectacular strike against the 'far enemy' fitted well with its internationalist mind-set. There were bombings in Somalia in December 1992, aimed at US troops that used the targeted hotels while deployed in the country; two people died but neither was American.[58] In November 1995, a car bomb at a US–Saudi joint training facility in Riyadh killed five Americans and two Indians, with the perpetrators admitting to having been inspired by Bin Laden.[59] In June 1996 a huge truck bomb deployed by Saudi Hezbollah killed nineteen Americans and injured 372 – the targeted complex, in Dhahran, Saudi Arabia, housed US air force personnel. There was suspected but never proven Al-Qaeda involvement.[60] 'Al-Qaeda's direct terrorist attacks against American targets began in 1998 with bombings of American embassies in Nairobi, Kenya and Dar es Salaam, Tanzania.'[61] Some twelve Americans and over 200 others were killed in the two attacks, with about 5,000 injured.[62] The American response to these atrocities lay primarily in the realms of diplomacy and intelligence rather than in law – the Antiterrorism and Effective Death Penalty Act of 1996 was more a response to the locally inspired Oklahoma bombing of 1995 than to any international threat, though its terms did include various powers to control manifestations of 'international terrorism' on US soil.

An early indication of what could be achieved was the attack on New York's World Trade Center in 1993, orchestrated by a small group led by Ramzi Yousef: '[t]he bomb that was planted created a seven-storey-deep crater, killing six people and injuring more than a thousand others when it exploded'.[63] Yousef does not appear to have been part of the Al-Qaeda network, though Khalid Sheikh Mohammed – a close associate of Osama bin Laden and a key member of Al-Qaeda – was his uncle. Mohammed has been identified by the 9/11 Commission as 'the principal architect'[64] of the devastating assault on the same location that took place on 11 September 2001. It was this event more than any other that transformed the various strands of anti-terrorism law we have been discussing up to now into the global movement that has indelibly embedded such laws in both liberal and authoritarian political cultures. Exploring exactly how this happened is the subject of the next part of this book.

PART TWO

SPREAD

SIX

The War on Terror

11 September 2001

On the morning of 11 September 2001, Al-Qaeda successfully executed its now infamous aerial assault on the United States. In early 1999 the organization's leader, Osama bin Laden, had begun planning the use of commercial aircraft to attack targets in the 'far enemy' (as Bin Laden conceived the US).[1] Shortly after this, the men selected to deliver on his plans began the process of securing the documentation to be able to enter the US. Many of them engaged in advanced planning in Germany where they were residents. In April 2001 the intended hijackers lawfully entered the US on tourist visas with cash and travellers cheques they had obtained in the Middle East, enrolling 'in flight schools and conduct[ing] cross-country surveillance flights in order to identify aircraft that would produce their desired impact'.[2] On the day of the attacks, the nineteen men successfully negotiated various security checkpoints at their chosen American airports, despite 'allegedly carrying knives, box cutters and concealed weapons on their person or in carry-on luggage'.[3] Eight of the men were randomly selected for additional screening and two were flagged as suspicious by a gate agent, despite which all nineteen were permitted to board their chosen aircraft. Five of the Al-Qaeda men boarded Boston's American Airlines Flight 11, bound for Los Angeles. In the same airport five others boarded United Airlines 175, also headed for Los Angeles. At the same time, in Washington's Dulles Airport, a further five successfully boarded yet another Los Angeles flight, American Airlines flight 77. In Newark New Jersey the same plan saw the final four board United flight 93, bound for the same west coast destination. The men planned 'to hijack these [four] planes and turn them into large, guided missiles, loaded with up to 11,400 gallons of jet fuel. By 8:00 A.M. on the morning of Tuesday, September 11th 2001, they had defeated all the security layers that America's civil aviation security system then had in place to prevent a hijacking.'[4]

One flight (United 93) crashed due to passenger resistance before it could attack its target, but the other three successfully propelled themselves onto the Pentagon and into each of New York's high-rise twin towers, integral parts of the city's World Trade Center. The Final Report of the National Commission on Terrorist Attacks Upon the United States summarized the effects of the attack in stark terms: '[m]ore than 2,600 people died at the World Trade Center; 125 died at the Pentagon; 256 died on the four planes. The death toll surpassed that at Pearl Harbor in December 1941.'[5]

The impact of this extraordinary set of coordinated attacks on the United States went far beyond the horror experienced by its direct victims and their grieving relatives: the country was both at a complete loss to understand the hate that it was assumed must have driven the suicidal perpetrators of these atrocities, and aghast at the apparent ease with which the hijackers had pulled off their violent spectacle. The insecurity of the American homeland had been brutally laid bare. The day after the attacks, the sitting US president George W. Bush addressed the nation, setting out a perspective on the atrocities that was political but also implicitly legal. He spoke of the 'deliberate and deadly attacks, which were carried out yesterday against our country'. These 'were more than acts of terror. They were acts of war.' In words that echoed those of his predecessor Ronald Reagan when addressing the problem of global terror at the start of his presidency,[6] the president continued:

> This will require our country to unite in steadfast determination and resolve. Freedom and democracy are under attack. The American people need to know we're facing a different enemy than we have ever faced.
>
> This enemy hides in shadows and has no regard for human life. This is an enemy who preys on innocent and unsuspecting people, then runs for cover, but it won't be able to run for cover forever. This is an enemy that tries to hide, but it won't be able to hide forever. This is an enemy that thinks its harbors are safe, but they won't be safe forever. This enemy attacked not just our people but all freedom-loving people everywhere in the world.

The pathway ahead was clear:

> Those in authority should take appropriate precautions to protect our citizens. But we will not allow this enemy to win the war by changing our way of life or restricting our freedoms.

This morning, I am sending to Congress a request for emergency funding authority so that we are prepared to spend whatever it takes to rescue victims, to help the citizens of New York City and Washington, D.C. respond to this tragedy, and to protect our national security.[7]

Reflecting the global nature of the threat, world leaders were quick to express their solidarity with the United States. Speaking within an hour of the attacks, explaining why he was cancelling a speech in southern England at short notice and returning to London, the British prime minister Tony Blair talked of '[t]his mass terrorism [as] the new evil in our world today. It is perpetrated by fanatics who are utterly indifferent to the sanctity of human life and we, the democracies of this world, are going to have to come together to fight it together and eradicate this evil completely from our world.'[8]

This fast-emerging idea of a new 'war on terror' that was global in nature was fleshed out further in a speech President Bush delivered to Congress on 20 September, just nine days after the attacks.[9] Declaring that '[w]hether we bring our enemies to justice or bring justice to our enemies, justice will be done', the president referred to 'the citizens of 80 other nations who died with our own. Dozens of Pakistanis, more than 130 Israelis, more than 250 citizens of India, men and women from El Salvador, Iran, Mexico and Japan, and hundreds of British citizens.' Bush went on to identify the assailants as practitioners of 'a fringe form of Islamic extremism that has been rejected by Muslim scholars and the vast majority of Muslim clerics; a fringe movement that perverts the peaceful teachings of Islam. The terrorists' directive commands them to kill Christians and Jews, to kill all Americans and make no distinctions among military and civilians, including women and children.' The danger was everywhere:

This group and its leader, a person named Osama bin Laden, are linked to many other organizations in different countries, including the Egyptian Islamic Jihad, the Islamic Movement of Uzbekistan. There are thousands of these terrorists in more than 60 countries. They are recruited from their own nations and neighborhoods and brought to camps in places like Afghanistan where they are trained in the tactics of terror. They are sent back to their homes or sent to hide in countries around the world to plot evil and destruction.

It is impossible to believe that any US president would have spoken or acted differently after such an attack. If Bin Laden believed that America's determination to maintain influence in Saudi Arabia and across the Islamic world would crumble as a result of the attacks, then this must go down as the greatest miscalculation in the history of asymmetrical political violence.[10] What worked in Beirut in 1983[11] and in Somalia in 1992[12] was never going to be effective after the scale of the violence wrought on 9/11. Instead, a 'war on terror' was unleashed which, as the president promised, was not 'to end until every terrorist group of global reach has been found, stopped and defeated'. This explicitly involved the pursuit of nations that provide aid or safe haven to terrorism: 'Every nation in every region now has a decision to make: Either you are with us or you are with the terrorists.' It also had a domestic aspect; at the end of his speech, Bush announced 'the creation of a Cabinet-level position reporting directly to me, the Office of Homeland Security'. It is remarkable how quickly the contours of the US response to the attacks of 11 September were defined, and how little the fundamentals were to change in subsequent years. Where the United States led, the world followed, and is still following. From the perspective of this book, the primary significance of the response to 9/11 was the way in which counter-terrorism was finally able to break free of its dependence on atrocity to explain and justify its actions. A new world of counter-terrorism law and practice – one that would eventually no longer need terrorism to sustain it – had begun to emerge.

Self-defence

Article 51 of the UN Charter has already been mentioned. The provision is expressed in the following terms:

> Nothing in the present Charter shall impair the inherent right of individual or collective self-defence if an armed attack occurs against a Member of the United Nations, until the Security Council has taken measures necessary to maintain international peace and security. Measures taken by Members in the exercise of this right of self-defence shall be immediately reported to the Security Council and shall not in any way affect the authority and responsibility of the Security Council under the present Charter to take at any time such

128

action as it deems necessary in order to maintain or restore international peace and security.

We have already seen how in 1985 Israel deployed this provision as the ostensible legal basis for its attack on Palestinian targets in Tunis, and how the US itself had echoed the same rationale when attacking Gaddafi's Libya the following year.[13] Both actions – the first against a sub-state entity; the second engaging a sovereign power – had been explicitly justified by reference to threats posed by what was described as international terrorism. At the time, these actions were not well received, even by the 'many leading American scholars' attending an international conference on terrorism when the Libyan attacks took place, 'few of [whom] were convinced supporters of their government's actions'.[14] The defensive explanation offered by the Israelis and Americans for what looked like aggression was to become a recurring if occasional theme in international affairs in the years after Tunis/Libya and before the 2001 attacks, only to come into its own after that date, in the form of a new 'imperialism as self-defence', as Antony Anghie astutely describes it.[15] During the autumn of 1987 and into the summer of 1988, article 51 was invoked on a number of occasions to legitimize US military action against Iran in the Persian Gulf. The following year, the US once more used the provision to justify the shooting down of two Libyan aircraft that had approached US fighter planes 'in a hostile manner' over international waters in the Mediterranean. In July 1993 Israel explained assaults on 'Hezbollah and "other terrorist organisations"' in Lebanon as part of its 'legitimate right of self-defence'.[16]

Perhaps inevitably, this expanded use of article 51 did not long remain exclusive to the Israelis and the Americans. In 1993, Iran went after 'armed and organised terrorist mercenaries' that it claimed were acting in Iraq's interests against it, and engaged once more against similarly constituted 'terrorist groups' on the same basis (this time implicitly) the following year, and again on three further occasions, in 1998, 1999 and April 2001. Turkey joined in, in 1995 recasting its violent engagement with Kurdish forces outside the state as a series of actions again terrorist organizations, confrontations necessitated by Iraq's failure to control forces hostile to Turkey acting within its jurisdiction.[17] In 1993, Kazakhstan, Kyrgyzstan, Russia and Tajikistan came together to justify attacks on 'the Tajik opposition and individual Afghan armed groups that support them' by reference (implicitly) to article 51 and (explicitly) to chapter eight of the UN Charter (on regional arrangements). The following year an emboldened Tajikistan, with Russian support, struck beyond its jurisdiction against '[a]rmed units from the intransigent wing of the opposition' based in Afghanistan. The government's explanation for the action, filed with the Security Council, included the following:

> In cooperation with the units and divisions of the Ministry of the Interior and the Ministry of Security of the Republic of Tajikistan the Russian Federation's frontier troops will continue to take energetic steps, using all troops and all equipment to put an end to hostilities on the border, in accordance with Article 51 of the Charter of the United Nations. The intransigent wing of the opposition bears full responsibility for the consequences of the escalation of violence, the pointless victims, the mothers' suffering and the orphan's tears.[18]

There was here a rationale for these sorts of attacks that, however flimsy, was capable of being presented to the international community as more coherent, or at least more plausible, than simple retaliation – Israel's (unsuccessful) explanation for its extra-jurisdictional engagements before 1985. The existence of article 51 meant that tactical incursions into foreign territory, conducted as part of a regional conflict, could be repackaged not as aggression but rather as necessary self-defence. There was no judicial mechanism to assess the justification for such state actions, or to evaluate their proportionality: if a country was strong enough to weather any resultant political storm, article 51 seemed to give it a blank cheque.

Nowhere was this made clearer than in relation to the United States' first deployment of the provision against Al-Qaeda, three years before 9/11. On 7 August 1998, the organization carried out devastating attacks on two US embassies in Africa that killed twelve American citizens and over 250 others. When the US response came on 20 August, it was carefully couched in the language of article 51, as the letter from the US ambassador to the United Nations Bill Richardson, filed on the day of the US action, made clear:

> The Bin Ladin organization maintains an extensive network of camps, arsenals and training and supply facilities in Afghanistan, and support facilities in

Sudan, which have been and are being used to mount terrorist attacks against American targets. These facilities include an installation at which chemical weapons have been produced.

In response to these terrorist attacks, and to prevent and deter their continuation, United States armed forces today struck at a series of camps and installations used by the Bin Ladin organization to support terrorist actions against the United States and other countries. In particular, United States forces struck a facility being used to produce chemical weapons in the Sudan and terrorist training and basing camps in Afghanistan.

These attacks were carried out only after repeated efforts to convince the Government of the Sudan and the Taliban regime in Afghanistan to shut these terrorist activities down and to cease their cooperation with the Bin Ladin organization. That organization has issued a series of blatant warnings that 'strikes will continue from everywhere' against American targets, and we have convincing evidence that further such attacks were in preparation from these same terrorist facilities. The United States, therefore, had no choice but to use armed force to prevent these attacks from continuing.

In doing so, the United States has acted pursuant to the right of self-defence confirmed by Article 51 of the Charter of the United Nations. The targets struck, and the timing and method of attack used, were carefully designed to minimize risks of collateral damage to civilians and to comply with international law, including the rules of necessity and proportionality.

It is the sincere hope of the United States Government that these limited actions will deter and prevent the repetition of unlawful terrorist attacks on the United States and other countries. We call upon all nations to take the steps necessary to bring such indiscriminate terrorism to an end.[19]

Doubts about the bombing of the chemical factory immediately surfaced, with many claims being made that it was in fact an ordinary pharmaceutical plant, entirely unconnected to terrorism.[20] The lack of coherent judicial processes to oversee the operation of the UN Charter (or at least this bit of it) had been made painfully clear.

There was therefore already considerable history to the use of article 51 against sub-state groups before the events of 11 September 2001. The Al-Qaeda actions of that day undoubtedly constituted an 'armed attack' against the United States, and the culpability of Osama bin Laden's organization for the strikes was conclusively established early on. Like

Palestine's Yasser Arafat in the 1970s and 1980s, Bin Laden was leader of no state, had no conventional territory over which he ruled; he was merely a guest in another country, albeit one that received and protected him and his supporters with far greater warmth than the Palestinians had ever enjoyed in their travels around the Middle East in search of sanctuary. That country was, of course, Afghanistan. The US president's congressional message on 20 September may have referred to 'places like Afghanistan', but there was no doubt in anyone's mind that it was there that Al-Qaeda operatives were being 'trained in the tactics of terror'. The invasion of Afghanistan that was launched in October 2001 by the United States and its ally the United Kingdom took place not under any specific UN authorization but rather in the more general terms of article 51. The explanation was laid out in the report filed with the UN (as required under article 51) on 7 October 2001, the day that President Bush announced the intention to engage militarily with Afghan targets, a campaign that was to go under the description 'Operation Enduring Freedom': 'my Government has obtained clear and compelling information that the Al-Qaeda organization, which is supported by the Taliban regime in Afghanistan, had a central role in the attacks [against the World Trade Center, the Pentagon and in Pennsylvania]'. It went on:

the attacks on 11 September 2001 and the ongoing threat to the United States and its nationals posed by the Al-Qaeda organization have been made possible by the decision of the Taliban regime to allow the parts of Afghanistan that it controls to be used by this organization as a base of operation. Despite every effort by the United States and the international community, the Taliban regime has refused to change its policy. From the territory of Afghanistan, the Al-Qaeda organization continues to train and support agents of terror who attack innocent people throughout the world and target United States nationals and interests in the United States and abroad. In response to these attacks, and in accordance with the inherent right of individual and collective self-defence, United States armed forces have initiated actions designed to prevent and deter further attacks on the United States. These actions include measures against Al-Qaeda terrorist training camps and military installations of the Taliban regime in Afghanistan. In carrying out these actions, the United States is committed to minimizing civilian casualties and damage to civilian property. In addition, the United States will continue its humanitarian efforts to alleviate the suffering of the people of Afghanistan. We are providing them with food, medicine and supplies.[21]

Somewhat ominously, the US declared that it also reserved the right to take other actions: 'we may find that our self-defence requires further actions with respect to other organizations and other States'.[22]

The United Kingdom took the same action on the same day. A succession of US allies followed with article 51 notifications of their own: Canada on 24 October; France and Australia on 23 November; Germany on 29 November; the Netherlands on 6 December; New Zealand on 18 December; and Portugal on 27 December and again on 15 March 2002. It was a considerable feat of diplomacy to achieve such solidarity, but its inevitable effect was to place great weight on a provision that had hardly been designed with such aggressive actions in mind. This would be proven in the years that followed. In June 2014, the article was relied upon to justify the seizure of Ahmed Abu Khattalah, a senior leader of the Libyan militant group Ansar al-Sharia-Benghazi, for trial in a US court on charges related to an attack in 2012 on a US mission facility in Benghazi during which the US ambassador to Libya and three other Americans were killed. The fact that 'he continued to plan further armed attacks against United States persons' was asserted to have brought the intervention within the realm of article 51.[23] (Khattalah was afterwards found guilty of offences related to the 2012 attack and sentenced to twenty-two years in jail.[24]) Three months later, on 23 September, the US struck against an emerging new threat in the region, Islamic State in Iraq and the Levant (ISIL/ISIS), and '"and other terrorist groups in Syria", including "al-Qaida elements in Syria known as the Khorasan Group"'; once again article 51 provided legal cover, with the defence on this occasion being mainly (but not exclusively) in support of the US's regional partners rather than the US itself.[25] Over the following fifteen months or so, article 51-based strikes against the same threat were notified to the United Nations by no fewer than nine member states, some on multiple occasions. On 14 November 2023, the US deployed its 'inherent right of self-defence, as reflected in Article 51', as a justification for its military action against 'militia groups affiliated with Iran's Islamic Revolutionary Guard Corps against United States personnel and facilities in Iraq and Syria', its sixth such engagement in three years.[26]

Meanwhile, and energized no doubt by the legal cover provided by the 'war on terror', the state that had initiated deployment of article 51 against sub-state entities had quickly returned to it in the years after the 11 September attacks. On 8 June 2005, Israel used it to justify striking against Hezbollah and the PFLP in Lebanon, and on 26 September that year against the 'terrorist organization Hamas'. The Al-Aqsa Martyrs Brigade, 'affiliated with Palestinian Authority President Mahmoud Abbas's very own Fatah movement', was a target in late 2005.[27] Israel's three-week military intervention in Gaza in December 2008/January 2009 was also purportedly legally insulated by two assertions that explicitly relied upon the right of self-defence and article 51. The first, on the day the operation began, explained that, 'after a long period of utmost restraint, the Government of Israel has decided to exercise . . . its right to self-defence. Israel is taking the necessary military action in order to protect its citizens from the ongoing terrorist attacks originating from the Gaza Strip and carried out by Hamas and other terrorist organizations.'[28] The second, heralding a new phase in the same action, asserted that '[i]n response to Hamas' continuous terrorist attacks, Israel has been acting in accordance with its inherent right to self-defence enshrined in Article 51'.[29] Approximately 1,400 Gaza inhabitants were killed, with thirteen Israelis losing their lives, four of whom died as a result of 'friendly fire'.[30] A year later, Israel once again used article 51 to launch attacks on Gaza, the explanation on this occasion being that '[i]n the past week, most notably on 7 January 2010, terrorists fired 20 mortars and rockets from the Gaza Strip towards Israel, including a Katyusha rocket that landed south of Ashkelon, a city with a population of over 100,000 individuals'. There was also a reference to 'an explosive device planted by terrorists along the Israel-Gaza border [that] was detonated while the Israeli army conducted a routine patrol on the Israeli side of the border'.[31] The bar for Israeli action was clearly dropping very low, the old policy of retaliation seeming to return under the flimsiest of self-defence covers: the letter from the Israeli ambassador to the UN Gabriela Shalev quoted 'Israeli Prime Minister Benjamin Netanyahu [who had] stated unequivocally on 10 January 2010: "Any firing at our territory will be responded to strongly and immediately."'[32] (Just three days before this action the Israelis had agreed with the UN to pay compensation for the damage done to its facilities during the 2008/9 military action.[33]) Israel did not formally invoke article 51 before responding to the Hamas attacks of 7 October 2023, although it did write to the Security Council on the day of the assaults, warning of the rigorous action that was to come.[34]

As we have already noted, it was not just Israel and the US and its allies who had spotted the potential utility of article 51. In the years following 9/11, opportunistic use of the provision by other international actors against non-state actors greatly increased. The Ivory Coast used the article in 2003 to justify assaults on 'rebel forces' in areas beyond the government's control, while twelve years later Bahrain and other Arab states deployed it to justify attacks on the Houthi militias based in Yemen. Turkey also renewed – and expanded – its reliance on the provision as part of its ongoing quarrel with Kurdish forces based outside the state, using it to justify attacks in February 2016 and again in April 2017, and then in January 2018 (showing, it might be cynically thought, great awareness of the international preoccupations of the day) linking the Kurds with the wider militant bodies in the area: the 'national security of Turkey has been under direct threat from the Syria-based terrorist organizations, among which Daesh and the PKK/KCK Syria affiliate, PYD/YPG, are at the top of the list'.[35]

The United States' use of the provision has continued to expand in recent years, in particular by deploying the idea of 'pre-emptive self-defence' against targets hosted by countries judged 'unable or unwilling' to assist in their capture. This has enabled the country to implicitly dress up such actions as article 51-compliant even if all they are is a way of assassinating their international opponents – the killing of Iranian military leader Qasem Soleimani on a visit to Iraq on 2 January 2020 being one example, that of the leader of Al-Qaeda Ayman al-Zawahiri, in Kabul on 30 July 2022, another.[36] Technical advances in the use of drone weapons have made this kind of targeted action more cost-free (in military and political terms) than ever before; a recent estimate of the fatalities caused by US drones and air strikes since the 11 September attacks has been put at over 22,000 civilians.[37] Agnes Callamard, the UN Special Rapporteur on extrajudicial, summary or arbitrary executions, protested in vain that the strike against Soleimani constituted a violation of international law.[38] Acknowledging the absence of any fora in which the article 51 assertion can be legally tested, Callamard's UN report fell back on the claim that 'even the legality of a strike under Article 51 of the Charter does not preclude its wrongfulness under international humanitarian or human rights law'.[39] The article 51 requirement for notification does not, however, demand the 'thorough justification' for which Callamard called: the reality is what is often a merely 'cursory report', one that (to make matters worse) is usually received in silence by the recipient UN organs.[40] Anticipatory self-defence is supposedly rooted in the imminence of the threat, but what is imminence and how can it be assessed? As Chris O'Meara observes: 'Without a common understanding of the term . . . assessing legality is extremely difficult, if not impossible.'[41] And no judicial body standing outside the fray has any capacity to evaluate either before or after a purportedly article 51-sanctioned action. The international law experts seek to keep up with state practice, providing academic nuance both to explain but at the same time mainly to seek to control this tendency to unaccountable excess.[42] In a world where global anti-terrorism enjoys such power as a driver of cross-border state violence, and where the controls available on the international stage are so meagre, it is an uphill task.

Detention

The action against Al-Qaeda in Afghanistan in the autumn of 2001 and beyond generated an immediate conundrum for the invading forces, made all the more urgent by their early and dramatic success: what to do with all the individuals who were inevitably taken into custody as the engagement proceeded? The authorization for the use of military force given by joint resolution of the US Congress on 18 September 2001 had allowed the president 'to use all necessary and appropriate force against those nations, organizations or persons he determines planned, authorized, committed or aided the terrorist attacks that occurred on 11 September 2001, or harbored such organizations or persons, in order to prevent any future acts of international terrorism against the United States by such nations, organizations or persons'.[43] The enemy here was not a state, with clearly marked combatants and an underlying shared commitment to long-established rules of war. Rather it was a state of mind: terror induced, instilled and deepened by a non-state entity (or entities) whose work was being done from within civil society by actors ('the terrorists') who were indistinguishable from the civilians by whom they were surrounded. This was old-style asymmetrical conflict, but now played out on a global scale and against the world's largest (conventional) military power. The ramifications of the 'war on terror' meant that the terrorists could be found anywhere, and not just in Afghanistan.

A later, critical report from several UN agencies acting together summarized the approach the Americans took to their detainee dilemma:

> individuals captured around the world were to be held neither as criminal suspects, put forward for federal court trials in the United States, nor treated as prisoners of war protected by the Geneva Conventions, irrespective of whether they had been captured on the battlefield during what could be qualified as an armed conflict in terms of international humanitarian law. Rather, they were to be treated indiscriminately as 'unlawful enemy combatants' who could be held indefinitely without charge or trial or the possibility to challenge the legality of their detention before a court or other judicial authority.[44]

Reflecting this line, on 7 February 2002, President Bush released a memorandum confirming his administration's view that 'common article 3 of Geneva [did] not apply to either Al-Qaida or Taliban detainees', that 'Taliban detainees [were] unlawful combatants and, therefore, [did] not qualify as prisoners of war under article 4 of Geneva', and that 'because Geneva does not apply to our conflict with Al-Qaida, Al-Qaida detainees also do not qualify as prisoners of war'.[45] Despite this liberation from legal orthodoxy, the president promised in the same memorandum that, nevertheless, 'as a matter of policy, the United States Armed Forces shall continue to treat detainees humanely and, to the extent appropriate and consistent with military necessity, in a manner consistent with the principles of Geneva'.[46] But the effect of the policy was that the United States felt able thereafter consistently to reject international, human rights based, oversight of its conduct.[47]

Detention of the sort that the 'war on terror' was now authorizing was not, of course, new. The critical UN report cited above traces the 'phenomenon of secret detention' to Nazi Germany but also detected forerunners of the practice in the Soviet gulags.[48] Secret detention was almost routine in Latin America in the late 1960s and through the 1970s, when the many authoritarian regimes then in power used it as a tool with which to destroy or undermine challenges to their rule. Of course, much of this was driven at the time by the Cold War-inspired threat of communist insurgency, while encompassing among its victims leftists of all descriptions. As in the late colonial period, the label 'terrorist' was bandied about as a kind of justificatory mantra for the brutality that such policies inevitably entailed – torture and (on many occasions) death were frequent consequences of the illicit or barely legal imprisonments in which such governments engaged. Nor were these Latin American abuses unique: successive UN Special Rapporteurs on torture as well as the UN's Working Group on Enforced or Involuntary Disappearances have deplored systemic disappearances of this sort in Africa and the Middle East and Asia across a time-line that stretches from the colonial period right through to the early 2000s. The victims of such actions have often, but not invariably, been described as terrorists: on many occasions mere political activism, trade union work or human rights advocacy have been enough to draw a state's hostile attention.[49]

If the actions taken by the Bush administration were not in themselves trail-blazing, what was new after 11 September 2001 was the direct and explicit engagement of the United States in these detention practices outside formal theatres of war (Korea in the 1950s, Vietnam in the 1960s and '70s, for example). 'Direct' and 'explicit' are important words here; the US had long trained military personnel from South America in, among other things, counter-insurgency at its 'School of the Americas', originally located in Panama and then (after 1984) at Fort Benning (now Fort Moore) in the state of Georgia. Successive administrations had taken an active interest in protecting many sovereign states from communism and this had without question involved advice on the darker arts of the sort that featured on the regular curriculum at the School. But wholesale detention of a kind that anticipated the 'war on terror' had only been tried once by the United States in the twentieth century, and that was itself during the global conflagration that was the Second World War. Even at the time, the incarceration without trial of large numbers of Americans of Japanese origin proved highly controversial, and remained so despite receiving legitimation in a wartime Supreme Court case.[50] The policy was brought to an end early in 1945, with the surviving victims eventually receiving an apology from President Clinton in 1993. In his letter, Clinton acknowledged that '[o]ver fifty years ago, the United States Government [had] unjustly interned, evacuated, or relocated you and many other Japanese Americans'. This had 'unfairly denied Japanese Americans and their families fundamental liberties during World War II'. The injustice was rooted 'deeply in racial prejudice, wartime hysteria, and a lack of political leadership', but, the wrong now having been acknowledged, the president could confidently 'guarantee a future with liberty and justice for all'.[51]

This rejection of executive detention from President Bush's predecessor proved short-lived, except that, importantly, the executive power of detention claimed by Bush under the powers Congress had given him did not extend to the detention of US citizens. The military order issued on 13 November 2001 made this crystal clear, being entitled the 'Detention, Treatment, and Trial of Certain *Non-Citizens* in the War Against Terrorism'.[52] Apart from this concession, the Bush memorandum was uncompromising in its tone and substance. Reflecting on the period immediately after the 11 September attacks, James Martel has observed that, '[i]n a sense, the use of procedure as a way to mask legal violence [was] even more fraught in the American empire than it was during the British'.[53] Bush's military order asserted that, so as to protect the US and its citizens, it was 'necessary for individuals subject to this order . . . to be detained, and, when tried, to be tried for violations of the laws of war and other applicable laws by military tribunals'; furthermore, for reasons of practicability, 'the principles of law and the rules of evidence generally recognized in the trial of criminal cases in the United States district courts' would not apply in any of their cases.[54] Death and life imprisonment were among the punishments that such tribunals were explicitly empowered to make.[55] The individuals to whom the order potentially applied were any non-citizens in respect of whom the president had in writing determined that they were in some way, however tangentially, involved in Al-Qaeda and/or terrorist threats against the US.[56] Persons so detained could be held 'at an appropriate location . . . outside or within the United States'.[57] In a way that was to be echoed in more legal language in the memorandum of 7 February 2002, humane treatment was promised, 'without any adverse distinction based on race, colour, religion, gender, birth, wealth or any similar criteria', and 'adequate food, drinking water, shelter, clothing, and medical treatment' were likewise guaranteed.[58] The 'free exercise of religion' was to be allowed, albeit only to the extent 'consistent with the requirements of such detention'.[59]

And so were born the various detention facilities situated on Guantánamo Bay, in a part of geographic Cuba that is on permanent lease to the United States (an arrangement dating from 1903). Cuba's 'ultimate sovereignty' asserted in the original agreement was trumped by the guarantee (in the same document) that the United States would enjoy 'complete jurisdiction and control' so far as what went on in the facility was concerned.[60] The attraction to the US was certainly the expectation that the activities at the military base would be beyond the reach of US national law while also being outside the jurisdiction of the Cuban authorities – a 'legal black hole' as it quickly came to be called, made even darker by the Americans' assertion that the way they managed detainees in the 'war on terror' was also beyond the reach of international law. The promise of humane treatment made by the president was the only guarantee Guantánamo inmates had against ill-treatment, and it can hardly therefore have been unexpected that allegations of brutal and arbitrary justice soon emerged from what the then General Secretary of Amnesty International was quick to describe as America's Gulag.[61]

In the twenty and more years since this naval base (the oldest overseas naval base in the US repertoire) was redeployed to these detention duties, many changes have been effected in the way in which it manages those incarcerated within its perimeter fences. Some of these have been imposed by court order, while others have been responses to critical international and domestic opinion (we look at how these changes came about in Chapter 8). All have tempered to some extent the arbitrariness that surrounded early iterations of the regime and the practical impunity that was enjoyed by the authorities in those early, fraught years. The base's current use has, however, survived presidential determination to see it brought to an end, and while at the time of writing the number being held in the facility has been sharply reduced,[62] there is no imminence about its current activities changing anytime soon. Far from it: as we shall see, the moves towards greater legal accountability introduced by the president (Obama) who had wanted the whole operation shut down have paradoxically entrenched it further, making the long-sought end to its detention role altogether less likely.[63]

The model of indefinite detention for terrorist suspects introduced by the Guantánamo regime both inspired and gave cover to detention regimes around the world. In the United Kingdom a system of

indefinite detention was introduced in the immediate aftermath of the
11 September attacks.[64] Analogous systems of control orders – once
unthinkable but now often welcomed as liberal alternatives to detention without trial – have since spread across the democratic world.[65]
The 'longstanding concern'[66] about arbitrary detentions in India was
deepened by the state's reaction to terrorism post-11 September, with
Human Rights Watch being recorded by a UN body as calling for India
'vigorously [to] investigate and prosecute officials who order, commit,
or tolerate human rights violations, including torture, custodial killings,
faked armed encounter killings, and enforced disappearances'.[67] Illiberal
governments have also naturally leapt upon the opportunity afforded
by the 'war on terror' to detain their political opponents in even greater
numbers,[68] without any longer (in the case of pro-US administrations)
the bother of American criticism. A UN report from early 2007 tells a
depressingly global story of enforced or involuntary disappearances, its
grim message encompassing much of the world and spread over more
than 500 paragraphs.[69]

If the Guantánamo model is one legacy of the 'war on terror' that
has embedded itself in many liberal and authoritarian states in the new
world order ushered in by America's reaction to the 9/11 attacks, then
secret detention around the world for the covert management of those
detained on suspicion of terrorism was another. These 'black sites' – loca-
tions scattered across the globe and entirely hidden from public scrutiny
in which not even a pretence of prisoner protection or accountability
was maintained – involved abuse which more closely resembled that
perpetrated by the worst of the South American juntas from the past
than the conduct of a democratic state ostensibly committed to the rule
of law.[70] It was the School of Americas run riot, but now in an organized
and premeditated way, mental and physical violence against suspects
being the core purpose of the curriculum rather than an occasional and
regrettable side-effect of otherwise legitimate activity.[71] Unsurprisingly,
the Bush administration was keen from the outset to keep these dismal
places entirely off the public radar – knowledge of their existence has
only been made possible by the scrupulous work of various international
and regional bodies,[72] allied to litigation that has forced the hand of the
states being sued, and above all by fearless journalism that has mixed the
dramatic (*The New Yorker* pictures of what was going on in Abu Ghraib,

for example[73]) with the scrupulous piecing together of a patchwork of data[74] to present an unanswerable case for their existence.

Three aspects of the operation of these sites have been particularly corrosive of our pre-9/11 understanding of right and wrong international conduct. First, and most obviously, there has been the direct involvement of US personnel in the organization and management of such sites and in the detainee abuse that has been consciously perpetrated within them – a kind of fleet of mobile Gulags that in the years after 11 September, and particularly following the invasion of Iraq in 2003, have popped up around the world, feeding into the Guantánamo central hub. Second, there has been the outsourcing of these operations to those US allies willing to do this dirty work on its behalf, and here we see such collusion not only from the 'usual suspects' with already dubious human rights records,[75] but from mainstream EU states as well, in particular Poland, Romania and Lithuania.[76] And, third, there has been the willing engagement of many US allies in the whole process, whether by facilitating the lawless kidnapping of suspects from within their own jurisdiction,[77] or by using the fact of such secret detention as an opportunity to secure intelligence of their own but without directly engaging in the brutality required to obtain it.[78] European states that see themselves as loud advocates of international human rights and the rule of law have been particularly engaged in the third of these, the chance to gain intelligence benefits from the dirty work of others being judged too good to let pass.

The effrontery of such state-engagement would have been impossible to anticipate in the decades of US-led liberal hegemony that preceded the 9/11 attacks. Since the end of the Second World War, the United States has made a virtue out of the principle of the rule of law and the protection of human rights – central themes in a world order largely constructed by it in the aftermath of that terrible conflict. Countries seeking to thrive (or even merely to survive) in the post-1945 age of American hegemony in the non-communist world could not risk subverting the values for which the US said it stood, values which if it were so minded it could enforce by the many national and international instruments, as well as economic tools, it had at its disposal. Of course, there has been some level of hypocrisy to this moral posturing – as with the School of the Americas and all it suggested about US means of control in South America. The Carter presidency of the late 1970s was particularly vulnerable on this score, and critics of America's engagement in the world have long made much of the 'culture of terrorism' which it has itself inculcated.[79] However, with the public establishment of the 'legal black hole' which Guantánamo represented, and its continued existence through multiple presidencies of various political persuasions, and above all with its use of these various 'black sites' around the world, the United States has signalled a dramatic change in its commitment to the rule of law. The contaminating effect on what is seen as 'normal' state practice has been immense – a change that has of course not gone unnoticed by those many states for whom adherence to the principles of fair procedures, the rule of law and human rights has always been at best difficult to stick with, at worst merely skin deep. As with the emasculation of the meaning of article 51, the US has led the way in the dilution of assumed standards of legal probity around the world – an opportunity that has been made possible by the 'war on terror' but which long outlives any of the serious violence at which that 'war' was, initially at least, not implausibly aimed. Counter-terrorism law has shed its rationale and now exists independently of the existence or non-existence of the violence to which it owes its foundation. Detention without trial and the emasculation of legal safeguards against severe restrictions on individual liberty have become common sense parts of the defence of democracy, not subversions of it.

The Joint Study from the key UN bodies working in this area from a human rights perspective, published in 2010, gives a sense of how the momentum has shifted away from the rule of law and in the direction of arbitrary detention.[80] Despite the advances made during the preceding decade in countering the threat from terrorism, '[o]n a global scale, secret detention in connection with counter-terrorist policies remain[ed] a serious problem, whether . . . through the use of secret detention facilities . . .; declarations of a state of emergency, which allow prolonged secret detention; or forms of "administrative detention", which also allow prolonged secret detention'.[81] The experts' long report details evidence of the practice in Asia ('in China, India, the Islamic Republic of Iran, Nepal, Pakistan, the Philippines and Sri Lanka, where anti-terrorist rhetoric is invoked to justify detention'[82]), the Middle East and North Africa (Algeria, Iraq, Israel, Jordan, Libyan Arab Jamahiriya, Saudi Arabia, the Syria Arab Republic and Yemen), central Asia (Turkmenistan and Uzbekistan), Europe (Russia) and sub-Saharan Africa (Democratic

Republic of the Congo, Equatorial Guinea, Eritrea, Gambia, Sudan, Uganda and Zimbabwe). As in the colonial and Cold War periods, the language of terrorism joins other inculpating labels to justify action against not only the violent but also those engaged in more traditional forms of protest, including political and trade union activity. There is also a new impunity so far as UN accountability is concerned, the Joint Study expressing in its concluding remarks its 'regret that, although States have the obligation to investigate secret detention, many did not send responses, and a majority of those received did not contain sufficient information'.[83] A further problem was a 'lack of access to States' territories [which] also meant that a number of interviews had to be conducted by telephone or Skype, with those interviewed fearing being monitored'.[84] In her follow-up report of 2022, the then UN Special Rapporteur on the promotion and protection of human rights and fundamental freedoms while countering terrorism, Fionnuala Ní Aoláin, lamented the lack of progress in this area, noting that '[t]he legacy of secret detention and torture does not exist in a distant past. Harms continue to be experienced to the present.'[85] Ní Aoláin observed 'with great concern that secret detention has evolved in the past two decades to encompass more complex and multifaceted forms of formally lawful transfer. Extradition, rendition to justice, extraterritorial operations, expulsion and the use of diplomatic assurance have become essential tools for States in counter-terrorism and national security contexts.'[86] With their newspaper sources, personal witness reports, annexes reporting individual cases, and multiple recommendations, these reports read like extremely well-informed Amnesty critiques of state practice in the field. They are clearly immensely valuable and extraordinarily well researched, but viewed together give an unavoidable impression of responding to states that have pulled down the shutters, regarding this human rights limb of the UN as being more akin to an aggressive NGO than an official human rights monitor.[87]

Conclusion

In a report to the United Nations filed in the week before Christmas 2001, the United States laid out the myriad legislative and executive actions it had already taken by way of response to the 11 September attacks.[88] As early as 26 October it had enacted (with minimal opposition) the USA

PATRIOT Act, which the report claimed 'significantly expanded the ability of US law enforcement to investigate and prosecute persons who engage in terrorist acts'. Additional powers related to the interception of communications were also extended to the authorities, and later revelations by the whistle-blower Edward Snowden showed how far federal intrusion into individuals' private lives had been taken.[89] There was also action against suspect organizations. On 5 October, the Secretary of State, in consultation with the Attorney General and the Secretary of the Treasury, 'redesignated 25 terrorist organizations (including Al-Qaeda) as foreign terrorist organizations pursuant to the Antiterrorism and Effective Death Penalty Act of 1996', the effect of this change being that '[g]iving material support or resources to any of these foreign organizations [became] a felony under US law'. On 7 November, the US added sixty-two new organizations and individuals to the list, all of whom were said to be 'either linked to the Al Barakaat conglomerate or the Al Taqwa Bank, [both of] which [had] been identified as supplying funds to terrorists'. On 5 December, the Secretary of State designated a further thirty-nine groups as '"terrorist organizations" under the Immigration and Nationality Act, as amended by the new USA PATRIOT Act, in order to strengthen the United States' ability to exclude supporters of terrorism or to deport them if they are found within our borders'. All of this was soon being mimicked across the democratic as well as the authoritarian world: assaults on civil society had been given the green light by the supposed imperatives of US counter-terrorism.[90]

It was the same with asset-freezing, which was central to the immediate response to the 11 September attacks by the Bush administration. On 23 September 2001, via Executive Order 13224, the authorities acted to freeze all the assets of twenty-seven foreign individuals, groups and entities said to be 'linked to terrorist acts or supporting terrorism' and 'authorized the freezing of assets of those who commit, or pose a significant threat of committing, acts of terrorism'.[91] Thirty-nine more names were added on 12 October, followed on 2 November by twenty-two 'terrorist organizations located throughout the world', thereby (it was asserted) 'highlighting the need to focus on terrorist organizations worldwide'. On 4 December, under the same executive order, the US froze the assets and accounts of the Holy Land Foundation in Richardson, Texas, whose funds, it was alleged, had been 'used to support the Hamas terrorist organization'. By this point no fewer than 153 entities had been included within the freezing regime. In a complementary move, on 29 October, the US created a Foreign Terrorist Tracking Task Force 'aimed at denying entry into the US of persons suspected of being terrorists and locating, detaining, prosecuting and deporting terrorists already in the US'.

The same pre-Christmas report also contained significant American undertakings aimed directly at supporting past UN initiatives: 'The US has signed and expects to ratify in the near future the UN Convention for the Suppression of the Financing of Terrorism and the UN Convention for the Suppression of Terrorist Bombings.' The Bush administration's mistrust of the UN – a prominent part of its international agenda in the first nine months of 2001 – had been replaced by a new awareness of its potential utility in the 'war on terror'. The report was only filed because of new international law requirements, obligations with which the US was happy to comply, not least because it had been responsible for them. 'On September 28, the US sponsored the UN Security Council Resolution 1373, calling on all UN members to criminalize the provision of funds to all terrorists, effectively denying terrorists safe financial haven anywhere.' With UN Security Council Resolution 1373 the US 'war on terror' went global in a legal as well as diplomatic way, now imposing these various American practices on the world by way of mandatory international law rather than mere exhortation. It is to this vital moment in the embedding of anti-terrorism laws in global practice that we now turn.

SEVEN

The United Nations

Defining terrorism

International concern about the threat posed by terrorism long predates the attacks of 11 September 2001. Even before the establishment of the United Nations in 1945, its predecessor body the League of Nations had in 1937 adopted a Convention for the Prevention and Punishment of Terrorism. The document reaffirmed 'the principle of international law' to the effect that it was 'the duty of every State to refrain from any act designated to encourage terrorist activities directed against another State and to prevent the acts in which such activities take shape, undertake as hereinafter provided to prevent and punish activities of this nature and to collaborate for this purpose'.[1] The drafters achieved an agreed definition of terrorism, set out in the first article: 'the expression "acts of terrorism" means criminal acts directed against a State and intended or calculated to create a state of terror in the minds of particular persons, or a group of persons or the general public'.[2] The duty to criminalize certain conduct (if not already criminal) then followed, revealing in its primary emphasis the reason the document had secured support, namely attacks on 'Heads of State', or the 'wives or husbands of the above-mentioned persons', or other '[p]ersons charged with public functions or holding public positions when the act is directed against them in their public capacity'.[3] There had been a rash of assassinations in the 1930s – including of the Austrian chancellor in 1934 and, just three months later, of the king of Yugoslavia on a visit to France – and it was to these that this Convention was reacting. The king's killers had fled to Italy, where they were able successfully to rely on the political exemption to avoid extradition, thereby heaping further pressure on the League to act.[4] The agreement never entered into force however, and the issues it tackled were soon overwhelmed by the outbreak of the Second World War, a conflagration that involved political violence on an altogether different scale. Despite its almost immediate redundancy, as Ben Saul remarks, 'the Convention is normatively significant in the debate about defining terrorism, since its drafting elucidated major substantive issues which remained relevant in the post-war period'.[5] Defining terrorism has proved what a euphemist might describe as a 'major challenge' for the UN, and more than twenty years on from the attacks of 9/11 it remains (as we will see shortly) a live one.

In Chapter 4, we described how terrorism as we know it today got underway in the late 1960s and early 1970s, noting there in passing how the UN organs (in particular the Security Council) responded from time to time with condemnation of state reaction to acts of violence of this sort. These Security Council resolutions were few and far between, and when they did come it was much more often in reaction to Israel's retaliatory responses against neighbouring states for their supposed support for Palestinian violence than to the sub-state violence that allegedly provoked the response. This was understandable: it was the job of the UN to monitor state action, not criminal engagements by individuals or associations. But the effect was inevitably to give an impression of partisanship. Not even the attack on the Munich Olympics by Palestinian militants in 1972 – the 9/11 of its day – drew comment from the Security Council, while the General Assembly resolution of 18 December 1972 that did address it coupled (as was earlier noted[6]) its condemnation of 'international terrorism which endangers or takes innocent human lives or jeopardizes fundamental freedoms' with an insistence on 'study of the underlying causes of those forms of terrorism and acts of violence which lie in misery, frustration, grievance and despair and which cause some people to sacrifice human lives, including their own, in an attempt to effect radical change' – language so important to the delegates that it found its way into the very title of the resolution lest it be lost in the longer text.[7] The balancing may have been awkward but was made inevitable by the UN's anti-colonial instinct, baked into its Charter with its commitment to the 'principle of equal rights and self-determination of peoples',[8] and deepening with each passing year as its membership grew to include ever-increasing numbers of previously subjugated imperial territories. The leadership in such countries was far from inclined to deny to others the techniques of violence that many of them had themselves used (as they saw it, not unreasonably) to bring freedom to their people.

Rather than grapple with the broad issue of terrorism in what was bound to be an ambiguous way, the early UN fell back on the security of the particular.[9] Throughout the period in which terrorism was emerging as an issue, the organization successfully generated numerous agreements aimed in a focused way on criminal acts of the sort that were occurring generally in the international sphere. These happened to be among the methods used by political activists to secure global attention for their cause, but such groups did not need to be explicitly mentioned in the more general condemnation of conduct of which the politically motivated were not the sole perpetrators. The Convention on Offences and Certain Other Acts Committed on Board Aircraft, adopted in 1963 and entering into force six years later,[10] is one such example; the Convention for the Suppression of Unlawful Seizure of Aircraft (adopted in 1970, entering into force a year later) another.[11] Old anxieties about the vulnerabilities of government leaders and officials were reflected in the Convention on the Prevention and Punishment of Crimes against Internationally Protected Persons, including Diplomatic Agents, adopted on 14 December 1973 and entering into force just over three years later.[12] This was later joined by an international agreement designed to protect the UN itself and its servants.[13] Aircraft hijacking continued to be a problem, both generally and (as we saw in Chapter 4) as a result of its use as a weapon of asymmetrical war by Palestinian groups, and it stimulated the Convention for the Suppression of Unlawful Acts against the Safety of Civil Aviation, adopted on 23 September 1971 and coming into force on 26 January 1973.[14] The continued vulnerability of airline transport hubs led in 1988 to a Protocol to that agreement covering 'the Suppression of Unlawful Acts of Violence at Airports Serving International Civil Aviation'.[15]

Some of these initiatives came close to being exclusively about 'terrorism' without explicit use of the term. As was the case with airports, particular atrocities often drove the UN into treaty-making action. An International Convention against the Taking of Hostages was produced a little over six weeks after the seizure of American embassy staff in Tehran in November 1979;[16] the hijacking by Palestinian militants of the cruise ship *Achille Lauro* on 7 October 1985 stimulated a push for what was to become, when adopted on 10 March 1988, the Convention for the Suppression of Unlawful Acts against the Safety of Maritime Navigation.[17] Experience of the dangers of plastic explosives led to a

Convention on the Marking of Plastic Explosives for the Purpose of Detection in 1991.[18] Sometimes the international community could be persuaded to act against potential rather than realized risks. Anxiety about the exposure of 'Fixed Platforms Located on the Continental Shelf' led to a Protocol to the Maritime Navigation Convention dealing with the issue specifically.[19] Analogous concerns about 'the potential dangers posed by the unlawful taking and use of nuclear materials' produced the Convention on the Physical Protection of Nuclear Material in 1980,[20] with an amendment following in 2005.[21]

Only once the term 'terrorism' had begun its successful embedding in international affairs did it start to make an explicit appearance in UN agreements, in the first instance among the preambular concerns with which this or that new initiative was being explained. The Maritime Navigation Convention adopted on 10 March 1988 alluded in its pre-amble to 'the world-wide escalation of acts of terrorism in all its forms, which endanger or take innocent human lives, jeopardize fundamental freedoms and seriously impair the dignity of human beings' – but note that even here the notion of some lives (those that do not count as 'innocent') being left without protection remained live, while another recital in the same preamble urged states 'to contribute to the progressive elimination of causes underlying international terrorism', paying special attention to, among other evils, 'colonialism, racism and situations . . . involving alien occupation'.[22] The plastic explosives Convention three years later likewise made reference to, this time, the 'implications of acts of terrorism for international security' but once again without feeling the need to define the phrase. Eventually the term seeped so fully into inter-national affairs that it secured a Convention explicitly engaging with it: the International Convention for the Suppression of Terrorist Bombings, adopted on 15 December 1997 and coming into force on 23 May 2001,[23] just three or so months before the 11 September attacks. The driver on this occasion was 'the worldwide escalation of acts of terrorism in all its forms and manifestations', despite which (and it might be thought remarkably) no definition of the term on which the entire agreement hinged was offered. Instead, the body of the document proceeded in the old way, identifying a set of mischiefs (e.g. detonating an explosive) which in certain circumstances were to attract the force of its provisions, but for none of which was the descriptor 'terrorist' needed to unlock its meaning. It is hard to resist the conclusion that the word was included in the title as a nod to its importance on the world stage while at the same time the drafters at the UN persisted in their belief in its vacuity.

The International Convention for the Suppression of the Financing of Terrorism, adopted on 9 December 1999 and coming into force on 10 April 2002,[24] seems initially to be striving to pull off the same feat, both deploring 'the financing of terrorism [as] a matter of grave concern' while refusing at any point across its twenty-eight articles and annexes to say what terrorism is. The agreement took things further in two important ways, however. First, it focused on prohibiting the financing of acts which constituted offences under the various conventions we have already discussed, and which are helpfully set out in an annex to the agreement.[25] Second, it introduced a set of circumstances, separately from those conventions, to which this Convention was nevertheless to apply. Article 2(1)(b) declared it to be an 'offence within the meaning of this Convention' where a person

> by any means, directly or indirectly, unlawfully and wilfully, provides or collects funds with the intention that they should be used or in the knowledge that they are to be used, in full or in part, in order to carry out . . . any other act [apart from those covered in the annexed conventions] intended to cause death or serious bodily injury to a civilian, or to any other person not taking an active part in the hostilities in a situation of armed conflict, when the purpose of such act, by its nature or context, is to intimidate a population, or to compel a government or an international organization to do or to abstain from doing any act.

Here, without being explicitly declared as such, was a definition of terrorism introduced under cover of an initiative on terrorist financing.

By the time of the attacks of 11 September 2001, it could be said by way of summary that the UN had been slowly feeling its way towards an agreed approach to terrorism, but one which – crucially – eschewed any direct confrontation with the ambiguities and uncertainties inherent in the term. This tentative mode of operating had long been unsatisfactory to the United States, whose influence at the UN was of course immense and whose capacity to debilitate the organization by the withdrawal of financial support hovered over all discussions between the two. The years since the aborted 1937 initiative by the League of Nations had seen various efforts to wrestle with the definitional issue in a more general way (for example, a draft code of offences drawn up by the International Law Commission in 1954,[26] as well as further efforts in the same direction in 1991 and again in 1996).[27] An ad hoc committee set up by the General Assembly in the second of these years had delivered the terrorist bombing and terrorist financing agreements mentioned above and had made progress on a much sought after Convention setting out a comprehensive definition of terrorism, with the attacks on US embassies in Nairobi and Dar es Salaam in 1998 providing further strong impetus for action. By 2000, a proposal from India for a wide agreement with a generic definition 'had been supported by the Non-Aligned Movement, the Group of Eight and the EU'.[28] But should not the Convention exclude (as Malaysia, speaking for the fifty-six countries of the Organization of the Islamic Conference, was later to put it) a 'people's struggle including armed struggle against foreign occupation, aggression, colonialism, and hegemony, aimed at liberation and self-determination'? [29] And, relatedly, should non-state entities engaged in such 'wars of liberation' be caught by the definition, groups like the PLO, Hamas, Islamic Jihad and Hezbollah? To global north countries, including them was the proposed Convention's main point; to others, the whole thing was yet another ruse to resist anti-colonial struggle. Not even the momentum behind the push for an International Criminal Court in the late 1990s could break the impasse, a resolution of the drafting conference regretting that 'despite widespread international condemnation of terrorism, no generally acceptable definition . . . could be agreed upon'.[30] By the summer of 2001, therefore, the search for an agreed universal definition was at an impasse, its promoters quite unable to resolve these various difficulties. It is not unreasonable to suggest that the insuperability of such obstacles was inevitable, given that the task was to pin down in law a term whose primary purpose was not rooted in reason at all (crucial to making a law coherent) but which was rather performative in its essence, to be deployed as a way of securing political advantage in a dispute with violent opponents. Its essential feature was its lack of essentiality.

The Security Council steps in

The twin towers in New York, destroyed in the 9/11 attacks, were situated close to the UN Plaza in the same city. From the start it was known that no conventional army had been involved in the attacks: the weapons used were self-evidently commercial airliners rather than state-supplied munitions, so the culpability of a non-state actor could be immediately assumed (even if it was not immediately known which non-state actor it was). Yet the UN Charter was rooted in the assumption that it was through nations that the peoples of the world would henceforth express their convictions, and it was through their governments that they would seek to achieve the maintenance of the 'international peace and security' and the 'larger freedom' that was that foundational document's promise. The day after the attacks, the General Assembly issued a short resolution strongly condemning 'the heinous acts of terrorism, which have caused enormous loss of human life, destruction and damage in the cities of New York, host city of the United Nations, and Washington DC, and in Pennsylvania'.[31] The resolution's urgent call 'for international coop-eration to prevent and eradicate acts of terrorism' was followed some two months later by a longer statement from the same body, setting out what were described as various 'measures to eliminate international terrorism'.[32] The General Assembly welcomed 'the important progress attained in the elaboration of the draft comprehensive convention on international terrorism' during recent meetings, and decided that this work should continue 'as a matter of urgency',[33] even going so far as to set out precise dates (28 January–1 February 2002) on which the relevant committee was to meet.[34] Certainly the 9/11 attacks were a spur to action, and the differences surrounding the draft agreement were narrowed considerably. But they were never to be removed: the slightly desperate optimism of the General Assembly's resolution of December 2001 just quoted proved misplaced. Saul summarizes what happened next:

> By 2003 . . . some states had reached their 'bottom line' on disputed matters. The Coordinator [of the ad hoc committee responsible for the work] believed that resolving outstanding issues – the preamble, definitions in Article 1 and definition of offences in Article 2 – would depend on resolving Article 18 (application to armed forces and armed conflict). The drafting mandate was

renewed again in 2004, 2005, and 2006. Negotiations were given further impetus by the recommendations to define terrorism in the High-Level Panel on Threats, Challenges and Change (2004), the UN Secretary-General's report *In larger freedom* (2005), the Madrid Summit (2005), and the UN World Summit (2005).[35]

For all the energetic words, the reality was that the draft comprehensive definition was stymied. It has remained lost in committee ever since, occasionally revived under the pressure of events, but going nowhere.

This was not true of the most powerful organ within the UN. As was the case with the General Assembly, the Security Council reacted to the events of 11 September in a short resolution issued on 12 September 2001, condemning these 'horrifying terrorist attacks', expressing 'the deepest sympathy and condolences to the victims and their families' as well as 'to the people and Government of the United States of America', and calling for states 'to work together urgently' and for 'the international community to redouble their efforts to prevent and suppress terrorist acts'.[36] All of this might have been thought somewhat routine, but the Security Council also went further, expressing 'its readiness to take all necessary steps to respond to the terrorist attacks of 11 September 2001, and to combat all forms of terrorism, in accordance with its responsibilities under the Charter of the United Nations'.[37] What these steps entailed became apparent before the end of the month, with the promulgation, on 28 September, of UN Security Council Resolution 1373 on 'Threats to international peace and security caused by terrorist acts'. We saw at the end of the last chapter how the US was to highlight its sponsorship of this resolution as one of the key pieces of evidence illustrating how seriously it was driving forward its 'war on terror'. It has had a dramatic and long-term effect on the balance between liberty and security across the world, tipping that balance sharply in the direction of security, and all with the imprimatur of the global institution charged with, among other goals, 'promoting and encouraging respect for human rights and for fundamental freedoms for all without distinction as to race, sex, language, or religion'.[38] A recent scholarly study on the subject was not overdoing its rhetoric when its editors chose as their subtitle 'How the UN Security Council Rules the World'.[39] If there is one reason why anti-terrorism law has embedded itself in the laws of nations in a way that is no longer dependent on the occurrence of 'terrorist' violence, it is UN Security Council Resolution 1373.

The resolution starts with the particular (the attacks of 11 September) before broadening out in its preliminary recitals to declare its concern at the 'increase . . . of acts of terrorism motivated by intolerance or extremism', and the need to 'combat . . . the threats to international peace and security caused by terrorist acts'. The usual international cooperation is called for, as well as 'full implementation of the relevant international conventions relating to terrorism'. But in a sign of what was to come, these preambular remarks reaffirmed 'the inherent right of individual or collective self-defence as recognized by the Charter of the United Nations', something the resolution of 12 September had also evoked but with 'recognized' by the Charter replacing in the 23 September version the 'in accordance with' it to be found on the 12th. Is there a subtle difference here, a suggestion in Resolution 1373 that this 'inherent right' stands apart from the rest of the Charter, uncontrolled by its other provisions? No mention of the Charter's obligations in the field of human rights appears in the preamble to the 23 September document, or indeed at any point apart from a passing single mention (in the context of the granting of refugee status). (The shorter 12 September resolution had also not referred to any UN human rights obligations.) What does appear in the meat of Resolution 1373 is a wide range of obligations imposed on states, covering not only a whole spectrum of potential anti-terrorist cooperation, but also many matters that the states are expected to pursue themselves which are largely or exclusively within their domestic legal orders. The broad thrust of 1373 is to require action against terrorism in the following areas: the mechanism by which terrorists secure funding for their actions; the organization and arming of terrorist groups; the effective enforcement of the criminal process against suspected terrorists; the inhibition of the movement of terrorists across borders; and (this is where international human rights standards get their singular shout as a qualifier) the toughening up of asylum laws to deny their abuse by terrorists. The imposition of these requirements on member states is declared to be taken under chapter VII of the Charter ('Action with respect to threats to the peace, breaches of the peace, and acts of aggression'); in other words, there is a mandatory duty on the part of all states to comply. The words 'terrorist', 'terrorism', 'terrorist organizations' and 'terrorist financing' are scattered across the document but without any guidance as to what they mean, even indirectly by reference to previously agreed conventions (such as that on financing from 1999). There is no reference to the ongoing effort to produce a comprehensive Convention with an agreed definition. With Resolution 1373, the Security Council appears to despair of its organization's primary legislative assembly, choosing to go down its own, quite different route. And so, remarkably, 'two decades of extensive global counterterrorism law and cooperation have proceeded from a normative black hole: the absence of a common definition of terrorism'.[40]

Declaring that 'acts, methods, and practices of terrorism are contrary to the purpose and principles of the United Nations and that knowingly financing, planning and inciting terrorist acts are also contrary to the purposes and principles of the United Nations',[41] the resolution establishes 'a Committee of the Security Council, consisting of all the members of the Council, to monitor implementation of this resolution, with the assistance of appropriate expertise, and calls upon all States to report to the Committee, no later than ninety days from the date of adoption of the resolution and thereafter according to a timetable to be proposed by the Committee, on the steps they have taken to implement this resolution'.[42] This Committee was then further directed 'to delineate its tasks, submit a work programme within 30 days of the adoption of this resolution, and to consider the support it requires, in consultation with the Secretary-General'.[43] Lest there be any doubts about this dramatic move of terrorism to the centre-stage of UN business, the final substantive paragraphs of 1373 put these at rest, the Council ending by expressing its 'determination to take all necessary steps in order to ensure the full implementation of the resolution, in accordance with its responsibilities under the Charter'[44] and 'to remain seized of this matter'.[45] The envisaged committee was speedily established as the 'Counter-Terrorism Committee' (CTC), its guiding principles being declared to be 'co-operation, transparency and even-handedness'.[46] Three years later, in spring 2004, a Counter-Terrorism Executive Directorate (CTED) was established 'so as to enhance the Committee's ability to monitor the implementation of resolution 1373 (2001) and effectively continue the capacity-building work in which it is engaged'.[47] Initially time-limited, the CTED mandate has been renewed on multiple occasions, most recently for a further four years on 30 December 2021.[48] By July 2021, the CTED had conducted more than 176 visits to some 114 UN member states on behalf of the CTC since it was declared operational.[49] Over twenty Security Council resolutions have engaged with its work, in the early years pushing for greater cooperation from member states, and in more recent times reflecting the very much greater range of work it is being required to do. The CTC and CTED have outgrown their origins to become the security lynchpins of the twenty-first-century UN.

Human rights legacies

The UN did not transform itself entirely into a vehicle for anti-terrorism regulation overnight – or indeed at all. Elements of the 'old UN' have remained in place from the start, making themselves awkward for the newcomer, sniping from the sidelines, and – eventually, when the time seemed right – moving near to centre-stage so inhibiting to some degree the emerging new regime with elements of this older, embedded personality. The UN – challenged by the changes after 11 September, and the de facto lèse-majesté of the Security Council that followed the attacks of that day – was an organization institutionally committed from its establishment to the idea of universal human rights. The preamble to its foundational Charter had in its second recital made clear the UN's determination to 'reaffirm faith in fundamental human rights, in the dignity and worth of the human person, [and] in the equal rights of men and women'.[50] This universalist idea had coursed through the work of the institution in the decades that followed, with the early Universal Declaration of Human Rights (1948) being embellished by more practical covenants on civil and political rights and on economic, social and cultural rights respectively, the two documents agreed in 1966 that collectively came to be understood as an international bill of rights.[51] Other rights instruments, more discrete in range, had preceded these landmark 1966 interventions, just as many were to follow, extending the reach of human rights into an increasingly wide range of human situations. Matching these various textual expansions were movements in the direction of oversight and enforcement. A Human Rights Commission and afterwards a Human Rights Council were from the start dedicated to (as the current Council's website puts it) 'the promotion and protection of Human Rights around the globe'.[52] A process of 'universal periodic review' subjects all member states to examination on their human rights records. Various treaty provisions allow individuals to do the same, challenging the validity of this or that state action by reference to their binding human rights obligations.[53] Of course there are many criticisms of the way the UN goes about its human rights business,[54] but for all its many faults, hypocrisies and institutional limitations, all agree that it has been a towering presence in the international firmament since the very dawn of UN time. This system has not been removed by the new terrorist-orientation of the UN – but it has had to learn to accommodate itself to it.

In doing so, it has needed to confront the influence of a second, equally foundational building block for the organization, one much closer to the heart of counter-terrorism: respect for national sovereignty. In the years after the 11 September attacks, countries in the global south were to find themselves threatened by disruption on a vast scale, often radical Islamist in nature but not only of that sort. The failure to agree a universal definition of terrorism did not indicate a lack of concern.[55] It was here, via the focus on states, that the CTC found its entry point. The evidence for it lies in the name: this is a united *nations*, not a united *people's* organization. Early aspirations for some kind of world government quickly drifted away when the diplomats of the world's sovereign powers addressed how to reconstruct the world order in the aftermath of the Second World War.[56] The pre-war League of Nations may have had to go, but its idea of a community of nations survived. The omitted line in the extract from the UN preamble's second recital quoted above refers to reaffirming faith not only in human rights but in 'nations large and small'. This promise found expression in the Charter's commitment to respect the autonomy of each and every state that joined its club. The seventh organizing principle to be found in article 2 of the Charter declares that '[n]othing contained in the present Charter shall authorize the United Nations to intervene in matters which are essentially within the domestic jurisdiction of any state or shall require the Members to submit such matters to settlement under the present Charter'. This was subject only to 'the application of enforcement measures under Chapter VII', covering 'actions with respect to threats to the peace, breaches of the peace, and acts of aggression'. But that caveat aside, and definitely so far as domestic human rights violations were concerned, the effect of article 2(7) was to insulate national governments from the threat of a collective global intervention to rectify local human rights abuses, however heinous. It is true that the Security Council had these various Chapter VII powers which could theoretically be deployed to promote human rights ends at the price of a particular state's sovereignty, but even here the justificatory language of the chapter was rather limited ('threats to the peace' and so on), and a perennially divided Security Council – with the veto on action enjoyed by the five permanent members (China, the Soviet Union/Russia, the United States, the UK and France) – ensured that robust action could rarely if ever be agreed even in those cases of undeniably egregious abuse where it was patently needed. True, countries had to put up with the occasional hostile report or critical visit by this or that UN human rights team, but here was a small price to pay for membership of an organization that offered so much in return.

How did this embedded UN human rights framework interact with the various initiatives on anti-terrorism that took effect after the attacks of 11 September? How did the foundational principle of human rights cope with a UN which was now driving anti-terrorism action by member states in ways that clearly had the potential to affect negatively many of the human rights guarantees to which the UN was committed? The problem may have been made possible by the tension between human rights and national sovereignty that was at the heart of the UN, but it was now manifest in an entirely new way. It was not states acting in anti-human rights ways which the UN needed to control; rather it was such states *being encouraged by the UN itself* to do exactly that. The 11 September attacks unleashed this new UN on the world, one keen to push legal change in order better to defeat 'global terrorism', mandated to do so by a Security Council that was in this case (and almost uniquely on an important matter) speaking with one voice. In the years since 11 September, the human rights personality of the UN has tried hard to stand up to this drive for counter-terrorism. The wins by its 'wing' of the UN have been on the detail rather than the substance. Just as is the case with another aspect of UN activities, the blacklisting of regimes (which is the subject of the next chapter), the UN anti-terrorism legal edifice has not only survived but emerged strengthened from its dialogue with the human rights advocates within the organization. As we will see in Chapter 8, it is the same with the human rights pushback against national anti-terrorism laws in democratic states. To anticipate the gloomy direction in which this book is headed, it is clear that the critical engagement with anti-terrorism laws that we are about to describe has served further to embed those laws (somewhat reformed it is true) in both the UN and the democratic states which have engaged in a similar way as the UN with the tension between liberty and security. Though anti-terrorism laws have been improved a bit, we have reached the point where their removal appears unthinkable and where they no longer need terrorism to justify their existence. They have all become a given.

The UN Rapporteur on counter-terrorism and human rights

In the early years of CTC and CTED activity, the security orientation of the UN ran very deep, breaking with old assumptions in the pursuit of the impossible: obliteration of a global mischief it could not even accurately define. The first signs of an invigorated human rights engagement came from the General Assembly. Like the Security Council it was, as we have seen, quick to respond to the attacks of 11 September, condemning these 'heinous acts of terrorism' on the day after the attacks.[57] Its 12 December 2001 resolution made the usual call for 'measures to eliminate international terrorism'[58] which were in this iteration required to be 'in accordance with the Charter . . . and the relevant provisions of international law, including international standards of human rights'.[59] One week later, a resolution on 'human rights and terrorism',[60] while mainly concerning itself with the human rights implications of the actions of the terrorists themselves, nevertheless also took the opportunity to reaffirm in one of its introductory recitals 'that all measures to counter terrorism must be in strict conformity with the relevant provisions of international law, including international human rights standards'.[61] The resolution was adopted with no votes against (albeit with the United States abstaining). Almost exactly one year later, on 18 December 2002, a further General Assembly resolution, on the 'protection of human rights and fundamental freedoms while countering terrorism',[62] reiterated earlier calls while also requesting the United Nations Commissioner for Human Rights to make use of existing mechanisms:

(a) To examine the question of the protection of human rights and fundamental freedoms while countering terrorism, taking into account reliable
information from all sources;

(b) To make general recommendations concerning the obligation of States
to promote and protect human rights and fundamental freedoms while
taking action to counter terrorism;

(c) To provide assistance and advice to States, upon their request, on the
protection of human rights and fundamental freedoms while countering
terrorism, as well as to relevant United Nations bodies.[63]

By now, the end of 2002, a head of steam was growing across the UN
about the potential effects of the US-led intervention in Afghanistan,
and in particular the reports of alleged human rights abuses for which the
occupying forces were said to be responsible and which were beginning
to receive publicity. There had long been some interest in the inter-
relationship between terrorism and human rights. Kalliopi K. Koufa, a
Special Rapporteur on the topic, had produced a long working paper as
early as June 1997,[64] and the UN Sub-Commission on the Promotion
and Protection of Human Rights had issued many resolutions on the
matter in the years before (and immediately following) the 11 September
attacks.[65] Koufa's follow-up paper of 17 July 2002 was stating the obvious
when it observed, nearly a year on from the attacks, that the response
to 9/11 had 'introduced new and unprecedented dimensions to the legal
issues and analysis' with the 'scale and scope of the mandate [having]
become almost unmanageable'.[66] This independent expert's interest in
definitional exactitude for the purposes of a UN-wide agreement on what
constituted terrorism seemed by then, however, to be somewhat besides
the point, though a stream of thoughtful reports were to follow from
her in the 2000s.[67] Meanwhile, taking up the prompt from the General
Assembly, and with the occupation of Iraq now an additional matter of
which to take account, the Commission on Human Rights established
for 'a period of one year' and 'from existing resources' an independent
expert to assist the Office of the UN High Commissioner on the topic.[68]
Building on work already done directly by the High Commissioner Mary
Robinson in response to the General Assembly's requests for her Office's
engagement,[69] the appointed expert, US Professor Robert K. Goldman,
duly submitted in February 2005 an extensive and penetrating analysis of

the deleterious impact on human rights of the UN's new and enthusiastic engagement with terrorism.[70] His recommendation of 'the creation of a special procedure with a multidimensional mandate to monitor States' counter-terrorism measures and their compatibility with international human rights law'[71] was taken up, and by a resolution dated 21 April 2005, the UN Commission on Human Rights established just such a Special Rapporteur for an initial three year term.[72]

The first holder of this position was Martin Scheinin, a law professor from Finland. His tenure was over six years, seeing through the first renewal. Subsequent renewals have continued the office, the later occupants of the position being Ben Emmerson KC and Fionnuala Ní Aoláin KC (Hon) (the first an English barrister, the second a law professor from Ireland), each having held the post for six years. (The fourth holder of the position, Professor Ben Saul, has recently been appointed.) All three undertook strong human rights work, engaging critically with the CTC and CTED. In his inaugural annual report,[73] Scheinin identified the problems for human rights that flowed from imposing duties of action in the field of counter-terrorism while leaving the question of what terrorism was to the member states. In Scheinin's view, here was a temptation to wield authoritarian power against one's domestic political opponents under cover not only of UN sanction but of positive UN obligation that many – especially those inclined against human rights in the first place – found impossible to resist. There was 'a risk that the international community's use of the notion of "terrorism", without defining the term, result[ed] in the unintentional international legitimization of conduct undertaken by oppressive regimes, through delivering the message that the international community wants strong action against "terrorism" however defined'.[74]

The practical consequences of this were then illustrated by Scheinin's review of what he had found when he had examined how the CTC was going about its business in those early years, trawling through the 640 or so reports that even by then member states had filed as part of their duty under Resolution 1373. True, there were some countries ('few in number') where the CTC engaged in a dialogue with the state that foregrounded human rights issues: Belgium was one, Kenya another.[75] Then there were countries that felt compelled to resist CTC recommendations on the ground that they ran counter to the state's human rights commitments. Paraguay, Peru and Austria fell into this category, the last of these being forced to explain some basic human rights law to the CTC: 'Austria defended its law with a reference to the need to comply with human rights in the fight against terrorism and the possibility of avoiding impunity for terrorist crimes.'[76] Scheinin found that in these cases the CTC had been pretty open to dialogue about how to resolve this human rights 'obstacle' to proper anti-terrorism law enforcement. But then there was the 'third and perhaps most problematic category' of cases, consisting of 'instances where subsequent reports by a State suggest[ed] that the CTC's questions and recommendations to the State in question might have been insensitive to human rights'. It appeared 'that the CTC, in its dialogues, ha[d] been routinely asking questions about a long list of crime investigation techniques that manifestly constitute[d] interferences with the right to privacy and family life'.[77] The Special Rapporteur found it

> problematic that the CTC seems to be recommending that the potential range of investigative techniques (such as 'controlled delivery', pseudo-offences, anonymous informants, cross-border pursuits, bugging of private and public premises, interception of confidential communications on the Internet and telephone, etc.) should be maximized. At least sometimes, safeguards required by human rights law (such as the requirement that only actual crime suspects may be subjected to the measures, the requirement of prior judicial authorization, and the requirement of limited duration) that may be in place under domestic law should be relaxed. Unless the applicable human rights standards are referred to in this type of question, States may get the impression that they are requested to expand the investigative powers of their law enforcement authorities at any cost to human rights.[78]

It was 'a matter of concern to the Special Rapporteur that this line of questions has been addressed also to regimes whose law enforcement authorities are known to violate human rights'.[79] His report was clear that '[l]aw enforcement practices that violate human rights do not deserve to be legitimized by the Security Council'.[80] It was even worse where – as in the case of Belarus (as Scheinin found) – this 'UN imprimatur' was being used to mount a fight back against human rights criticisms from other parts of the UN.[81] The root of the problem lay in the failure to define the remit of Resolution 1373, with the CTC showing 'little, if any, interest in the definition of terrorism at the national level'.[82] This was despite its being 'well known that States frequently apply terrorism definitions that either do not meet the requirements of [criminal justice] or, even worse, are designed in bad faith to outlaw political opposition, religious entities, or minority, indigenous or autonomy movements that have never resorted to violence against persons'.[83]

This inaugural Scheinin report is an important snapshot of how things stood at the end of December 2005, with a rampant CTC and CTED roaming the globe in search of ever tighter domestic action against terrorism, without bothering to inform itself particularly as to what terrorism was, and barely acknowledging the existence of other institutions within the UN with historic missions pointing in a different direction to themselves. Scheinin has written of how his period in office 'allowed first-hand exposure to the colossal negative and lasting impact that counter-terrorism measures can have on a whole range of human rights, including political, civil, economic, social and cultural rights'.[84] Ben Emmerson's tenure saw the emergence of a new concern about foreign fighters,[85] and a vast increase in the use of drones as counter-terrorism killing machines – both the subject of critical reports.[86] Fionnuala Ní Aoláin's engagement with the subject has been wide-ranging but also deep, displaying a refreshing willingness to engage with the underlying causes of terrorist violence and the gendered way in which the subject is so frequently presented.[87] The position of Special Rapporteur seems now as embedded as the CTC itself has become – part of the furnishing delivered to the new anti-terrorism rooms of the UN by the older human rights suites scattered about.

Has the post made any difference, and if so of what sort? Certainly the days are long gone when a chair of the CTC could say (as the inaugural chair Jeremy Greenstock did, in a briefing to the Security Council on 18 January 2002) that '[m]onitoring performance against other international conventions [apart from Resolution 1373], including human rights law, [was] outside the scope' of the Committee.[88] Atrocities in 2002 (in Bali, Moscow and Kenya) kept the subject at the forefront of the international agenda and led to further Security Council calls for countries to discharge their various Resolution 1373 duties,[89] but with no effort being made to develop any human rights obligations at this time.[90] In the years since that low-point of 2001–2, however, and reflecting no doubt the increased pressure from the human rights interest, the CTC has slowly but surely introduced such a dimension to its work. Change has been slow – as we have just seen, even by 2005 Scheinin had found next to no human rights sensitivity in the CTC and (the then newly established) CTED engagements with states. But at least the High Level Meeting of the Security Council on Combatting Terrorism, held on 20 January 2003, had accompanied the Council's usual demands for greater anti-terrorism activity with calls for states to ensure that their actions under this head 'comply with all their obligations under international law' and that all measures thereby adopted are 'in accordance with international law, in particular international human rights, refugee, and humanitarian law'.[91] It was the immediate aftermath of the Madrid bombings on 11 March 2004 (erroneously attributed at the time to the Basque group ETA[92]) that saw the establishment of CTED,[93] and two years later policy guidance for this new organ relating to the human rights aspects of its work was laid out. This guidance required it to advise the CTC on the human rights dimensions to its dealings with states when discussing with them implementation of Resolution 1373, and also to advise on how to ensure that measures taken by those states under a later core intervention, Resolution 1624, complied with, as that resolution put it (echoing the High Level group), 'their obligations under international law, in particular international human rights law, refugee law, and humanitarian law'.[94] Preliminary implementation assessments, or PIAs, were developed as a way of highlighting potential problem areas in advance of a CTC visit to this or that country.[95] In 2008, the Security Council endorsed the establishment within the CTED of a working group on the human rights aspects of counter-terrorism,[96] and two years later it embraced the language of the recently finalized UN Global Counter-Terrorism Strategy and Plan of Action,[97] which had acknowledged the importance of respect for human rights as part of effective counter-terrorism. The Security Council also further toughened up the requirement for human rights to play a prominent part in the daily work of the CTED.[98]

Despite all this busy human rights activity, the inaugural Special Rapporteur under whose watch these changes had occurred remained somewhat sceptical. Writing in 2018, Scheinin identified various gaps in the system as it had developed, and – echoing his inaugural report – wondered aloud whether some states might 'have used this mechanism to obtain international recognition – even a stamp of approval – for rights limiting measures which they would possibly not have otherwise taken, or not otherwise have adopted so openly'.[99] This is the key point: how much have these improvements bedded down a system that might otherwise have become unsustainable with the decline of international terrorism as a matter of central global concern? Emmerson used one of his reports to point out that, for all the eloquence of its human rights commitments, '[b]etween 2005 and 2013, [the CTED] employed only one Human Rights Officer to cover its entire global mandate; a second was appointed in 2013'. Emmerson went on to observe that '[t]aken alone, these staffing levels might not suggest that human rights protection has been a high priority in the Executive Directorate's programme of work'.[100] Indeed, despite its best efforts, 'it would be difficult to categorize the human rights input in the Executive Directorate's programme of work as central or systematic'.[101] Fionnuala Ní Aoláin has been even more forthright, zooming in as Scheinin had earlier done on the fundamental problem of definitional uncertainty:

> Despite agreement on 19 universal counter-terrorism instruments, international counter-terrorism regulation remains a normative 'black hole', precisely because, in resolution 1373 (2001) and successive counter-terrorism resolutions, the Security Council has deliberately failed to advance a consistently used definition of terrorism . . . The Special Rapporteur observes that extraordinary leeway is granted to States in defining a far-reaching range of actions, including expression, religious practice, assembly, relationships and association (many protected by international human rights law) as 'terrorism' subject to expansive legislative and executive action . . . The result is that the provision of capacity-building and technical assistance is carried out in a definitional vacuum; a permissive environment that is human rights 'lite' by design and practice.[102]

Ní Aoláin acknowledged that by the summer of 2021, 'the Counter-Terrorism Committee Executive Directorate ha[d] expanded its human rights in-house expertise and [now had] a small number of highly expert human rights legal advisors', and that its engagement with human rights had 'deepened in recent years'.[103] But the process of country review remained immersed in secrecy:

> One key challenge in evaluating the nature, scope and adequacy of the human rights advice given to States through the Counter-Terrorism Committee

and the Counter-Terrorism Committee Executive Directorate monitoring and reporting processes is that only one State has made its report public since 2006, and, while a few reports are now available through the Global Counter-Terrorism Coordination Compact, regrettably, they cannot be assessed publicly . . . The Special Rapporteur notes that the deep-dive process which the Counter-Terrorism Committee Executive Directorate undertakes, engaging directly in capacity-building and technical assistance with States, constitutes a unique opportunity to address the profound human rights deficits amply demonstrated in national counter-terrorism practice. It remains unclear, precisely because of the opacity of process and the narrow reliance on Security Council resolutions without full engagement with the totality of States' international law obligations, how effective this process may be in practice.[104]

Ní Aoláin described herself as 'profoundly concerned that such a lack of transparency occludes the compatibility of advice given by the Executive Directorate with the assessment of human rights deficits in counter-terrorism practice by authoritative entities and processes (such as the universal periodic review, determinations of the United Nations treaty bodies and country assessments by the Special Rapporteur)'.[105] This 'shortcoming' was 'of particular concern given the political weight of recommendations issued by the Counter-Terrorism Committee and its Executive Directorate and the comparatively high rate of compliance with counter-terrorism related soft and informal norms and relevant guidance by member states, compared with the lacunae in human rights and humanitarian law compliance identified in the present report and elsewhere'.[106]

Conclusion

How plausible is the idea that human rights safeguards may do valuable work, but that in doing so they copper-fasten a regime that might otherwise have been exposed for its extremist nature, particularly when the threat of terrorism loses its capacity to compel rapt attention on the world stage? To answer that question more fully, the next chapter turns to another aspect of the UN's work, blacklisting, and then (in the chapter following) to the ways in which important strands within liberal democratic society have sought to resist the counter-terrorism juggernaut. Here we find the same process of embedment, the same story of a code of anti-terrorism that is solidified by its engagement with liberal values. This is not to say that it is a bad thing that such engagement has occurred, but it has certainly made possible the entrenched global counter-terrorism laws that exist today.

EIGHT

UN Blacklists

Introduction: The 1267 regime

Economic sanctions have a long history at the United Nations. In 1965, a non-binding Security Council resolution responded to the declaration of independence by the 'illegal authorities in Southern Rhodesia' (now Zimbabwe) by calling upon all states 'to refrain from any action which would assist and encourage the illegal régime and, in particular, to desist from providing it with arms, equipment and military material, and to do their utmost in order to break all economic relations with Southern Rhodesia, including an embargo on oil and petroleum products'.[1] The matter was later made the subject of compulsory action under Chapter VII of the UN Charter, and a committee set up to manage the sanctions system effectively.[2] After the end of the Cold War, the use of sanctions became a routine weapon in the UN's arsenal when faced with state malfeasance: Iraq following its invasion of Kuwait in 1990; and various bodies, governmental and non-governmental, in Afghanistan, Haiti, Liberia, Rwanda, Sudan and components of the former Yugoslavia. Sudan found its diplomatic presence on the international stage forcibly scaled back and certain commodities (such as illicitly sourced 'blood diamonds') used to fund insurgencies were taken off the market. The idea that 'targeted' sanctions were a better idea than those aimed in an indiscriminate way at the general population of a state took hold quite early on: in the 1990s travel was inhibited for local elites in Iraq, the former Yugoslavia, Libya, Haiti, Angola, Sudan, Sierra Leone and Afghanistan, with the assets of individuals assessed as culpable being as vulnerable as those of government entities in most of these countries as well. As early as 1993, a Turkish airline company found itself enmeshed in a long-running legal action against Ireland after an airplane it leased from Yugoslav Airlines was impounded under a UN sanctions regime that had been put in place against the former Federal Republic of Yugoslavia.[3]

The key escalation in these sanctions regimes came nearly two years before the 11 September attacks, on 15 October 1999. This was when the UN Security Council acted against the Taliban government in Afghanistan for its 'harbouring of international terrorists and their organizations' and – more specifically – for its ongoing refusal to turn over Osama bin Laden for trial. As we saw in Chapter 6, Bin Laden's Al-Qaeda group had already been involved in aggressive attacks on the US around the world, and had in the Taliban's Afghanistan found a 'safe haven'[4] from within which such actions could be planned. Promulgated under Chapter VII (as the second Rhodesian resolution had been), UN Security Council Resolution 1267 set out various punishments that were to be implemented against the Taliban regime if it continued to flout the will of the international community as epitomized in the demands of the UN, of which controls on aviation and on a range of financial transactions were the most intrusive.[5] A special oversight committee consisting of all the members of the Council was established to effectively implement the sanctions and to propose further action where they appeared to have been breached. Anticipating the Counter-Terrorism Committee's obligations of two years later, the committee was required to make regular reports to Council,[6] and a monitoring group to oversee implementation of the whole system was set up in the summer of 2001. This was based in New York and consisted of up to five experts (including a chairman).[7]

And so was born the UN Resolution 1267 sanctions framework.[8] The number and range of listed entities exploded after the 11 September attacks, not least due to the impetus given by Resolution 1373.[9] An expansion of the system in a Security Council resolution in late January 2002 was absolutist in its demands on states while still (as with Resolution 1373 four months earlier)[10] failing to qualify its calls by reference to any of the UN's pre-existing (and as already noted long-standing) human rights obligations.[11] Like the CTC, the expert monitoring group quickly established itself as an advocate for ever tougher measures to deliver better (equated with, inevitably, 'more effective') sanctions. The group's early reports reflect how hurried the whole process was, and how uncertain, with governments complaining that they knew nothing about the 'consolidated' lists which the committee was seeking to adopt in these very early years and being told in response to have a look at the committee's website.[12] State officials charged with implementation also raised problems 'at the technical level';[13] in a number of cases there were 'insufficient identifiers' of who was actually intended to be included, while 'in others the "cultural construction" of the names' ran the risk of 'implementation of the resolution [being] open to possibilities on non-compliance'.[14] Governments may not have known about the UN lists, but many were aware – as they regularly made clear in their interactions with the group – of the US equivalent.[15] This was US Executive Order 13224,[16] issued by President Bush as early as 23 September 2001. Following the additions to it made in the months following, the result was that by 4 December 2001 the number of entities affected by this measure had reached 153.[17]

With a British chair (Michael Chandler) and an American and Jordanian presence on the inaugural UN monitoring group (Michael Langan and Hasan Ali Abaza, respectively), it was always likely that there would be a strong connection between US and UN action on the monitoring group as well as in the 1267 committee proper. The listing and delisting processes at the committee were in these very early days extremely opaque. There were immediate concerns over 'fundamental acts of compliance',[18] with the group observing in late 2002 that '[o]ne of the most significant failings observed' by it was 'the apparent reluctance of many countries, for various reasons, to submit the names of persons or entities they have identified as al-Qa'idah members, associates or associated entities'.[19] A new set of guidelines adopted on 7 November 2002 was said by the monitoring group to 'provide a clearer indication of the procedures for the listing and de-listing of individuals and entities on the list'.[20] It was hoped that these changes would 'serve to alleviate concerns that some Member countries have expressed about the need to consider humanitarian factors in determining whether to provide the Committee with information relating to the possible listing of individuals or entities'.[21] Updates to the lists followed the flow to it of 'relevant information'[22] with 'a narrative description of the information that forms the basis or justification for taking action' being supplied only 'to the extent possible'.[23] It was the same with the provision of 'relevant and specific information to facilitate [the] identification' of those on the list – again only 'to the extent possible'.[24] Delisting was almost impossible: it could only occur through governmental channels and in practice required support from the government originally behind the designation that was being challenged.[25] The regular reports filed by the group in the immediate post-9/11 years reflect the uncertainties that surrounded the listing process and in particular the accuracy of the names entered, with a consequent 'continuing reluctance' on the part of states fully to engage.[26] By mid-2004 it was clear even to the bureaucratic managers of the scheme that their list had 'begun to lose credibility and operational value and now need[ed] updating in terms of its relevance and accuracy'.[27]

The Kadi revolution

In his last annual report as Special Rapporteur, Martin Scheinin queried the legality of Resolution 1373, arguing that the whole edifice had been created by a Council that had in doing so exceeded its powers under the UN Charter.[28] Scheinin thought that the same might well be true of the sanctions regime introduced under Resolution 1267, pointing to the criticism the system had been exposed to and the concerns that had been expressed by the Security Council itself.[29] Fionnuala Ní Aoláin followed his lead with biting critiques of her own, based on the challenge to human rights that the whole framework represents.[30] The argument deployed by Scheinin in his assessment was a plausible one, rooted in a close analysis of international law and of the UN Charter, the sort of opinion that would legitimately expect to be tested in a court of law. But which court? The International Court of Justice long ago acknowledged 'that, in the absence of any specific procedure to clarify the validity of the acts of UN organs, each of them must determine its own jurisdiction'.[31] The Security Council seemed to stand resolutely above the standards of behaviour which the UN felt able to impose on the rest of the world. Could such a position survive the negative impact on human rights and the rule of law that was an inherent part of the organization's choice to engage in counter-terrorism in the way that it did, and in particular in relation to the egregious breaches of due process and human rights that were self-evidently entailed in the blacklisting system?

The answer turned out to be no, or at least no insofar as the whole world was concerned. It came as a result of one individual and an assertive regional court, and was possible because the sanctions system depended on the actions of states or groups of states acting together – the UN had no direct intrusive capacity of its own. On 17 October 2001,

Yasin Abdullah Kadi had been identified as 'an individual associated with Usama bin Laden and the Al-Qaeda network'[32] and placed on the UN sanctions committee's consolidated list. European regional action had then followed. The European Union (EU) already had its own sanctions system in place, and on 19 October Kadi was 'added to the list in Annex I to Council Regulation (EC) No 467/2001 of 6 March 2001 prohibiting the export of certain goods and services to Afghanistan, strengthening the flight ban and extending the freeze of funds and other financial resources in respect of the Taliban of Afghanistan'.[33] When the legal basis for the EU sanctions changed about six months later, he also found his way onto the new list, 'imposing certain specific restrictive measures directed against certain persons and entities associated with Usama bin Laden, the Al-Qaeda network and the Taliban'.[34] By then Mr Kadi – who had presumably been finding his life suddenly narrowing all around him – had already instituted legal proceedings. He wanted all these EU regulations annulled 'in so far as [they] concerned him', on the basis that they 'were, respectively, infringement of the right to be heard, the right to respect for property and the principle of proportionality, and also of the right to effective judicial review'.[35]

His action was initially unsuccessful: the UN takes priority, said the first EU tribunal to consider the matter, the General Court. Short of the extreme situation of a violation of the fundamentals of international law known as *jus cogens* (not found to be the case here), the Security Council could do what it wanted, immune from the procedural tribulations that affected lesser bodies. Then, as an appeal to the most senior European Court got under way, along came an opinion from a key adviser to that body whose job it was to set out his view as to how the court should tackle the matter. Advocate General Maduro took a different line from the lower court, arguing that the EU simply couldn't do what it liked (*jus cogens* apart) to people within its jurisdiction simply because another international organization (albeit a powerful one) seemed to require it to do so. The Grand Chamber of the Court of Justice agreed, holding in 'essence . . . that the obligations imposed by an international agreement cannot have the effect of prejudicing the constitutional principles of the EC Treaty, which include the principle that all European Union acts must respect fundamental rights, that respect constituting a condition of their lawfulness which it is for the Court to review in the framework of the complete system of legal remedies established by that treaty'.[36] It followed, as the judgment made crystal clear, 'that the Courts of the European Union must ensure the review, in principle the full review, of the lawfulness of all European Union acts in the light of fundamental rights, including where such acts are designed to implement Security Council resolutions, and that the General Court's reasoning was consequently vitiated by an error of law'.[37]

This decision was issued on 3 September 2008. The immediate problem was what to do with Mr Kadi. The Court gave some hints about how best to proceed – Kadi needed to have the grounds behind his listing communicated to him and should, as well, have an 'opportunity to be heard in that regard'.[38] This should have happened 'as swiftly as possible'[39] after the listing, and the EU was now given three months to sort things out, during which time the annulled regulation would be maintained. There then began a search for compromise. Responding to the internal and state criticisms discussed earlier, the UN sanctions regime had already been tempering some of its more draconian aspects even before the 2008 ruling in *Kadi*. A 'focal point' within the Security Council had been established in March 2007 as somewhere for those affected by these decisions to turn, especially if they were minded to try to get off the list.[40] This was made more potentially effective by a decision made at around the same time that states suggesting additions to the list must provide a 'statement of case' which should 'provide as much detail as possible on the basis(es) for the listing, including (i) specific information supporting a determination that the individual or entity meets the criteria . . .; (ii) the nature of the information; and (iii) supporting information or documents that can be provided'.[41] States were also asked to identify parts of their statements that they would be comfortable passing on to the listed entity and any other parts that they might show interested states upon request.[42] In June 2008 the publicity element was ratcheted up a bit, with a new obligation being imposed on the sanctions committee to make accessible on its website 'a narrative summary of reasons for listing' decisions.[43]

Then, after *Kadi* in September 2008, a new functionary emerged, not a judge or other independent decision-making body, but rather an 'Ombudsperson . . . of high moral character, impartiality and integrity with high qualifications and experience in relevant fields',[44] whose job it now was to assist the sanctions committee in relation to delisting requests. As envisaged in the relevant resolution, this involved a lot of information gathering, consultation, handholding of the appealing party, the preparation for the sanctions committee of a 'comprehensive report' and assisting that body in its determinations – but no independent decision-making authority.[45] In the summer of 2011 the requirement that there be unanimity on the sanctions committee before a delisting could take effect was removed, and at the same time the opportunity was taken to make further procedural tweaks so as to give the ombudsperson a somewhat stronger grip on procedures, albeit without yet securing any kind of original decision-making power.[46] By this time, 'there were 485 entries on [a now] Consolidated List: 137 individuals associated with the Taliban, and 256 individuals and 92 entities associated with Al-Qaida'.[47]

So far as Mr Kadi himself was concerned, on 21 October 2008 a narrative summary of the reasons for his listing was sent to him. This contained many very damaging assertions about his role both as a banker financially entangled with Osama bin Laden and also as someone deeply implicated in terrorism, one who 'funnelled money to extremists' and (even) someone in one of whose premises '[p]lanning sessions for an attack against a United States facility in Saudi Arabia may have taken place'.[48] No further details were supplied; we should note the 'may', as well as the pejorative term 'funnelling'. There was much deeply prejudicial assertion of culpability along these lines. Mr Kadi responded by asking to see the evidence, asserting that none of what was said about his terrorist inclinations was true, and that 'whenever he had been given the opportunity to express his point of view on the evidence said to inculpate him, he had been able to demonstrate that the allegations made against him were unfounded'.[49] This cut no ice with the EU Commission officials. Kadi-duty duly discharged, the listing was confirmed on 28 November 2008.[50] Mr Kadi went back to court, arguing – hardly surprisingly – that the process which he had undergone since his legal victory could hardly be described as the kind of 'full review' that the Grand Chamber had had in mind. The General Court agreed.[51] It was 'obvious' that it had been the intention of that court that 'judicial review, in principle full review, should extend not only to the apparent merits of the contested measure but also to the evidence and information on which the findings made in that measure are based'.[52] Citing another important EU decision, *Organisation des Modjahedines du people d'Iran v Council,* the General Court expressed confidence that the Court in *Kadi* had

> approved and endorsed the standard and intensity of judicial review determined in that judgment, namely that the Courts of the European Union must review the assessment made by the institution concerned of the facts and circumstances relied on in support of the restrictive measures at issue and determine whether the information and evidence on which that assessment is based is accurate, reliable and consistent, and such review cannot be barred on the ground that that information and evidence is secret or confidential.[53]

The result followed inevitably from such remarks. The EU Commission was sent back to the drawing board. Before going there, however, the authorities rolled their final dice: an appeal back to the EU's top court, the Grand Chamber. All the big beasts weighed in. The Commission took a case, as did the Council of the EU, each asking for the judgment to be set aside and an order for costs made against Mr Kadi. They were supported by a dozen or so member states; over fifty names appeared among the lawyers assigned responsibility to win the appeal. Against them, five UK-based lawyers were left to argue Kadi's point of view.[54] A line taken by some of the appellant and intervening parties was that the first *Kadi* decision had been ill-considered and should now be disregarded. The Court was unsurprisingly unsympathetic, swatting away arguments that had been rejected in that earlier decision. The case-law was now entirely clear that 'European Union measures implementing restrictive measures decided at international level enjoy no immunity from jurisdiction',[55] and that, 'without the primacy of a Security Council resolution at the international level thereby being called into question, the requirement that the European Union institutions should pay due regard to the institutions of the United Nations must not result in there being no review of the lawfulness of such European Union measures, in the light of the fundamental rights which are an integral part of the general principles of European Union law'.[56] As for the substance of the human rights themselves, the Court resisted the opportunity offered it by the scores of government and EU lawyers before it to dilute the level of procedural safeguards upon which Mr Kadi could rely – in other words, to restrict

Kadi I in a way that ignored at least its spirit and possibly also (though not implausibly so) the actual words used in that ruling. There were to be no double standards so far as fairness in the EU was concerned.

The Grand Chamber achieved this outcome, startlingly at odds with all the parties before it except for Mr Kadi, and in defiance as well of the United Nations institutions (of which, of course, the judges could hardly have been unaware), by the simple but highly effective device of taking the rhetoric of human rights seriously. The judges were obliged 'in accordance with the powers conferred on them by the Treaties' to 'ensure the review, in principle the full review, of the lawfulness of all Union acts in the light of the fundamental rights forming an integral part of the European Union legal order'. Quite naturally (indeed inevitably), this 'included review of such measures as are designed to give effect to resolutions adopted by the Security Council under Chapter VII of the Charter of the United Nations'.[57] This obligation was 'expressly laid down by the second paragraph of Article 275 TFEU'.[58] The fundamental rights guaranteed in this way included 'respect for the rights of the defence and the right to effective judicial protection'.[59] The first of these included 'the right to be heard and the right to have access to the file, subject to legitimate interests in maintaining confidentiality',[60] while the second ('affirmed in Article 47 of the Charter'[61]) required

> that the person concerned must be able to ascertain the reasons upon which the decision taken in relation to him is based, either by reading the decision itself or by requesting and obtaining disclosure of those reasons, without prejudice to the power of the court having jurisdiction to require the authority concerned to disclose that information, so as to make it possible for him to defend his rights in the best possible conditions and to decide, with full knowledge of the relevant facts, whether there is any point in his applying to the court having jurisdiction, and in order to put the latter fully in a position to review the lawfulness of the decision in question.[62]

Phrased like this, it would have made no difference if all EU states had joined the case or pooled their resources to secure the best advocate in the world: there could only be one winner.

The Court pointed out that Mr Kadi had got stuck on the list in the first place because the US had decided as early as 12 October 2001 (through its 'Office of Foreign Asset Control') that he was a 'Specially Designated Global Terrorist'.[63] It was this that had produced the UN action which in due course had generated the summary of reasons upon which the EU had to rely, having nothing apart from that to go on.[64] His family and working life had been turned upside down and he had suffered the 'public opprobrium and suspicion' which such measures as these inevitably provoked.[65] Kadi had been rolling about in this echo chamber of insinuation and innuendo for nearly twelve years, but as every criminal lawyer learns early in law school, the repetition of an allegation multiple times does not make it more true. Where was the 'sufficiently solid factual basis'[66] to explain Kadi's elevation to this role of 'global terrorist'? The European judges' law required that they check whether the 'reasons [given], or at the very least one of those, deemed sufficient in itself to support that decision, [was] substantiated'.[67] The final sections of the judgment are a devastating critique, allegation by allegation, of the unsubstantiated nature of the claims that had led to the listing of the applicant.[68] If security requires secrecy, then that could easily have been arranged: there were available to be deployed by the court various 'techniques which accommodate on the one hand, legitimate security considerations about the nature and sources of information taken into account in the adoption of the act concerned and, on the other, the need sufficiently to guarantee to an individual respect for his procedural rights, such as the right to be heard and the requirement for an adversarial process'.[69] But none of this had been suggested as a route out of the impasse. True, the UN system had improved since Kadi had been listed, but it still fell far short of what EU law required.[70] The appeal was dismissed with costs.

Nowhere is Kadi's nationality mentioned. Who is this Yasin Abdullah Kadi who had caused such a stir? He was born in Cairo, Egypt in 1955, but is described by the EU Commission as a Saudi Arabian national.[71] If we are to believe the web, he appears to have trained as an architect in Egypt, after which he moved to Chicago. He is (or perhaps was) extremely wealthy, has ties to the Saudi royal family, and became involved in banking in the 1990s. He would seem also to have been associated with the Muslim Brotherhood, a very strong opponent of the Egyptian regime headed (during the *Kadi* litigation) by Hosni Mubarak, a president strongly supported by the United States and with whose security apparatus Mubarak would have had very close links, not least in his role as the region's most important Arab defender of Israeli interests.[72] The 2001 designation sparked a range of actions against Kadi and his financial interests around the world.[73] Intriguingly, he had disappeared from the sanctions list some months before the Grand Chamber ruling:[74] he had escaped the echo chamber before it could be explained to him why he had been there. The issue remained an important one for the Court despite this: there were sure to be future individuals for whom, like Mr Kadi, delisting would not be judged possible. The Court addressed this in an obscure couple of paragraphs well into the substance of its ruling:

> if it turns out that the reasons relied on by the competent European Union authority do indeed preclude the disclosure to the person concerned of information or evidence produced before the Courts of the European Union, it is necessary to strike an appropriate balance between the requirements attached to the right to effective judicial protection in particular respect for the principle of an adversarial process, and those flowing from the security of the European Union or its Member States or the conduct of their international relations. In order to strike such a balance, it is legitimate to consider possibilities such as the disclosure of a summary outlining the information's content or that of the evidence in question. Irrespective of whether such possibilities are taken, it is for the Courts of the European Union to assess whether and to what extent the failure to disclose confidential information or evidence to the person concerned and his consequential inability to submit his observations on them are such as to affect the probative value of the confidential evidence.[75]

The judicial review – which according to the Grand Chamber is 'indispensable to ensure a fair balance between the maintenance of international peace and security and the protection of the fundamental rights and freedoms of the person concerned . . . those being shared values of the UN and the European Union'[76] – was not exactly the same as guaranteed rights to see evidence, to be heard, to put the other side to proof and avail oneself of the principles of open justice. But it was substantially more than had been available under the sanctions regime to which Kadi had been subjected.

Kadi was followed by further challenges in other cases arising out of the implementation of the UN sanctions regime at national and regional levels.[77] Around the time of the first *Kadi* ruling in 2008, the UN Human Rights Committee had already identified rights violations in the 1267 regime.[78] Both the Special Rapporteur and the UN Human Rights Commissioner had long expressed concern,[79] as had a host of bodies drawn from civil society. But of course none of these judicial, quasi-judicial or political interventions had the power to direct a change of heart on the part of the Security Council. Despite *Kadi*, the system has been further expanded, reorganized and even more deeply embedded in the architecture of the UN.[80] At the time of writing, there are '14 ongoing sanctions regimes which focus on supporting political settlement of conflicts, nuclear non-proliferation, and counter-terrorism. Each regime is administered by a sanctions committee chaired by a non-permanent member of the Security Council. There are 10 monitoring groups, teams and panels that support the work of 11 of the 14 sanctions committees.'[81] True, there are now directions to the key sanctions committee concerned with Isil and Al-Qaeda 'to continue to ensure that fair and clear procedures exist for placing individuals, groups, undertakings and entities' on the relevant lists 'and for removing them as well as for granting exemptions',[82] as well as detailed rules on how the Office of the Ombudsperson (now extended into 2024) should manage delisting requests.[83] Annual reports by the Ombudsperson are issued, and a critical perspective rooted in respect for human rights and due process does on occasion appear in these.[84] The system is vastly better than it was, albeit still reposing the decision-making power in the sanctions committee – with a stark reminder of this in a recent Security Council intervention reiterating that 'the measures referred to . . . are preventative in nature and are not reliant upon criminal standards set out under national law'.[85] The sanctions system thrives. No independent framework of the sort that the *Kadi* case required has been forthcoming.

Conclusion

More than twenty years after the attacks of 11 September 2001, the engagement of the UN in the 'struggle against terrorism' has become fully embedded within the UN system. The week of 19–23 June 2023 was designated 'counter-terrorism week' at the UN, the third such gathering of its type. This involved a high-level conference of terrorism specialists from member states, a plenary session of the General Assembly, and no fewer than twenty-six side events 'jointly organized by Member States, United Nations Global Counter-Terrorism Compact entities, intergovernmental organizations, civil society organizations, academia and the private sector'.[86] The range of activities was made possible by the driving force behind the conference, the UN Counter-Terrorism Centre (UNCCT). The UNCCT has an advisory board chaired by the Saudi Arabian ambassador: it was that state's voluntary contribution that had made establishment of the centre possible in 2011.[87] Its support since has been unstinting. In August 2014, Saudi Arabia donated a further $100 million to UNCCT, and by the end of 2021,

> UNCCT had received generous contributions amounting to $159.8 million from 32 donors. This accounted for 56 per cent of the total resources of $286.8 million mobilized by the UNOCT [United Nations Office of Counter-Terrorism] for the United Nations Trust Fund for Counter-Terrorism from 35 donors. The Kingdom of Saudi Arabia remained the largest donor to UNCCT, with a total contribution of $110 million or 69 per cent of the total contributions allocated to UNCCT, while the remaining 31 donors contributed $49.8 million or 31 per cent.[88]

It would not be at all fair to deduce from this funding arrangement that human rights are totally ignored: the UNCCT annual report for 2021 makes clear that mainstreaming human rights and gender are at the heart of its mission. A global human rights programme is being rolled out during 2022–4 and it is intended that this 'will serve as key guidance for UNCCT in the implementation of human rights compliant capacity building and technical assistance support to Member States'.[89] The Council of Europe has unveiled its own revised counter-terrorism strategy for 2023–7.[90] No less a figure than the UN Secretary-General António Guterres gave a keynote address on the topic in London in November in 2017,[91] and while the programme for the high-level conference held in 2020 might have included sessions with evocative titles such as 'the global scourge of terrorism' and 'the plight of victims of terrorism', it also devoted one session to human rights (entitled 'Protecting and promoting Human Rights as a cornerstone of building resilience against terrorism', and featuring among others the UN Special Rapporteur on human rights and terrorism, Fionnuala Ní Aoláin).[92] The programme for 2023 saw the human rights session appear as the first substantive session of the week.[93] Ní Aoláin's recent reports on, among other topics, the increased terrorism (rather than peace) focus of the UN[94] and the closing down of civic space under cover of counter-terrorism[95] suggest, however, that the struggle between the old human rights/peace-oriented UN and the new anti-terrorism model remains intense. Which 'side' is winning out? Writing towards the end of her term in office, Ní Aoláin observed that 'the normative eruption in counter-terrorism' that has been evident since 2001 has also been accompanied by 'massive investment in a global counter-terrorism architecture, both within and outside the United Nations'.[96] Can the momentum behind this resource-rich counter-terrorism drive be resisted? Is there a risk that it will reduce the original purpose of the UN to a distant memory, a necessary ethical assessor to a new brutalism? Is *Kadi* the future or a quirky outrider from the past? Part of the answer lies in assessing how democratic states have dealt with the issue within their own jurisdictions, which is the focus of the next chapter.

NINE

Liberal Fightback?

Reasserting the rule of law

It might be thought that democratic states have a large advantage over the United Nations when it comes to asserting the values of human rights and the rule of law in the face of security-based pressures: their systems of government allow for oversight of executive action by an independent judicial branch. This can often permit the striking down of legislative measures found to offend basic constitutional rights, but at the very least it empowers the courts to rein in the excessive exercise of governmental power. Despite the theoretical controls this would appear to offer, however, the reality of judicial practice across twentieth-century democracies has pointed squarely in the direction of judicial passivity, at least so far as national security was concerned.[1] The key challenges have arisen in the context of war, hot and cold. In neither situation have judgments about what a state's interest required been seriously undermined by judicial actors. We saw this in Chapter 2 when we discussed the way in which the Cold War embedded the idea of an 'enemy within' in democratic states,[2] and it was equally true of judicial engagement with power during the two world wars.[3] True, there were a few outriders: Lord Atkin's famous dissent in the English wartime case *Liversidge v Anderson*,[4] for example, or the Indian courts' efforts to resist Mrs Gandhi's emergency of the mid-1970s.[5] But the general position has been one of passivity.

This restraint was also evident in early judicial engagement with executive responses to terrorism when this kind of political violence became more prominent at the end of the 1960s. In a case heard before but decided after the 11 September attacks, a senior Law Lord in the United Kingdom, Lord Hoffmann, summed up the general mood across the democracies when he observed that, '[u]nder the constitution of the United Kingdom and most other countries, decisions as to whether something is or is not in the interests of national security are not a matter for judicial decision. They are entrusted to the executive.'[6] The events of 9/11 provoked a postscript from the same judge to the effect that the attacks were 'a reminder that in matters of national security, the cost of failure can be high', and that they tended 'to underline the need for the judicial arm of government to respect the decisions of ministers of the Crown on the question of whether support for terrorist activities in a foreign country constitutes a threat to national security'.[7]

Lord Hoffmann's personal perspective was, as we shall see, to alter in the years that followed. By the time the exact nature of the changes wrought by governmental responses to 11 September had begun to sink in, the wider judicial mood in the liberal democracies had also begun to change. A strong and growing confidence in the assertion of judicial power in constitutional democracies emerged in the first decade of the twenty-first century, one marked by the fast growth of human rights instruments at local as well as regional and international levels. As Lord Hoffmann's remarks remind us, this was initially challenged in the security field by the events of 11 September. But it was to become apparent fairly quickly that the Al-Qaeda assault was more of a one-off than had been initially feared, at least so far as the advanced democratic economies were concerned. True, the violence continued around the world and was often horrific when it did occur (including from time to time in global north countries like England and Spain), but the bursts of destruction were sporadic rather than systematic. 9/11 did not prove to be a new Pearl Harbor. At the same time as the magnitude of the terrorist threat appeared to be receding, the rigorous nature of the international response to the initial attacks on the US came under the spotlight. Thus began a shift in focus away from sub-state (Al-Qaeda) malfeasance and onto state conduct, first as a result of the invasion of Afghanistan but then – and mainly – the assault on Iraq in 2003. The latter was an operation at least partly justified by reference to supposed links between Iraqi president Saddam Hussein and various terrorist organizations. Even quite early on, critical voices were being raised.[8] Stories about conduct in violation of international norms (of both war and human rights) quickly began to circulate.[9] The harrowing pictures of the ill-treatment of prisoners at Abu Ghraib that appeared in *The New Yorker* on 30 April 2004 made the issue impossible to avoid.[10] The critical scholarly response began slowly but surely to outweigh the supporters of President Bush's approach.[11]

This was accompanied by a series of interventions by reputable non-governmental authorities.[12] Books emerged expressing great concern about the new anti-terrorism powers, but wondering in a positive way whether human rights could 'fight back'.[13]

Among lawyers, the especial concern was over the challenge to the rule of law that government responses to terrorism appeared increasingly to present.[14] This concern percolated upwards to senior judges, the matter crystallizing less and less (as time went on) as a matter of national security and more and more as one of a challenge to judicial authority. This question of whether a court is competent to oversee the actions of the executive branch goes to the core of judicial identity. The belief that courts must have some capacity to rein in governmental excess, that they must not be shut out entirely from oversight of the exercise of this or that power however sensitive, is one that unites judges across the political spectrum in functioning democracies. They may agree on little else, but that they have a role as guardians of the rule of law is something to which they can all generally subscribe without difficulty (albeit without necessarily meaning the same thing when such a commitment is given). We have already seen this trend exemplified in the case of *Kadi*, discussed in the last chapter. In practice, this idea of 'the rule of law' entails the assertion of procedural fairness where individuals are adversely affected by executive action. The judges are rarely confident about outcomes – but they are invariably sure that individuals should be given a chance to hear the case against them and to put their own point of view before facing irretrievably negative outcomes at the hands of state power. Courts in a constitutional democracy rooted in the rule of law find it difficult to submit to notions of collective justice, no longer accepting (as one judge put it back during the First World War) that the safety of the state is the greatest good,[15] or at least that it is so great that individuals can be marooned beyond the law without any explanation. The Al-Qaeda attacks challenged this perspective, but courts across the liberal democracies gradually battled back, asserting *Kadi*-like that national security could never give the state carte blanche to do whatever it desired. Strong enough to insert themselves but not strong enough to eliminate the whole architecture of anti-terrorism law, courts have pulled off a series of admirable coups for due process, but at a price of embedding further the legal changes wrought by the laws they have been determined to scrutinize.

Indefinite detention: Belmarsh and its consequences[16]

In the autumn of 2001, under pressure both from the United Nations and the wider public, the UK government introduced into Parliament a new Anti-terrorism, Crime and Security bill that had as its centrepiece the proposal to detain indefinitely and without charge persons suspected by the Home Secretary of being 'international terrorists'.[17] The initiative required a derogation from the right to liberty that is to be found in the European Convention on Human Rights, a regional charter of rights that had been incorporated into domestic UK law only the previous year.[18] To work effectively as a matter of law, this human rights exemption required both that there be a 'public emergency threatening the life of the nation' and that all measures taken under it should be 'strictly required by the exigencies of the situation' whilst also not 'inconsistent with its other obligations under international law'.[19] The bill became law on 14 December 2001, after which a handful of men were picked up and detained in Belmarsh prison in London: eight on 19 December, a ninth on 5 February the following year, two in April 2002, one in October 2002, and a few more in 2003. The key characteristic of all the detainees was that they were foreign and Muslim. Their non-national status meant that they could in theory be removed from the country but they were in practice impossible to expel: either no country would take them or those that could (their home countries for example) would be places in which they were vulnerable to being ill-treated, or (in the language of the European Convention) put at real risk of death or torture or inhuman or degrading treatment or punishment.[20]

In the very early years after 11 September, the necessity of the legislation was widely accepted, with a challenge to it being seen off in the Court of Appeal in a judgment handed down on 25 October 2002.[21] The power was supported by government ministers as a crucial way of defending the security of the state.[22] The decision to root this part of the statute in immigration law inevitably entailed that only foreigners ('suspected international terrorists') were affected, and while this reduced the political heat it meant that there was an irrationality at the core of the law: if the emergency was so severe and the danger so palpable, why deal with only one potential set of terrorists (the international) while leaving their domestic equivalents entirely untouched? The answer to this question could not be that there were no UK-born radicals willing to follow the Al-Qaeda path, an assertion that was too incredible ever to have been made – and if it had been, would have been shown to be false by the suicide attacks on London's transport infrastructure by English-born bombers on 7 July 2005. By then, however, the detention power had been destroyed by a combination of political and legal hostility. During the process of enacting the measure in the autumn of 2001, concerned parliamentarians had inserted a clause mandating a committee of senior figures (in Britain's antiquated constitutional parlance, 'privy counsellors') to review the operation of these controversial parts of it. When the resulting review was published at the end of 2003, it constituted a devastating attack on the whole system, and called on Parliament to think again before it continued to support such a radical departure from the country's basic principles of liberty and due process.[23] Within a year, the then most senior judicial body in the United Kingdom had agreed, overturning the courts below in holding that the breach of the European Convention that the law entailed could not be said to be lawful due to its eccentric – indeed partisan – focus on foreigners alone.[24] While a majority of the judges did not challenge governmental assertions about the existence of an emergency,[25] they were emphatic that the discriminatory dimension to the measure took it outside what was 'strictly required' and so was beyond the protection afforded by the derogation that had been deployed on its behalf. Though the government did not have to change the law as a result (due to a curiosity of Britain's constitutional arrangements of no relevance to this story), ministers moved to do so anyway. The Prevention of Terrorism Act 2005, enacted shortly after the court ruling and just a few months before the 7 July bombings,[26] brought to an end this phase of preventive detention in the UK.

As the title of the new law suggested, however, it did not lead to an end of this kind of administrative anti-terrorism power: it merely took the power out of the prisons and more indirectly into the everyday lives of those subject to it. Crucially, these new powers could be deployed against British and non-British people alike: this was what made enactment of the law so difficult to achieve at the time, with long debates in both Houses of Parliament leading to important modifications before final agreement was eventually achieved. And even so, the measure was revisited six years later, when a new framework, the Terrorism Prevention and

Investigation Measures Act,[27] replaced the system put in place in 2005 with measures carrying the acronymic name of their parent Act, TPIMs. That modified framework is still in force and there is little likelihood of any political or legal head of steam now being generated to remove it.[28] The brute power of detention has been replaced by a subtler set of controls, accompanied by a variety of safeguards, the combined effect of which has been to inoculate society to changes that would have been seen as entirely unacceptable only a generation before. Yet the powers in the new regime are plain: in its early iteration forced relocation could be required, and even the modified TPIM system continues to permit state intrusion into private life on a grand scale. Those subject to such orders are able to challenge them on legal grounds, and the courts have also insisted on a degree of due process, a certain basic level of fairness to be accorded to those affected. There are not many TPIMs in place at the time of writing (a mere handful during 2021, for example); the whole system is also overseen by a 'terrorist watchdog' independent of government with a brief to ensure that the powers are not abused.[29] These liberal modifications may dilute the impact of the scheme, but it could be argued that in doing so they have ensured its survival.

Schemes such as these were rolled out across many democracies in the first decade of the 2000s. This was against a wider backdrop of frenetic anti-terrorism legislative activity: in Australia, for example, there were no fewer than forty-four anti-terrorism-related statutes enacted between 2001 and 2007, including legislation establishing a framework of control orders.[30] That country also has a preventive detention power whereby 'terrorist' suspects can be detained on the basis of a risk of future crime.[31] Other countries followed similar pathways.[32] During this time a new functionary, called a 'Special Advocate', became part and parcel of the UK's quasi-judicial system of accountability in the field of anti-terrorism. First developed in the late 1990s as a way of offering some element of independent representation to persons facing expulsion as security risks from their country of residence,[33] the idea was taken up by the UK in the Anti-terrorism Crime and Security Act as a useful adjunct to the detention power, enabling those affected by it to have their cases put to a special tribunal constituted to hear their cases (the Special Immigration Appeals Commission). This was retained in the control order/TPIM system that followed, and similar functionaries are now to be found scattered across the democratic world, providing succour to those whose lives are suddenly transformed for the worse by administrative sanctions which are analogous to criminal sanction but can be imposed without the discipline imposed on officials by the need to prove their case in open court.[34] In the usual model, Special Advocates are security cleared lawyers, independent of government, whose job it is to represent the 'accused' and who are equipped with all the relevant information that underpins the state action against him or her. The price of such informed engagement is, however, high: the Special Advocate may represent the interests of the individual concerned, but they do not represent them in the traditional way. That is the job of the ordinary lawyer: the one who meets the client, takes the case and tries their best to feed the views of the client back into the decision-making chain via the Special Advocate – but without any knowledge of the security case that has been made against them and without the right to engage in the proceedings insofar as these trespass into the territory of national security (which, inevitably in cases of this nature, will be often).

Detention: Guantánamo

The system just described grew out of a rejection of indefinite detention but in managing that decision generated a framework of administrative control which, if not as swingeing, was nevertheless unprecedented in its effect when considered from the perspective of the ordinary criminal law. Unlike the Belmarsh powers, the system of detention introduced by the United States after 11 September has survived the two decades plus since those attacks, albeit in a different form to that which was first introduced. Gone are the absolutes of the early years when an apprehended suspect could be lost in America's legal 'black hole' for years on end, incapable of challenging their incarceration and wholly at the mercy of their (often brutal) jailor. Instead, in a move similar to that which we have just been discussing in relation to control orders, and to what we have already seen with regard to the UN's sanctions system, the framework has been modified in important ways, and humanized to a degree – in other words, made durable, rebuilt to last, at least until the deaths of its remaining inmates. Indeed, it could be in place possibly even longer if a future US administration should find a use for its facilities; a scenario that is not impossible as the shame caused by early revelations about its operations gradually recedes in the public mind, and new anxieties – about terrorists once again, or asylum seekers, or (even) internal political opponents – bubble to the surface.

The story about how the US system of detention of suspected terrorists changed in the decade after 11 September is a frequently told one, with the US Supreme Court in the starring role. An early indicator of what was to come were three dramatic decisions, all handed down on the same day, 28 June 2004. First there was *Rumsfeld v Padilla*.[35] The petitioner was being held as a material witness in an anticipated trial, and when judicial review proceedings were being mustered to challenge this, a presidential order decreed that he should now be detained as an enemy combatant – an association with Al-Qaeda was alleged. Because Padilla was a US citizen, the Guantánamo facility was unavailable, so the authorities moved him to a military brig in South Carolina waters where he was denied access to the outside world and subjected to intense interrogation. The Supreme Court dodged the issue of the lawfulness of his detention when the case reached it – the suit had been filed in New York when it should have started in South Carolina, where the commander of the ship (and so in this case the jailor) lived and worked. But only the narrowest of margins – five to four – could be mustered to support this procedural sleight of hand, with one of the dissentients (Justice Stevens) asserting in dramatic terms that 'if this Nation is to remain true to the ideals symbolized by its flag, it must not wield the tools of tyrants even to resist an assault by the forces of tyranny'.[36] (Padilla was eventually charged with a broad range of criminal offences linked to terrorism, but unrelated to the reasons why he had been originally detained.)

There was, secondly, the case of Yaser Hamdi.[37] Here was another US citizen who on this occasion was captured in Afghanistan and moved to Guantánamo, only to be relocated to a naval brig (initially in Virginia and afterwards in South Carolina) when his citizenship became known. The justices agreed that in his case some rudimentary due process was owed to him. But in a remarkable dissenting opinion the most conservative member of the court Antonin Scalia joined with its most venerable liberal John Paul Stevens – the same man who had written in such rhetorical terms in the *Padilla* case – to assert that the 'very core of liberty secured by our Anglo-Saxon system of separated powers has been freedom from indefinite imprisonment at the will of the executive'[38] and this had been breached by the action taken against Hamdi. The implications of this took these two justices much further than the court was prepared to go – their view was that Hamdi was entitled to be released unless criminal proceedings were initiated against him in a prompt matter or the writ of habeas corpus to which he was otherwise entitled was suspended by Congress. Hamdi was afterwards deported to Saudi Arabia on condition that, among other requirements, he disavow his citizenship.

These two cases were decided early in the phase of apex court engagement with the exercise of post-11 September counter-terrorism powers; it would be a further six months before the path-breaking Belmarsh detention ruling, discussed above, would be handed down by the UK House of Lords. Both US cases wrestled (from opposite factual perspectives) with the fundamental distinction that each jurisdiction was making between non-citizens and citizens. This was eventually to prove as uneasy a point for the US justices as it had been for their British counterparts. Pressure was ratcheted up still further by the third case decided on that same day, *Rasul v Bush*.[39] Here the Supreme Court asserted its jurisdiction over the detentions in Guantánamo despite the fact that the people held there were by definition not American citizens (Rasul was British). Once again the formal court ruling was quite narrow, rooted in a fairly small point of statutory interpretation. The US legislature responded to it by enacting a Detainee Treatment Act the following year. Purporting to provide a series of safeguards for detainees in Rasul's position as someone without US citizenship, the Act conceded the establishment of Combatant Status Review Tribunals. It gave the Washington DC Federal Circuit Court oversight over them, in return for which the Act stipulated that all habeas corpus proceedings be directed through the avenue being offered by this new legal initiative. A general prohibition on 'cruel, inhuman or degrading treatment or punishment' of any prisoner of the US government (in Guantánamo or further afield) was also offered. A churlish signing statement accompanying the Act (reasserting the president's duty 'of protecting the American people from further terrorist attacks') tended to show that the administration's heart was not in what Congress had demanded and successfully brought into law.[40]

There then began a brief period of ping-pong between the legislative and judicial branches. On 29 June 2006, in *Hamdan v Rumsfeld*, the Supreme Court condemned the military commissions that had been painstakingly erected under the Detainee Treatment Act. They were judged to have failed to deliver the levels of procedural protection required by both the international laws of war and (more prosaically) America's own Uniform Code of Military Justice.[41] Within four months Congress had retaliated with the Military Commissions Act, signed into law by President Bush on 17 October 2006. This sought to undo the effects of *Hamdan*, not least by reasserting the procedural correctness of the tribunals set up under the earlier Act but also (and in particular most urgently) by choking off the array of habeas corpus cases that were even then making their way to the federal courts or had already been lodged there.

There matters stood for only a short time. The Supreme Court's concerns about due process were clearly now at odds with both other branches of government. But the Court had one card left to play, and it was a trump. Up to this point in the legislative/litigation process it had always been assumed that habeas corpus was a matter of legislative discretion – it was mentioned in the constitution but whether it was therefore to be assumed to be a constitutional right was left uncertain. The matter was resolved in *Boumediene v Bush*, decided on 12 June 2008.[42] Here the Supreme Court found a geographically unrestricted right to habeas corpus within the constitution, something that needed to be hewn out of the fairly oblique language of this foundational document. The political atmosphere around the case changed over the summer and autumn that followed. Reflecting the strong distaste in liberal America for the whole edifice of executive detention, the Democratic candidate for president, Barack Obama, made closure of the Guantánamo base one of his key campaign themes.[43] Almost immediately upon assuming office, in his first full day in the job, Obama issued an executive order requiring that Guantánamo be closed within one year 'consistent with the national security and foreign policy interests of the United States and the interests of justice'.[44]

Despite appearances, however, this did not mean an end to Guantánamo. Strong efforts to release, transfer or try all the detainees and so empty the place in a rational manner proved impossible fully to pull off. A rump remained, for whom a country willing to take them could not be found and who could not be prosecuted (often because the evidence against them was tainted by their earlier ill-treatment), but who were nevertheless judged too dangerous simply to be released into the United States. In place of closure, a new system of detention was introduced by presidential order dated 7 March 2011.[45] This explicitly recognized the 'constitutional privilege of the writ of habeas corpus' and promised periodic reviews of the legitimacy of each detention. But the test of the necessity for detention remained very broad, being permitted if it was judged 'necessary to protect against a significant threat to the security of the United States'. Gone were the old military commissions, to be replaced by a periodic review board, with a full review of each detention being promised every three years together with a lighter 'file review' every six months. Humane treatment was promised and a fairly basic appeal system was constructed. The presidential order also contained a vaguely worded directive to continue to seek criminal prosecution wherever feasible. At the review hearings, however, classified documentation could be withheld from a detainee, with (as in the British system) a 'personal representative' with the right security clearance being appointed by the government to put the prisoner's case. Not even this official could be certain of getting the whole circumstances underpinning the continued incarceration of their 'client' (as the Order does not describe the detainee). If the detainee instructed private counsel, then a raft of disadvantageous consequences could follow, including the denial of access to relevant documentation when said to be required by 'the need to protect national security, including intelligence sources and methods, or law enforcement or privilege concerns', with the lawyer receiving a 'sufficient substitute or summary of the information' instead.

Guantánamo remains operative today as a camp of indefinite detention. Of the 780 or so that have been through its gates, some thirty remain. 'Of those, 11 have been charged with war crimes in the military commissions system – 10 are awaiting trial and one has been convicted. In addition, three detainees are held in indefinite law-of-war detention and are neither facing tribunal charges nor being recommended for release. And 16 are held in law-of-war detention but have been recommended for transfer with security arrangements to another country.'[46] Each of the three being held indefinitely (Abu Zubaydah, Mustafa Faraj Masud al-Jadid Mohammed and Muhammad Rahim) has had his detention upheld by decision of the periodic review board. The first of these was captured on 28 March 2002, and 'became the first black site prisoner of the Central Intelligence Agency to undergo "enhanced interrogation," including waterboarding, forced nudity, sleep deprivation, confinement to a coffin-size box and other methods of extreme isolation'.[47] Given the likely evidential worthlessness of any admissions secured under such circumstances, it is not surprising that the prosecution recommended by the Guantánamo task force that looked at his case in 2009–10 was not acted on. Mohammed is in the same position, and Rahim (the last man ever to be admitted to Guantánamo, on 4 March 2008) is similarly stuck in a permanent lawless limbo. Like these men, those facing charges before a military commission will often argue for the inadmissibility of evidence on the basis of their earlier ill-treatment: the UN Working Group on Arbitrary Detention, in a report made public in June 2023, called for the release of one such prisoner, Abd al Rahim al-Nashiri, who was held in black sites in six countries before eventually being transferred to Guantánamo, and whose trial – begun over ten years ago – has been long delayed by various procedural issues.[48] Al-Nashiri has already obtained damages from Poland by order of the European Court of Human Rights for its having facilitated the operation of a CIA-run 'black site' on its territory.[49]

Security versus liberty

There does appear to be one irreducible value left in the liberal democratic locker, evidenced not only by al-Nashiri's victory in Strasbourg but also by the disinclination of ordinary courts and military commissions alike to deploy evidence secured by torture to achieve the convictions sought by prosecuting authorities. This is the unqualified wrongness of state torture in all circumstances. This is not to say, of course, that torture has not occurred – the post-9/11 counter-terrorism story makes it impossible to deny the centrality of the practice.[50] But early efforts to create new frameworks of legally sanctioned 'coercive interrogation' have not proved successful.[51] 'Torture warrants', under which a legally sanctioned (and therefore in the eyes of its supporters accountable) regime of judicially overseen ill-treatment would have been possible, never took off as a persuasive idea, even at the very height of terrorism-induced anxiety in the three or four years immediately following 9/11. The Council of Europe's unequivocal ban on torture and related behaviour, in a set of guidelines issued as early as the summer of 2002, can now be seen to have had history on its side.[52] The unqualified prohibition of this sort of behaviour is, however, something of an outrider. The lesson of both Belmarsh and Guantánamo is that liberalism can square its conscience so far as anti-terrorism law is concerned by legalizing the exercise of raw executive power, by inserting a degree of legal process into the deployment of that power but in a way that does not entirely (or perhaps even partly) subvert its deployment.

It is surprising how our ideas of liberty have changed in only a lifetime of exposure to 'terrorism'.[53] Of course, as we have seen in earlier chapters, 'abroad' has always been a place where the liberal writ has not necessarily run, and the Cold War also familiarized democratic culture to some extent with the idea of an 'enemy within'. But even allowing for such historic attenuations of liberty, the changes wrought by terrorism have been dramatic. Whereas in the United Kingdom in 1974, seven-day pre-charge detention was thought to be an unacceptable breach of civil liberties and was only achieved off the back of a series of shocking terrorist actions, by the mid-2000s, long pre-trial detention had become so much the norm for terrorism suspects that even the then statutory limit of twenty-eight days was widely considered by government to be altogether too lenient. The then prime minister Tony Blair had argued for ninety days in the immediate aftermath of the London bombings of 2005. Pushback by the junior coalition party in government after 2010, the Liberal Democrats, reduced the limit to fourteen days, with power in emergency situations to double that limit without recourse to Parliament.[54] Special procedures now routinely limit the material that can be made public in the course of litigation where the disclosure can be presented as threatening security interests.[55] In a way that mimics the detention powers we have just been discussing, there are various safeguards in terms of police and judicial oversight, and also in rights of access to legal advice.[56] The European Court of Human Rights too has had a moderating role, insisting on a judicial presence far earlier than the common law's adversarial system would normally allow (in contrast to the civil approach where judicially sanctioned detention is altogether more routine).

The long-standing freedom of association with others has been badly affected by counter-terrorism law. It was once thought central to liberal democratic values that you could not be banned for belonging to a political organization – that membership of something was different from personal criminal action. As late as 1974, membership of the IRA was entirely lawful in Great Britain (though not it should be said in the ambiguous homeland of Northern Ireland), and it took an Act of Parliament to change things in late 1974, in the shape of an emergency Prevention of Terrorism (Temporary Provisions) Act, passed against police advice on this point. Now some years on, proscription of associations deemed unacceptable has become almost routine in the UK: in late 2021, no fewer than seventy-eight such organizations were banned under the UK Terrorism Act 2000, with a further fourteen being caught by Northern-Ireland-specific laws.[57] Nor is the UK unique here. The change is evident in, among other places, Australia,[58] the United States,[59] in the European Union generally[60] and not least in Germany (where even the strong constitutional assumption in favour of association now takes second place to security in terrorism-related cases[61]). Nor need the banned group be itself engaged in a criminal enterprise: it is enough that it indirectly supports such activity, as was the case in one of the three associations involved in the German ruling.[62] Of course, all these democratically legitimated schemes have safeguards, not just judicial but also on occasion (as in the UK) via specially constituted independent oversight bodies, serviced (in the UK case) by the Special Advocates that have become such a feature of anti-terrorism law in recent years.[63]

Sometimes the shape that the liberal reaction to terrorism takes serves to increase rather than diminish state power, to reduce rather than protect freedom. It has long been taken for granted that whatever else might be sacrificed, at least freedom of thought and the liberty of expression that flows from it remain fundamental to liberal democratic society. Of course, as we have seen earlier in this book, neither has survived unscathed concerns about the colonial enemy without or the radical subversive within: as the Indian nationalist Vinayak Damodar Savarkar found to his cost when he had the temerity to take to print to praise the assassination of an official of the Raj,[64] and as the experiences of the communists in democratic society recounted in Chapter 2 also testify. But despite these evident hypocrisies, the ideas of freedom of thought and expression have clung on in democratic homelands as important identity markers. Despite their entrenched value, they have recently yielded yet further ground to the anti-terrorism juggernaut.[65] The emerging idea, echoing old Cold War tropes, has been of a muscular democracy that has needed to defend its values by (it might be said without irony) the temporary suspension of some of them: in this way is the supposed strength of liberal society used as a cover for its own dilution. Such changes have been noted in a critical report issued by the UN Special Rapporteur on human rights and terrorism, Fionnuala Ní Aoláin.[66]

Concerns about the misuse of speech have led to a significant broadening in the remit of counter-terrorism powers. Post-9/11 attacks, such as those in Madrid in March 2004 and London in July 2005, have led to an increased focus on 'terrorist Godfathers', the men and women behind the scenes who seduce the otherwise innocent into politically motivated atrocity. The idea taps into a long-accepted image of the terrorist as the mere dupe of a brutal orchestrator behind the scenes, now exacerbated by the advances in online technology which have made non-criminal 'hate speech' more accessible and harder to track than in the past.[67] The modus operandi here has been to deplore 'violent extremism', though in some jurisdictions, such as the UK, the 'violent' qualifier has been dispensed with, leaving only the bar on 'extremism', a word that is obviously dependent on the wider political context for its meaning[68] and which has the potential to be used interchangeably with terrorism in ways that are potentially damaging from a civil liberties point of view.[69] The term has also produced absurd results: in the UK for example, 'extremism' is defined as an affront to such 'British values' as (among others) individual liberty and the rule of law. Criminalizing 'extremist' speech on such a basis has been a step so obviously too far that it has not even secured a space in the country's statute book: its chilling effect has been via secondary legislation and codes of practice and the like, arenas of activity which its promoters hope will not be looked at too closely while its repressive intent (primarily the curbing of political speech by radical Muslims) can be quietly realized. Constitutional oversight has not prevented other jurisdictions – even those that ostensibly bask in their commitments to free speech – from deploying controls on extremism so as to narrow political debate in a nakedly partisan manner.[70]

Finally, we should note the technological advances that have given law enforcement and national security officials opportunities for investigation that would have been unthinkable a generation before. Concerns about terrorism have played a large part here in driving change, making acceptable the hitherto unthinkable. Data collection and retention has become the new front in the balancing of liberty and security, and once again there is evident the compromise between the exercise of state power and the preservation of liberal values, a reconciliation which both moderates the impact of the law and so at the same time ensures its survival. The German Federal Constitutional Court set out the dilemma very well in a judgment from 2013. Its analysis reflects the dilemma of apex courts throughout the liberal constitutional world:

> When assessing the significance of such a database, it must be taken into account that the effective fight against terrorism carries great weight for a democratic and free society. Criminal acts that qualify as terrorism, against which the [German] Counter-terrorism Database Act is directed . . ., aim to destabilise society and, to this end, comprise attacks on the life and limb of random third parties, in a ruthless instrumentalization of others. They are directed against the pillars of the constitutional order and society as a whole. Our constitutional order requires that such attacks not be considered acts of war or a state of emergency, which would lead to a suspension of certain requirements derived from the rule of law, but that they be qualified as criminal acts that must be countered with the means available to the state under the rule of law. At the same time, the proportionality assessment required under the principle of the rule of law must accord considerable weight to the fight against terrorism.[71]

Conclusion

There have of course been many reductions in the protection afforded individual and political liberty across the democratic world over the past forty years which have not been solely or even (on occasion) partly derived from the political impetus generated by anxiety about terrorism: our subject does not have sole claim as the source of all change in this area. Rights of protest and of dissent generally have been in decline, while many societies have shown an appetite for the more vigorous punishment of offenders than would have been the case in the liberal heyday, even if 'terrorism' as a problem had never become a concern. As noted above, law enforcement and national security officials, aided by technological advances, have for sure made the best of the opportunities the needs of anti-terrorism law have afforded them, but some kind of regulated power was bound to come here in any event. Anti-terrorism law has throughout been going with the grain of this authoritarian-inclination. The central message of this chapter is twofold: first that respect for the rule of law in general and human rights considerations in particular have modified the arbitrary impact of many elements of the anti-terrorism legal frameworks that were constructed in response to the attacks of 11 September 2001; but, second, that such moderation has embedded these frameworks in our liberal systems of law, making their survival no longer controversial, and – critically – no longer dependent on terrorist atrocity for their preservation. Anti-terrorism law has shaken off its origins in tragedy and become a permanent, relatively uncontroversial part of our liberal democratic polity.

Conclusion: Depth Charges

Counter-terrorism continues to serve as a rationale for Israeli military actions against its neighbours, such as that against the Palestinian town of Jenin in early July 2023 (to remove a 'nest of terrorists', according to prime minister Netanyahu[1]), and, above all, the wholesale assault on Gaza that followed Hamas's brutal actions in southern Israel on 7 October 2023. This latter Israeli operation appears to mark a return to the sort of savage retaliation that was to the fore in the late 1970s and early 1980s, when efforts to destroy Palestinian resistance led to the death of many thousands of civilians in Lebanon, not least in the merciless siege of Beirut through the summer of 1982. The Israeli notification of the 7 October attack, filed with the United Nations on the day it occurred, spoke in general terms of the country's right to take defensive action but did not explicitly invoke article 51 of the UN Charter.[2] This may or may not have been due to a reluctance to define the nature of the territory from which the attacks emanated, but even if it had been invoked the legal basis for these latest Israeli actions would have remained uncertain, and at the time of writing it is by no means inevitable that Israel's military and political commanders will escape indictment before the International Criminal Court, or avoid condemnation for the commission of genocide before the International Court of Justice.[3]

Few quibble with Israel's right to act against those who committed the brutal wrongs of 7 October, but the legal justifications for what has followed have felt perfunctory and formulaic, in stark contrast to the violent language of destruction and reconquest voiced by many of those at the very top of Israel's military and governmental commands. The International Criminal Court's assertion of its jurisdiction over Palestine, determined before the conflict began, was condemned as antisemitic by Mr Netanyahu, and it is to this language of antisemitism that the country increasingly turns when it feels the need to dampen international criticism of it, a tendency that has been especially evident recently in relation to the conduct of its operations in Gaza.[4] Terrorism law may continue to provide a useful basis on which to castigate its Palestinian opponents and to hound its foreign critics in the courts,[5] but is no longer as useful as it once was in the wider campaign to rebut non-violent international criticism. Whether either label, terrorist-sympathizer or antisemite, is able to bear the burden of explanation being increasingly demanded of Israel as its conduct of the Gaza hostilities deepens remains to be seen. The risk from Israel's point of view is that painting all their critics as one or other of these simply collapses into implausibility in the face of fact.

Outside the Middle East, the deployment of the phrases 'terrorist' and 'terrorism' in contemporary contexts feels increasingly odd. The Russian-Ukraine conflict is instructive here. On 24 February 2022, the Russian president Vladimir Putin launched a 'special military operation' in the neighbouring state of Ukraine. In his initial reasoning for what was to all intents and purposes an invasion, Mr Putin did not mention terrorism, other than in the context of errors made by the West which had led to increased terrorism and to his own actions in having broken 'the back of international terrorism in the Caucasus' in the first decade of the 2000s.[6] As the conflict has progressed, however, both sides have used the language of terrorism with abandon to describe the actions of their opponents in what they hope (and expect) are disparaging terms: drone attacks on Moscow were 'obviously a sign of terrorist activity' according to Mr Putin;[7] Russia was a 'terrorist state' said Ukraine's ambassador-at-large at the Hague Anton Korynevych at the start of proceedings against the country launched at the International Court of Justice;[8] the Wagner Group was not just a paramilitary ally of Russia but a 'terrorist group'[9]; and so on. Perhaps some of the incidents identified as terrorist can plausibly be described as such, fitting the bill so far as this or that academic definition is concerned. But the terrorist narrative as a whole feels unsuited to the gravity of what is occurring, which is in truth altogether more serious than the deployment of symbolic acts of violence in order to communicate a political message. For sure, that is occurring from time to time, but so too are vast movements of tanks and troops, sieges and counter-sieges, and extensive aerial bombardment: all these may have a terrorizing effect but their main purpose is to break the military capacity of the enemy or to make that capacity unusable due to the price required to be paid in terms of civilian devastation.

This book has explored those places in which the language of terrorism has always felt comfortable, where the fit seems there for all to see, without the need for energetic advocacy or persuasive engagement by anyone. It is true that that fit has broadened in the years since the 11 September attacks. The world is awash today with singular threats of subversive violence emanating from many sources and threatening destruction on a vast scale, with such sources of danger being found in hostile sole actors, isolated groups without any recognizable political creed, and malignant users of social media.[10] The laws that seek to counter such violence in its many forms are wide-ranging, with deployment of the legal framework of anti-terrorism offering a route through liberal obstacles to state action that manages both to run with the grain of liberal sentiment while at the same time undermining it. But as with Russia/Ukraine, the terrorist label has been given a weight that, in many of the circumstances in which it is deployed, it cannot bear. Great efforts have been expended in recent years to extend the reach of the descriptor to the killings of persons of colour by white extremists where these are motivated by racial and/or religious hatred – in other words, to explain these acts of violence as driven not only by hatred but by a terroristic mentality that the state needs to acknowledge and treat as such.[11] It is the same with the public campaign to characterize as 'terrorist' the deliberate choice made by a small number of the men committed to the 'incel' cause to kill young women so that their anguish over their sexual isolation can be better known and (as they hope) understood.[12]

These latter examples may well fit academic and legal definitions of terrorism, with the protagonists of such labelling seeking to have their opponents designated in this way in order to generate the energetic hostility (and subsequent legal action) towards such terrible behaviour that they believe will follow. Perhaps this is a sort of progress. It is now easier than ever to have right-wing, politically motivated violence not only classified as 'terrorism' but understood in those terms. The darker side to this is the use democratic power makes of the term when confronted by progressive dissent. Climate activists are often forced to resist the description, pointing to state-sponsored destruction of eco-systems as the real terrorism,[13] turning the tables just as Gandhi did with regard to the conduct of his prosecutors at his trial in 1922,[14] or as the public intellectual Noam Chomsky has done consistently with regard to US foreign policy over many decades.[15] Such disputed expansions of the language show the success of its embedment within our society. But anti-terrorism law remains in its essence about identity, about those who buy into our (liberal democratic) society and those who would destroy it and so must be stopped and/or punished. For all its spread, the language still lacks high levels of salience outside its contemporary home base of Israel/ Palestine, and the violence that radiates out of that troubled region.

Understanding beginnings helps explain how the rise of anti-terrorism law can continue to be so irrepressible. There is a key point about meaning (and therefore origins) that is missed by many who take academic definitions of terrorism at face value. The singular guide as to whether there is a fit between incident and terrorist label lies not in the nature of the act itself but in the kind of actor who is engaging in it. To Victoria Sentas, quoting Michel Foucault, the '"juridico-moral concept of the dangerous individual" is inscribed in the very idea of the crime, facilitating censure based on who the individual is rather than what they do'.[16] Many people kill for political advantage but not all are so easily presented as terrorists. Those who are so described are the 'others' among us, the different, 'the enemy without' or 'the enemy within'. The white guy murdering women or the white supremacist shooting Black Americans simply because of the colour of their skin[17] may be charged with terrorism-related offences nowadays, but such wrongdoers are at bottom part of the dominant culture – a disordered criminal part for sure, but a part nevertheless. They challenge authority to make the system work for them, or to 'restore' some contrived version of the past to which they are committed. They are insiders running rampage, not outsiders seeking to knock everything down. It is to the origins of 'othering', to an exploration of what causes some people to be seen as 'in' and some as 'out', that we need to turn if we want to get under the skin of what is meant by terrorism, in practice if not in legal theory.

In the genealogy that it has been this book's aim to explore, there are four main staging posts in the creation of what we take for granted today as the 'terrorist' crisis. The book sees, first, the construction of the 'terrorist' other and the problem of terrorism more generally as rooted in the long practice that European liberalism has had (both before and into the democratic era) in castigating its anti-colonial opponents in exactly these (or closely analogous) terms. Vastly more coercive treatment was always legitimately available to the authorities once the 'terrorist' route was opened to them. There has always been one rule for the true homeland, and another (more vicious, altogether disdainful of liberal principle) for the 'home-away' of the colonies: double standards have been baked into liberalism from the start.

Then, secondly, with colonialism increasingly falling away as an effective tool of control, the Cold War embraced its hypocritical legacy, building for this new era on the discriminatory way in which liberalism had long distinguished between good and bad people, this time rooted in the threat the latter posed from the Left.[18] An old trope derived from past anxieties about anarchists and Russian revolutionaries was revitalized in the shape of concern about the 'enemy within'. In this new post-1945 context, this 'enemy' was now composed of those for whom colonial agitation had been a route not only to independence in constitutional theory but to a different kind of world altogether, one in which it would be possible to build a thoroughly new society, even if this involved challenging established Western/capitalist power. The old colonial security laws were repurposed in these newly established nations, and new ones added, so that these new states (or those amongst them allied to the US) could play their part in the West's battle against communist influence while presenting a democratic veneer to the world. 'Terrorism' was not the only concern here – sedition generally was the focus. But it was an important one, especially when an ambitious, Left-oriented radicalism took its turn towards violence in South America and Western Europe itself during the 1960s.

The third major shift in our genealogy comes with the internationalization of the term in the 1970s, when the state of Israel successfully (indeed, I might say brilliantly if I can avoid the normativity that's usually inherent in the term) persuaded the world that the Palestinian question was one of global terrorism rather than national liberation. All these violent groups scattered about the 'civilized world' became not discrete fighters to be assessed on their merits but offshoots of one dramatic scourge, the terrorism whose proponents were waging war on the West. No longer was terrorism a part of this or that branch of area studies; it became a psycho-criminal activity full of malice but thoroughly decontextualized, a kind of anti-colonial madness from an earlier generation, but now writ large globally.

The fourth and final stop takes us right up to 2001, by which time Islam had become the central focus of terrorist-related anxiety. This brand of violence combined aspects of all three of the earlier stages. It was anti-imperial (seeking to challenge Western power in its continued control of post-colonial states, especially in Iran where this stage began in 1979); it was Cold-War-like in generating a fear of 'the Muslims' lurking as domestic enemies within our liberal society seeking to destroy us; and it was also profoundly anti-Israeli in its worldview (reflected in the support shown by Iran and its surrogates for Palestinian resistance to Israeli coercion, the continued totem-power of hostility to Israel as a galvanizing force in the Muslim world through the 1990s, and militant Islam's willingness to use asymmetrical violence to achieve its aims).

The attacks of 11 September 2001 in their turn contained elements from all four of these stages in the evolution of the language of terrorism: that internal enemy 'the Muslims' moving about freely in our liberal society, determined to drive Western violence out of the Arab world and convinced in the religious rightness of their cause, while in Israeli-occupied Palestine there was 'dancing in the streets' in celebration of the blow struck against the Israeli/American foe.[19] The Hamas attacks of 7 October repeated these conventional descriptors of classic terrorism to a near-haunting degree.

A nagging question remains, even for those who find the analysis thus far persuasive. It is one that has echoed throughout this book, an informing theme from the outset. To revisit the questions set out in the introduction, why were the double standards that were deepened after the 11 September attacks so easy to maintain? To put this in other ways: How had they become embedded in the way that they had? What explains the ease with which the West has distinguished between people in the way that it clearly has, to which distinction (on this book's argument) our subject of anti-terrorism law owes its existence? Here we get to the essence of what this book has been about. Liberal democracy has been rooted in double standards since before even the democratic idea was added to the liberalism that was embraced with the West's move away from rival theocracies and into empire in the late eighteenth and nineteenth centuries. Since division on the basis of identity has always been in the pot, it has been relatively easy to add a bit more, especially if those now on the wrong side of such state power resembled those who had long been the traditional victims of such hypocrisy.

Two further points emerge as this longish study draws to a conclusion. First there is the unavoidable (though up to now, it is true, mainly avoided) correlation between 'the other' that we have been discussing in this book and that 'big elephant in the room',[20] race. Ilyas Mohammed has written convincingly recently about the need to 'decolonise' the whole terrorism industry, a world that he argues has been dominated by the priorities of the global north for generations.[21] A recent report into 'extremism' in Britain tends to prove his point, with its misjudged laments over how little attention is being paid to radical Islamist ideas (or 'Islamism' as the report calls it) as compared to white-based violence, when in fact – according to the report – the greater threat by far is posed by the former.[22] To the author, 'the present boundaries around . . . extremist Islamist ideology are drawn too narrowly while the boundaries around the ideology of the Extreme Right-Wing are too broad'.[23] A detailed American study has found 'that selective counterterrorism enforcement allocates disproportionate resources targeting Muslim communities',[24] with '[c]ounterterrorism enforcement [being] one of the many contexts in which the racial disparities are glaring' in the United States.[25] The scholar Fatima Ahdash has warned against deploying the language of terrorism in family courts in the UK, in a way that she argues leads to discrimination against Muslim families.[26] The Australian-based scholar Victoria Sentas sees 'counter-terrorism as a mode of racial subjection' where race is 'made invisible yet orders counter-terrorism law and policing'.[27] It has been noted that traditional approaches such as human rights and anti-discrimination law 'construct racism as being an aberration from legal norms and as perpetuated by individuals, rather than being structurally produced and sustained in part through law'.[28] While the point quoted here was made in relation to immigration law, it could just as easily have been said of terrorism law.

The anti-colonial agitators were invariably of a different skin colour to the European masters to whom they took such exception. There were, of course, other differences, rooted in unfamiliar cultural, social and religious habits, and even on their own these would have marked the peoples and communities subject to colonial subjugation as different, not part of our (Western, cosmopolitan, Christian) club. In the UK context, the Irish were white but (as the nineteenth-century descriptions in the British press constantly reminded their readers) behaved like savages, were drunk most of the time, feckless, dirty, given to over-breeding, and so on, as the revolutionary leader Michael Collins noted when he lived in London in the early 1900s,[29] and as was unattractively recalled by a *Times* cartoon caricaturing the US president Joe Biden as a drunken Irish leprechaun as late as 2023.[30]

Race was the key extra ingredient, the factor that made possible acceptance of the brutality of, first, colonial expansion (by unrelenting military power) and then the retention of these territorial gains (by the robust application of coercive laws). Of course, Islam is a religion and not a race, but the fact that the followers of this faith are overwhelmingly of a different skin colour to the great majority of the people of the West has made it easy to ignore this fact.[31] As Sentas observes, 'religious difference forms part of the social construction of race'.[32] To Nadine El-Enany, 'dismissals and brutal crackdowns on struggles for self-determination in the colonies necessitated justifications that rested on constructions of difference and their accentuation in official discourse'.[33] The violence by Islamist militants that has been such a feature of the 'terrorist' challenge over the past thirty years has invariably emanated from regions previously colonized by Western power, all overwhelmingly non-white in their ethnic make-up. To take one local example which speaks to the wider point, the link between anti-terrorist coercive action against British Muslims and assaults on an earlier embattled British community, the Irish in England, was made clear in an excoriating essay, published in April 2008, by the civil liberties lawyer Gareth Peirce, the woman who had been key to exposing the miscarriages of justice to which the latter community had been subject in the 1970s.[34]

The plausibility enjoyed by the double standards which underpin so much of this story derives at least in part from a gigantic failure in human rights thinking, or more accurately its coherent application on the ground, something we see being repeated in real time during Israel's re-conquest of the Gaza Strip, ongoing as this book goes to press. Right at the start of Europe's colonial adventures, Bartolomé de Las Casas, a Jesuit priest alive to the brutality of Spanish forces in Mexico, wrote a famous defence of the humanity of the native peoples being subject to such oppressive treatment. Knowing his audience, he emphasized that these peoples were not created by God as 'stupid or barbarous', but having seen the behaviour of their Spanish conquerors they surely 'commit no sin and do not deserve punishment if they do not accept the gospel. Nor would any nation have been guilty for not accepting the faith of Christ if, supposing the impossible, the Apostles had behaved like the Spaniards.'[35] This lesson about their own potential for barbarity remained one unlearnt by the colonial amd settler-colonial powers through the four centuries that followed.

Are things different today? Western culture is altogether more alive to the iniquities of the conduct of its colonial predecessors than it was at the time or for many years after. In Chapter 1, the scholar Deana Heath was referred to, citing Ann Stoler: '[t]he violence of empire is rediscovered . . . when it is deemed safe for public consumption and scholarly investigation'.[36] As we have seen from the extensive pushback against this kind of critical appraisal, it is still not entirely safe.[37] Strong traces of the racism that flows from a denial of humanity, or (in its modern form) a denial of the equality of humanity, remain in Western culture. Israel, self-described outpost of the 'civilized' West, continues to destroy the life chances of the effectively colonized Palestinians living under its control, using the anti-terrorist trope as cover for the imposition of its will on a neighbouring people; and it has enjoyed wide support in Europe and the United States for doing so, not least but perhaps most obviously in its latest efforts to destroy the communities living in the Gaza Strip. Anti-terrorism discourses and the laws that flow from and make possible such discourses offer to those who have not been able to reconcile themselves to human rights and equality thrilling opportunities if not to say, then at least to imply, the unsayable: that the person of colour is different, inferior, was properly subjugated and should never have been released from Western captivity; that their savagery threatens our civilized values. The barbarian conquistador excoriated by de Las Casas lives on, disguised as a protector of civilized values against the terrorist jihadist. (And sometimes, as with the current Israeli political and military leadership, such sentiments are no longer left unsaid.[38])

If the imperfection of the reception of the idea of human rights in the former colonizing states is a key part of understanding anti-terrorism law, then the flawed reception of democratic values is another. This book has finally mentioned race and it should also now in the same spirit confront another unmentionable – money. Ntina Tzouvala's work, referred to in passing earlier, has driven home in a highly effective manner the relationship between corporate power and anti-terrorism, between the profit-making entities that thrive on the panic induced by the 'war on terror' and the blank cheques for anti-terrorism that flow from that panic.[39] This connection does not have to have been direct to have become highly entrenched. The political economy of counter-terrorism reveals a source of profit that makes an end to the global war on terror (or whatever it happens to be called) practically impossible to envisage.

But why should this be so? Here I come to my second, and final, large-scale point: the complacent way in which we assume the success of the democratic turn in one-time-colonial powers hides how truncated that success has been in general – how shallow it remains across the West (as we have been calling what we now think of as the 'global north') and indeed the world as a whole. Economic power may have surrendered control of the formal levers of power, but this has been a strategic move designed to retain the (economic) power that counts. Just as human rights have never entirely broken the colonial mindset, so democratic advance has never been able to shed the structures of power that were embedded for centuries before its arrival and whose defenders held many cards when it came to their retention, even if none of these was democratic in any meaningful sense.[40] The nineteenth-century conservative mind thought that democracy meant socialism and had to be explicitly fought on that ground. The twentieth century proved that democratic freedom need not mean radical change to existing power distributions. Those who seek to challenge this are the other 'other' whose existence is a running theme in this book. These 'others' did not need a different skin colour to qualify for particular persecution.

The decline of first Al-Qaeda and then Islamic State, together with a combination of the Russia-Ukraine conflict and gross overuse of the term, have, it might be claimed, surely left 'terrorism' seeming more yesterday's crisis than that of today or tomorrow. Perhaps, perhaps not – Gaza and its possible consequences around the world are a sharp indicator of the latter. The salience of the subject has always depended on atrocity: as 7 October demonstrated, and as yet could prove to be the case further afield, a few more serious incidents involving mass casualties that can plausibly be assigned to a terrorist 'other' could lead to a renaissance in relevance. But this book is not about terrorism as such; rather its focus is on anti-terrorism laws, and there is no sign of any abatement in the reach of such laws or in the enthusiasm with which they are enforced, atrocity or no atrocity. The sheer irrepressibility of our subject has been an underlying theme. Anti-terrorism laws provide a code for the efficient management of so much more than mere terrorist threats. We have seen in earlier chapters the monumental bureaucratization of anti-terrorism law and practice across the UN and the many states that constitute its membership. In authoritarian states, anti-terrorism laws become a catch-all sledgehammer with which to smash opponents of all shapes and sizes, from the genuinely violent to the merely politically sceptical. In democracies, such laws offer a tempting shortcut through the often procedurally complex (and, some believe, overly defendant-sensitive) criminal law, while also being very useful in the control of protests whose energy takes their participants closer to the (expanded) world of anti-terrorism law than they will often realize.

True, human rights ideals and imperatives rooted in the rule of law have successfully tempered the worst excesses of terrorism law. This is an unambiguously good thing so far as those exposed to the operation of such coercive laws are concerned. But, as this book has argued, in doing so these liberalizing initiatives have helped embed such laws further in democratic culture: the regulation becomes not so extreme as to be entirely unpalatable without being so mild as to be (from the state's point of view) ineffective. But human rights constraints do not always work, even in countries describing themselves as democracies. The Indian Catholic priest Fr Stan Swamy, who died in prison aged eighty-four (suffering from Parkinson's disease as well as Covid) after being charged with terrorism offences in October 2020, was described by the president of the Federation of Asian Bishops' Conferences as 'the latest saint of modern India's poor [who] shone a damning light on the injustice that is becoming a norm in the world'.[41] He also stands in this book as a secular martyr to the oppressive power of this persecutory label.

Fiona de Londras has recently observed that 'transnational counter-terrorism has been removed from the realm of politization, and developed into an order of great scale, depth, influence and opacity – a powerful framework that is remarkably resistant to being dislodged as a pillar of global governance'.[42] Supposedly democratic states like India (as we have

just seen) and Turkey seem increasingly able to expand their authoritarian ambitions under cover of the demands of anti-terrorism. As the world
encounters the unique threat of global climate change, with its horrific
effects generating conflict (over scare resources) and the mass movements
of peoples (to avoid the uninhabitability it causes), it would be very
optimistic not to anticipate a new harder edge developing among post-
colonial and neo-imperial powers, manifested in an equation between
climate instabilities and terrorist threats.[43] The human rights insights
of the past are at risk of being shed completely, with explicit brutality
returning to the centre-stage in place of the ambiguous universality that
has been to the fore since 1945. The reaction to the 11 September attacks
weakened but did not destroy the human rights ideal – but that does not
mean it is safe. Mark Condos has described 'a widespread colonial culture
of insecurity' in British India, with fear helping to explain how colonial
decision-makers could 'enact such frightening regimes and displays of
brutality against their fellow men and women'.[44] If the multiple crises
the world faces in the decades ahead do lead to the ideal of human rights
being jettisoned, then anti-terrorism law may be the rationale of choice
for their eviction.

Notes

Introduction

1 *Re Castioni* [1891] 1 QB 149.
2 Extradition Act 1870 s 3(1).
3 V.E. Hartley Booth, *British Extradition Law and Procedure* (Alphen ann den Rijn: Sijthoff and Noordhoff, 1980), vol. 1, p. 79.
4 *Re Castioni* [1891] 1 QB 167.
5 Ibid., p. 168.
6 In the United Kingdom the Suppression of Terrorism Act 1978 and the Extradition Act 2003.
7 *R v F* [2007] EWCA Crim 243, [2007] QB 960 (Judge P; Forbes, Irwin JJ) para 32.
8 Ibid., para 7.
9 Ibid., para 9.
10 Ibid., para 26.
11 Through belonging to organizations that are proscribed under anti-terrorism law, a common feature of contemporary legal systems, as we shall see.
12 Note that residual constitutional rights to overthrow a government are still to be found in many constitutions worldwide: Tom Ginsburg, Daniel Lansberg-Rodriguez and Mila Versteeg, 'When to Overthrow Your Government: The Right to Resist in the World's Constitutions' (2013) 60 *University of California Law Review* 1184–1260. The fairly minimal operation of these clauses is not something I probe in what follows.
13 Conor Gearty, *Terror* (London: Faber and Faber, 1991).
14 Fiona de Londras, *The Practice and Problems of Transnational Counter-Terrorism* (Cambridge: Cambridge University Press, 2022); Ben Saul (ed.), *Research Handbook on International Law and Terrorism* 2nd edn (Cheltenham: Edward Elgar, 2020); Aniceto Masferer and Clive Walker (eds.), *Counter-Terrorism, Human Rights and the Rule of Law: Crossing Legal Boundaries in Defence of the State* (Cheltenham: Edward Elgar, 2013); Clive Walker (with Alex Carlile, Ken McDonald and David Omand), *Terrorism and the Law* (Oxford: Oxford University Press, 2011); Genevieve Lennon and Clive Walker (eds.), *Routledge Handbook of Law and Terrorism* (Abingdon: Routledge, 2015); Laura Donohue, *The Cost of Counterterrorism: Power, Politics, and Liberty* (Cambridge: Cambridge University Press, 2008); Andrew Lynch, Nicola Hensley McGarrity and George Williams (eds.), *Counter-Terrorism and Beyond: The Culture of Law and Justice after 9/11* (London: Routledge, 2010).
15 See respectively Richard English, *Does Counter-Terrorism Work?* (Oxford: Oxford University Press, 2024) and Thomas Renard, *The Evolution of Counter-Terrorism since 9/11: Understanding the Paradigm Shift in Liberal Democracies* (Abingdon: Routledge, 2022).

16 True even among the finest (Alex P. Schmid (ed.), *The Routledge Handbook of Terrorism Research* (Abingdon: Routledge, 2011)) and the most innovative (Richard Jackson, Marie Breen Smyth and Jeroen Gunning, *Critical Terrorism Studies: A New Research Agenda* (London: Routledge, 2009)) of the genre. For a snapshot of the vast increase in post-9/11 scholarship see Brian J. Phillips, 'How Did 9/11 Affect Terrorism Research? Examining Articles and Authors, 1970–2019' (2023) 35 (2) *Terrorism and Political Violence* 409–432.

17 Christos Boukalas, *Homeland Security, its Law and its State. A Design of Power for the 21st Century* (Abingdon: Routledge, 2014).

18 Christos Boukalas, 'No Exceptions: Authoritarian Statism. Agamben, Poulantzas and Homeland Security' (2014) 7 (1) *Critical Studies on Terrorism* 112–130.

19 Michael Livesey, 'Historicising "Terrorism": How, and Why?' (2021) 14 (4) *Critical Studies on Terrorism* 474–478. See further Bart Schuurman 'Topics in Terrorism Research: Reviewing Trends and Gaps, 2007–2016' (2019) 12 (3) *Critical Studies on Terrorism* 463–480.

20 Audrey Alejandro and Mattia Pinto, *Law and Discourse; Law as Discourse* (unpublished; copy with author).

21 Charlotte Heath-Kelly, 'Critical Approaches to the Study of Terrorism' in *The Oxford Handbook of Terrorism* (Oxford: Oxford University Press, 2019), 224–237, p. 229.

22 *Critical Terrorism Studies: A New Research Agenda*, n 16 above. Pathbreaking works included Stuart Croft, *Culture, Crisis and America's War on Terror* (Cambridge: Cambridge University Press, 2006) and Richard Jackson, *Writing the War on Terrorism* (Manchester: Manchester University Press, 2005).

23 My *Liberty and Security* (Cambridge: Polity Press, 2014) approached this subject in a way that highlighted the relationship between democracy and the false claims (rooted in the security imperative) of what I there called 'neo-democracy', but it did not delve into the origins of the language of terrorism and anti-terrorism, one of the central themes of this book.

24 Mark Neocleous, 'Security, Liberty and the Myth of Balance: Towards a Critique of Security Politics' (2007) 6 (2) *Contemporary Political Theory* 131–149.

25 Jessica Wolfendale, 'The Narrative of Terrorism as an Existential Threat' in Richard Jackson (ed.), *Routledge Handbook of Critical Terrorism Studies* (Abingdon: Routledge, 2016), ch. 11.

26 As I called these aspirant nationalist fighters in my book, *Terror* (London: Faber and Faber, 1991).

27 Lisa Stampnitzky, *Disciplining Terror: How Experts Invented 'Terrorism'* (Cambridge: Cambridge University Press, 2013).

28 Nadine El-Enany, *(B)ordering Britain. Law, Race and Empire* (Manchester: Manchester University Press, 2020), p. 27.

29 Ntina Tzouvalu, 'The "Unwilling or Unable" Doctrine and the Political Economy of the War on Terror' (2023) 14 (1) *Humanity* 19–38. See also her *Capitalism as Civilization: A History of International Law* (Cambridge: Cambridge University Press, 2020).

30 See Oliver Wainright, '"War is Back. People Want to Stock Up": Inside Europe's Biggest Arms Fair', *Guardian*, 20 September 2023.

Chapter 1

1 Randall D. Law, *Terrorism: A History* 2nd edn (Cambridge: Polity Press, 2016), pp. 40–46.
2 Mia Bloom, *Dying to Kill: The Allure of Suicide Terrorism* (New York: Columbia Press, 2005), pp. 4–11. Bloom includes the Hindu Thugs with the Jewish Zealots and the Muslim Assassins as 'early examples of terrorism and religiously inspired sacrifice' (p. 11). A typical treatment is Gérard Challiand and Arnaud Blin, 'Zealots and Assassins' in the same authors' edited collection *The History of Terrorism: From Antiquity to Al Qaeda* (Berkeley and Los Angeles: University of California Press, 2007), ch. 3. Note that Michael Burleigh, *Blood and Rage: A Cultural History of Terrorism* (London: Harper Press, 2008) includes (ch. 4 'Death in the Sun: Terror and Decolonisation', pp. 88–151) an extensive treatment of Palestine, Algeria and South Africa, but does not cover earlier colonial engagements. David C. Rapoport, *Waves of Global Terrorism: From 1879 to the Present* (New York: Columbia University Press, 2022), designates the anti-colonial as the second of his four waves, but his treatment of its various manifestations is almost entirely free of any particular context, or of the state coercion that may or may not have been occuring at the time the violence discussed took place. Writing as a political historian, Richard English's *Does Terrorism Work? A History* (Oxford: Oxford University Press, 2016) neatly avoids the pitfalls of over-generalized accounts by 'adopting a profoundly context-specific approach to explanation' (p. 20). For a stimulating analysis of the wider field, see Mikkel Thorup, *An Intellectual History of Terror: War, Violence and the State* (London: Routledge, 2010).
3 Alexander Berkman, who in 1892 attempted to kill the industrialist H.C. Frick, manager of the Carnegie Steel Company, described himself as a 'terrorist by conviction': *Prison Memoirs of an Anarchist* (New York: Schocken Books, 1970 (originally published in 1912)), p. 10, cited by D. Novak, 'Anarchism and Individual Terrorism' (1954) 20 (2) *The Canadian Journal of Economics and Political Science* 176–184, p. 178.
4 Brenda J. Lutz, 'Historical Approaches' in Erica Chenoweth, Richard English, Andreas Gofas and Stathis N. Kalyvas, *The Oxford Handbook of Terrorism* (Oxford: Oxford University Press, 2019) 194–206, pp. 198–199.
5 Conor Gearty, *Terror* (London: Faber and Faber, 1991).
6 George P. Fletcher, 'The Indefinable Concept of Terrorism' (2006) 4 (5) *Journal of International Criminal Justice* 894–911.
7 Joshua Tschantret, 'Social Origins of Modern Terrorism' (2023) 32 (1) *Security Studies* 66–100.
8 Angela Woollacott, 'Making Empire Visible or Making Colonialism Visible: The Struggle for the British Imperial Past' (2009) 1 (2) *British Scholar* 163, cited in Deana Heath, *Colonial Terror: Torture and State Violence in Colonial India* (Oxford: Oxford University Press, 2021), p. 16, text at n 83.
9 Ann Laura Stoler, 'Colonial Aphasia: Race and Disabled Histories in France' (2011) 23 (1) *Public Culture* 121–156, p. 125, quoted by Heath, *Colonial Terror* n 8 above, pp. 16–17.
10 Quoted by Heath, *Colonial Terror* n 8 above p. 17.
11 Nasser Hussain, *The Jurisprudence of Emergency: Colonialism and the Rule of Law* (Anne Arbor: University of Michigan Press, 2003), p. 3. A second pathbreaker here, published around the same time, was Antony Anghie, *Imperialism, Sovereignty and the Making of International Law* (Cambridge: Cambridge University Press, 2004).
12 Hussain, *The Jurisprudence of Emergency* n 11 above, p. 4.

13 Ibid., p. 6.
14 Caroline Elkins, *Legacy of Violence: A History of the British Empire* (London: Penguin Random House, 2022).
15 James Martel, 'The Law of Rules: Hyperlegalism, Emergency and the Violence of Procedure' (2021) 17 (1) *Law, Culture and the Humanities* 53–70, p. 57. See further on the international law side the excellent book by John Reynolds, *Empire, Emergency and International Law* (Cambridge: Cambridge University Press, 2017). On the rule of law in nineteenth-century India, see Keally McBride, *Mr Mothercountry: The Man Who Made the Rule of Law* (Oxford: Oxford University Press, 2016).
16 Joseph McQuade, *A Genealogy of Terrorism: Colonial Law and the Origins of an Idea* (Cambridge: Cambridge University Press, 2021), p. 28. The quote is from Laleh Khalili, *Time in the Shadows: Confinement in Counterinsurgencies* (Stanford CA: Stanford University Press, 2013), p. 5.
17 Richard Reid, 'Terrorism in African History' in Richard English (ed.), *The Cambridge History of Terrorism* (Cambridge: Cambridge University Press, 2021) 199–222, p. 205.
18 See generally Roy F. Foster, *Modern Ireland 1600–1972* (London: Allen Lane, 1988).
19 Rory Miller, 'Terrorism: History and Regionalisation' in English (ed.), *The Cambridge History of Terrorism* 81–105, p. 84.
20 Sathnam Sanghera, *Empireland: How Imperialism Has Shaped Modern Britain* (London: Penguin Random House, 2021), chs 3 and 4 for a highly readable account and a good review of the literature. On post-colonial influences, Elleke Boehmer and Stephen Morton (eds.), *Terror and the Postcolonial* (Oxford: Blackwell, 2010) is an invigorating read covering its subject from a variety of disciplinary perspectives albeit not (or at least not directly) including law.
21 Heath, *Colonial Terror* n 8 above, p. 66 citing Nathan K. Hensley *Forms of Empire: The Poetics of Victorian Sovereignty* (Oxford: Oxford University Press, 2016), p. 2.
22 Ranabir Samaddar, 'Law and Terror in the Age of Colonial Constitution Making' (2006) 212 *Diogenes* 18–33, p. 19.
23 Reid, 'Terrorism in African History' n 17 above, p. 206.
24 Ibid., p. 207. See Thorup, *An Intellectual History of Terror* n 2 above, pp. 70–71 where General von Trotha's chilling message to the Herero people is set out.
25 Reid, 'Terrorism in African History' n 17 above, p. 206.
26 Elkins, *Legacy of Violence* n 14 above, p. 54.
27 Ibid., p. 85.
28 Nicholas Dirks, *The Scandal of Empire: India and the Creation of Imperial Britain* (Cambridge MA: Harvard University Press, 2006).
29 Charles Townshend, *The British Campaigns in Ireland 1919–1921: The Development of Political and Military Policies* (Oxford: Oxford Historical Monographs, Oxford University Press, 1975).
30 McQuade, *A Genealogy of Terrorism* n 16 above, pp. 2–3, citing Priya Satia, 'Drones: A History from the British Middle East' (2014) 5 (1) *Humanity: An International Journal of Human Rights, Humanitarianism, and Development* 1–31.
31 Khalili, *Time in the Shadows* n 16 above, p. 12, citing Geoffrey Parker, *The Military Revolution: Military Innovation and the Rise of the West 1500–1800* 2nd edn (Cambridge and New York: Cambridge University Press, 1996). See Parker, p. 119: 'The logic of Western superiority in fixed encounters had been thoroughly digested by the Indians:

after their costly initial defeats, they were scrupulously careful to avoid pitched battles – much to the fury of the Europeans – because they always lost them.'

32 Elkins, *Legacy of Violence* n 14 above, p. 77.

33 Stan Cohen, *States of Denial: Knowing about Atrocities and Suffering* (Cambridge: Polity Press, 2000).

34 McQuade, *A Genealogy of Terrorism* n 16 above, p. 3 quoting from Mark Condos, 'License to Kill: The Murderous Outrages Act and the Rule of Law in Colonial India, 1867–1925' (2016) 50 (2) *Modern Asian* Studies 479–517, p. 504.

35 Elkins, *Legacy of Violence* n 14 above, p. 134.

36 131 HC DEB 1725 (8 July 1920).

37 See this important early critical account: Brijen K. Gupta, *Sirajuddaullah and the East-India Company, 1756–1757: Background to the Foundation of British Power in India* (Leiden: E.J. Brill, 1962), pp. 70–80; Dirks, *The Scandal of Empire* n 28 above, pp. 1–4.

38 McQuade, *A Genealogy of Terrorism* n 16 above, p. 7, citing John Pincince, 'De-centering Carl Schmitt: The Colonial State of Exception and the Criminalization of the Political in British India, 1905–1920' (2014) *Politica Comun* 5. 'Sedition as a criminal offence was introduced into the Indian Penal Code (IPC) in 1870 as the offence of "exciting disaffection" against the Colonial government': Janaki Bakhle, 'Savarkar (1883–1966), Sedition and Surveillance: The Rule of Law in a Colonial Situation' (2010) 35 (1) *Social History* 51–75, p. 53.

39 McQuade, *A Genealogy of Terrorism* n 16 above, p. 16, citing Daniel Brückenhaus, *Policing Transnational Protest: Liberal Imperialism and the Surveillance of Anticolonialists in Europe, 1905–1945* (New York: Oxford University Press, 2017), pp. 8–41. See also Bakhle, 'Savarkar' n 38 above.

40 Elkins, *Legacy of Violence* n 14 above, p. 77.

41 Ibid., pp. 77–78.

42 Heath, *Colonial Terror* n 8 above, p. 10.

43 McQuade, *A Genealogy of Terrorism* n 16 above, p. 25 citing Partha Chatterjee, *The Black Hole of Empire: History of a Global Practice of Power* (Princeton: Princeton University Press, 2012), p. 119.

44 On which see Radhika Singha, *A Despotism of Laws* (Oxford: Oxford University Press, 1998) 168–228. For an interesting contemporary account dealing with India, see Walter Russell Donogh, *A Treatise on the Law of Sedition and Cognate Offences in British India, Penal and Preventive: With an Excerpt of the Acts in Force Relating to the Press, the Stage, and Public Meetings* (Calcutta: Thacker, Spink & Co, 1911).

45 Colm Campbell, *Emergency Law in Ireland 1918–1925* (Oxford: Clarendon Press, 1994). On the UK wartime legislation see Keith Ewing and Conor Gearty, *The Struggle for Civil Liberties: Political Freedom and the Rule of Law in Britain 1914–1945* (Oxford: Oxford University Press, 2000), ch. 2.

46 Mark Condos, *The Insecurity State: Punjab and the Making of Colonial Power in British India* (Cambridge: Cambridge University Press, 2017) 199–201.

47 Ewing and Gearty, *The Struggle for Civil Liberties* n 45 above, ch. 7. See below Chapter 3.

48 Heath, *Colonial Terror* n 8 above, pp. 180–181 (notes omitted). For a gripping account of the punishment meted out to three Indian nationalists for the assassination of a police officer see Satvinder Singh Juss, *The Execution of Bhagat Singh: Legal Heresies of the Raj* (The Hill, Stroud: Amberley Publishing, 2020).

49 McQuade, *A Genealogy of Terrorism* n 16 above, p. 123.
50 Ibid., p. 81 and generally ch. 1. Donogh, *A Treatise on the Law of Sedition* n 44 above abounds with various disparaging ways in which to describe Indian opponents of British control. For a full review of recent scholarship on India and revolutionary violence, see Andrew Amstutz, Daniel Elam, Rishad Choudhury, Mou Banerjee, Rohit De, Michael Silvestri, Kama Maclean and Durba Ghosh, 'New Histories of Political Violence and Revolutionary Terrorism in Modern South Asia' (2019) 10 (3) *South Asian History and Culture* 340–360.
51 Explaining the Murderous Outrages Act passed in India by way of response to the challenge of governing at the empire's frontier, see Mark Condos, 'License to Kill' n 34 above.
52 Sedition Committee 1918 (Calcutta: Superintendent Government Printing, 1918), i.
53 Ibid., especially paras 171–172, 181 from which the quotes in the text are drawn. For an interesting personal account see Justin Rowlatt, 'The Sins of the Great-Grandfather: The Rowlatt Act and the Amritsar Massacre' (2019) 50 (3) *Asian Affairs* 296–304.
54 McQuade, *A Genealogy of Terrorism* n 16 above, p. 18.
55 For Tegart see https://www.s-asian.cam.ac.uk/?papers-collection=tegart (last visited 5 May 2022).
56 McQuade, *A Genealogy of Terrorism* n 16 above, p. 18.
57 Cited in ibid., p. 169.
58 Bakhle, 'Savarkar' n 38 above, p. 73.
59 McQuade, *A Genealogy of Terrorism* n 16 above, p. 203.
60 Amstutz et al., 'New Histories' n 50 above, p. 343. See Durba Ghosh, *Gentlemanly Terrorists: Political Violence and the Colonial State in India, 1919–1947* (New York: Cambridge University Press, 2017).
61 On the Rowlatt committee see generally McQuade, *A Genealogy of Terrorism* n 16 above, pp. 154–162.
62 McQuade, *A Genealogy of Terrorism* n 16 above, p. 179.
63 Ibid., p. 30.
64 For evidence of how prominent the language of terrorism was as a way of describing anti-colonial action at this time see David French, *The British Way in Counter-Insurgency 1945–1967* (Oxford: Oxford University Press, 2011), ch. 2.
65 Elkins, *Legacy of Violence* n 14 above, p. 221.
66 Christopher A. Bailey and Tim Harper (eds.), *Forgotten Wars: The End of Britain's Asian Empire* (London: Allen Lane, 2007), p. 453. A full account of the incident is at pp. 449–456. Efforts years later to force a public inquiry were unsuccessful: *Keyu v Secretary of State for Foreign and Commonwealth Affairs* [2014] EWCA Civ 312, [2015] 1 QB 57, [2015] UKSC 69.
67 Quoted by Elkins, *Legacy of Violence* n 14 above, p. 513.
68 Ibid., p. 524.
69 536 HC DEB 119 (written answer) (2 Feb 1955).
70 Reid, 'Terrorism in African History' n 17 above, pp. 208–209.
71 David M. Anderson, 'Guilty Secrets: Deceit, Denial, and the Discovery of Kenya's "Migrated Archive"' (2015) 80 *History Workshop Journal* 142–160, p. 142; Caroline Elkins, 'Looking Beyond Mau Mau' (2015) 120 (3) *The American Historical Review* 852–868.
72 Reid, 'Terrorism in African History' n 17 above, p. 209 (footnote omitted). After the decision in *Mutua v Foreign and Commonwealth Office* [2011] EWHC 1913 (21 July 2011),

the then Foreign Secretary William Hague acknowledged that 'Kenyans were subject to torture and other forms of ill-treatment at the hands of the colonial administration': 563 HC DEB 1692 (6 June 2013). Later cases were not successful: *Mutua and others v Foreign and Commonwealth Office* [2012] EWHC 2678 (QB). For the denial of litigation on the basis of the law of limitations see *Kimathi and others v Foreign and Commonwealth Office* [2018] EWHC 2066 (QB); *Kimathi and others v Foreign and Commonwealth Office* [2018] EWHC 3144 (QB).

73 594 HC DEB 1131 (6 November 1958).
74 Ibid.
75 Quoted in French, *The British Way in Counter-Insurgency* n 64 above, p. 107.
76 These were the descriptions used by the Secretary of State for the Home Department Sir Samuel Hoare when introducing the Prevention of Violence (Temporary Provisions) Bill in the House of Commons in July 1939: 350 HC DEB 1047–1049 (24 July 1939).
77 Peter Fitzpatrick, *The Mythology of Modern Law* (London: Routledge, 1992). The quote is from Hussain, *The Jurisprudence of Emergency* n 11 above, p. 28.
78 Beatrice de Graaf, 'Terrorism in the Netherlands' in English (ed.), *The Cambridge History of Terrorism* 333–360, p. 345 (footnote omitted).
79 Ibid., p. 346.
80 Ibid. (footnote omitted)
81 Ibid.
82 Roger Levy, 'Indochina: A Keystone in Asia – a French View' (1952) 8 (1) *India Quarterly* 31–38, p. 32.
83 Ibid., p. 37.
84 Elkins, *Legacy of Violence* n 14 above, p. 620.

Chapter 2
1 Ekaterina Stepanova, 'Terrorism in the Russian Empire: The Late Nineteenth and Early Twentieth Centuries' in Richard English (ed.), *The Cambridge History of Terrorism* (Cambridge: Cambridge University Press, 2021) 284–312, p. 299.
2 Martyn Frampton, 'History and the Definition of Terrorism' in English (ed.), *The Cambridge History of Terrorism* 31–57, p. 39. See generally Richard Bach Jensen, *The Battle Against Anarchist Terrorism: An International History, 1878–1934* (Cambridge: Cambridge University Press, 2014). For anarchism in the US at this time see Mary S. Barton, 'The Global War on Terrorism: The United States and International Anarchist Terrorism, 1898–1904' (2015) 39 (2) *Diplomatic History* 303–330.
3 Stepanova, 'Terrorism in the Russian Empire' n 1 above, p. 302.
4 Bach Jensen, *The Battle Against Anarchist Terrorism* n 2 above, ch. 10.
5 Stepanova, 'Terrorism in the Russian Empire' n 1 above p. 304.
6 For an interesting study of this point see Gareth Jenkins, 'Marxism and Terrorism' (2006) *International Socialism* 110.
7 James Martel, 'The Law of Rules: Hyperlegalism, Emergency and the Violence of Procedure' (2021) 17 (1) *Law, Culture and the Humanities* 53–70, p. 70.
8 Dennis Dworkin, 'Terrorism: An American Story' in English (ed.), *The Cambridge History of Terrorism* 361–386, p. 374.
9 Ibid.
10 Frampton, 'History and the Definition of Terrorism' n 2 above, p. 46.

11 Stepanova, 'Terrorism in the Russian Empire' n 1 above, p. 317.
12 See Eric Waldman, *The Spartacist Uprising of 1919 and the Crisis of the German Socialist Movement: A Study of the Relation of the Political Theory and Party Practice* (Milwaukee: Marquette University Press, 1958), pp. 56–65.
13 Frampton, 'History and the Definition of Terrorism' n 2 above, p. 40.
14 Edwin P. Hoyt, *The Palmer Raids, 1919–1920: An Attempt to Suppress Dissent* (New York: Seabury Press, 1969).
15 Dworkin, 'Terrorism: An American Story' n 8 above, p. 376.
16 See e.g. in the US the laws discussed in Samuel Walker, *In Defence of American Freedom: A History of the ACLU* 2nd edn (Carbondale and Edwardsville: Southern Illinois University Press, 1999); and in the UK: Keith D. Ewing and Conor A. Gearty, *The Struggle for Civil Liberties: Political Freedom and the Rule of Law in Britain, 1914–1945* (Oxford: Oxford University Press, 2000), chs 3–5.
17 For Debs himself see *Debs v United States* 249 US 211 (1919).
18 341 US 494 (1951). Frankfurter used an article by the distinguished diplomat George Kennan to illustrate the gravity of the threat as he saw it: 554–556.
19 Ewing and Gearty, *The Struggle for Civil Liberties* n 16 above, p. 148.
20 *German Communist Party v Federal Republic of Germany*, European Commission on Human Rights, app 250/57 (20 July 1957).
21 341 US 494 (1951).
22 See generally Conor Gearty, 'No Golden Age: The Deep Origins and Current Utility of Western Counter-Terrorism Policy' in Richard English (ed.), *Illusions of Terrorism and Counter-Terrorism* (Oxford: Oxford University Press, 2015) 73–93.
23 Constitution of the Irish Free State (Saorstát Eireann) Act 1922, sched 1, arts 73 and 75, building on the Agreement between the British and Irish leaders that had led to a cessation of hostilities; see Sched 2, art 17.
24 Irish Constitution 1937, art 50.
25 Indian Independence Act 1947, s 18.
26 The Kenya Order in Council 1963 (SI 791 of 1963), art 4; Kenya Independence Act 1963; The Constitution of Kenya.
27 Commonwealth of Australia Act 1900, ss 7 and 9 and the Constitution s 108; British North America Act 1867 s 129.
28 John Dugard, *Human Rights and the South African Legal Order* (Princeton: Princeton University Press, 1978), chs 2 and 10B.
29 Dated 23 September 1948; see https://www.jewishvirtuallibrary.org/israel-s-prevention -of-terrorism-ordinance-no-33-september-1948#0 (last visited 17 January 2023).
30 State of Israel, Report to the Counter-Terrorism Committee pursuant to Paragraph 6 of Security Council Resolution 1373 (2001) of 28 September 2001: https://documents-d ds-ny.un.org/doc/UNDOC/GEN/No2/229/21/PDF/No222921.pdf?OpenElement (last visited 18 January 2023).
31 Colm Campbell, *Emergency Law in Ireland, 1918–1925* (Oxford: Clarendon Press, 1994), p. 193. See Chapter 3 generally for a full account.
32 Dayyab Gillani, 'The History of Terrorism in Pakistan' in English (ed.), *The Cambridge History of Terrorism* 223–253, p. 248. For a fascinating essay on the difficulty of developing a rigorous study of terrorism in decolonized states that uses Pakistan as its case study see Muhammad Feyyaz 'The Discourse and Study of Terrorism in

Decolonised States: The Case of Pakistan' (2016) 9 (3) *Critical Studies on Terrorism* 455–477.

33 Jeremy Harding, 'You're With Your King' (2022) 44 (3) *London Review of Books*, 10 February 2022: https://www.lrb.co.uk/the-paper/v44/n03/jeremy-harding/you-re-with-your-king (last visited 18 January 2023).

34 See p. 74.

35 Joseph McQuade, *A Genealogy of Terrorism: Colonial Law and the Origins of an Idea* (Cambridge: Cambridge University Press, 2021), p. 240.

36 Susan Williams, *White Malice: The CIA and the Neocolonisation of Africa* (London: C Hurst and Co, 2023), p. 137. The politician quoted is Richard Nixon, at the time US vice-president.

37 Fatemah Alzubairi, *Colonialism, Neo-Colonialism, and Anti-Terrorism Law in the Arab World* (Cambridge: Cambridge University Press, 2019), p. 78.

38 Article 314 of the Lebanese Penal Code (No 340 of 1943), cited in ibid., pp. 78–79.

39 Alzubairi, ibid., p. 79.

40 Ibid.

41 An excellent overview is provided in Victor V. Ramraj and Arun K. Thiruvengadam (eds.), *Emergency Powers in Asia: Exploring the Limits of Legality* (Cambridge: Cambridge University Press, 2010). For a country that escaped colonial domination but which nevertheless was exposed to these Cold War pressures, see Mara Malagodi, 'Nepal's Constitutional Foundations Between Revolution and Cold War (1950–60)' (2023) 41 (2) *Law and History Review* 273–294.

42 See Nathan J. Brown, 'Retrospective: Law and Imperialism: Egypt in Comparative Perspective' (1995) 29 (1) *Law and Society Review* 103–126, p. 111.

43 Article 98(b) of the Egyptian Penal Code added by Law No 117 of 1946, as set out in Alzubairi, *Colonialism, Neo-Colonialism, and Anti-Terrorism Law* n 37 above, p. 79.

44 Alzubairi, ibid., p. 134.

45 Ibid.

46 See Tareq Y. Ismael, *The Communist Movement in Egypt, 1920–1988* (New York: Syracuse University Press, 1990) cited in Alzubairi, ibid., p. 135. The details are in Ismael, ch. 4.

47 Alzubairi, ibid., p. 137.

48 Ibid., p. 114.

49 Ibid., p. 184.

50 Ibid., p. 7.

51 Ibid., p. 9.

52 Ibid.

53 Ibid., p. 18.

54 David A. Dyker and Ivan Vejvoda (eds.), *Yugoslavia and After: A Study in Fragmentation, Despair and Rebirth* (London: Longman, 1996).

55 Chris Ogden, *A Dictionary of Politics and International Relations in India* (Oxford: Oxford University Press, 2019): see the entry for 'Naxalites'. See further Alpa Shah, *Nightmarch: Among India's Revolutionary Guerrillas* (Chicago: University of Chicago Press, 2019).

56 Williams, *White Malice* n 36 above.

57 Richard Reid, 'Terrorism in African History' in English (ed.), *The Cambridge History of Terrorism* 199–222, p. 199.

58 Ibid.
59 On Israel and Palestine see Chapter 4 below. So far as the Irish-international terrorist/ communist links are concerned, it is clear that General Gadaffi's Libya was a generous supplier of weaponry to the IRA during the second half of the 1980s. See Conor Gearty, *Terror* (London: Faber and Faber, 1991), pp. 119–120.
60 Jonathan Hartlyn and Arturo Valenzuela, 'Democracy in Latin America since 1930' in Leslie Bethell (ed.), *The Cambridge History of Latin America, Vol. 6: Latin America since 1930: Economy, Politics and Society* (Cambridge: Cambridge University Press, 1994), pp. 99–100.
61 BBVA Research, *Urbanisation in Latin America* (July 2017); Joana Xavier Barros, *Urban Growth in Latin American Cities*, UCL PhD thesis, October 2004: https://core.ac.uk/do wnload/pdf/78076244.pdf (last visited 20 September 2023).
62 Frampton, 'History and the Definition of Terrorism' n 2 above, p. 43.
63 Gearty, *Terror* n 59 above, pp. 36–37.
64 Randall D. Law, *Terrorism. A History* 2nd edn (Cambridge: Polity, 2016), p. 247 and generally ch. 13.
65 Ibid., p. 248.
66 Gearty, *Terror* n 59 above, pp. 41–43.
67 Law, *Terrorism: A History* n 64 above, p. 248.
68 See respectively David Macey, *Frantz Fanon: A Biography* 2nd edn (London: Verso, 2012) and Jon Lee Anderson, *Che Guevara: A Revolutionary life* (New York: Grove Press, 1997).
69 Stepanova, 'Terrorism in the Russian Empire' n 1 above, p. 299.
70 Ibid., p. 297.
71 Reid, 'Terrorism in African History' n 57 above, p. 211.
72 See https://www.marxists.org/archive/marighella-carlos/1969/06/minimanual-urban-gu errilla/ch38.htm (last visited 22 January 2023).
73 The grim consequences are detailed in Gearty, *Terror* n 59 above, pp. 42–43.
74 Roddy Brett, 'Political Violence and Terrorism in Colombia' in English (ed.), *The Cambridge History of Terrorism* 387–419, pp. 400–401.
75 Cecilia Méndez, 'The Paths of Terrorism in Peru' in English (ed.), *The Cambridge History of Terrorism* 420–452, p. 427.
76 Ibid.
77 Law, *Terrorism: A History* n 64 above, p. 251.
78 Dworkin, 'Terrorism: An American Story' n 8 above, p. 377.
79 Kurt Groenewold, 'The German Federal Government's Response and Civil Liberties' (1992) 4 (4) *Terrorism and Political Violence* 136–151.
80 Karrin Hanshew, 'Daring More Democracy? Internal Security and the Social Democratic Fight against West German Terrorism' (2010) 43 *Central European History* 117–147, p. 117. See generally Stefan Aust, *Baader-Meinhof: The Inside Story of the RAF* (London: The Bodley Head, 2008).
81 Hanshew, 'Daring More Democracy', p. 117.
82 John Schmeidel, 'My Enemy's Enemy: Twenty Years of Co-operation between West Germany's Red Army Faction and the GDR Ministry for State Security' (1993) 8 (4) *Intelligence and National Security* 59–72.
83 Hanshew 'Daring More Democracy' n 80 above, p. 117. A further influence was the

German philosopher Herbert Marcuse; see his *An Essay on Liberation* (1969), available at https://www.marxists.org/reference/archive/marcuse/works/1969/essay-liberation.htm (last visited 3 February 2023).

84 Leith Passmore, 'The Ethics and Politics of Force-Feeding Terror Suspects in West German Prisons' (2012) 25 (2) *Social History of Medicine* 481–499, p. 482.

85 *Klass and Others v Germany*, European Court of Human Rights, 6 September 1978.

86 Hanshew 'Daring More Democracy' n 80 above, pp. 133–134 (footnote omitted).

87 Chapter 3 below.

88 Markus Rau, 'Country Report on Germany' in Christian Walter, Silja Vöneky, Volker Röben, Frank Schorkopf (eds.), *Terrorism as a Challenge for National and International Law: Security versus Liberty?* (Springer: Heidelberg, 2004), pp. 313–314.

89 Hanshew, 'Daring More Democracy' n 80 above, p. 143 (footnote omitted).

90 On the role of Helmut Schmidt see Hanno Balz, 'Head of State of Exception: Federal German Chancellor Helmut Schmidt and the Supralegal Crisis Management During the 1970s' (2018) 28 *Politikwiss* 469–483.

91 Hanshew, 'Daring More Democracy' n 80 above, p. 144.

92 Ibid., p. 119.

93 Ibid., p. 128.

94 *Glasenapp v Federal Republic of Germany*, European Court of Human Rights, app 9228/80 (28 August 1986).

95 *Vogt v Germany*, European Court of Human Rights, app 17851/91 (26 September 1995).

96 Quoted in an interview in *Espresso*, 19 May 1974, included in Lorenzo Bosi, 'A Processual Approach to Political Violence. How History Matters' in English (ed.), *The Cambridge History of Terrorism* 106–123, p. 116. See generally pp. 113–14 on the Red Brigades and state reaction at pp. 114–115.

97 Carr Gordon, *The Angry Brigade: The Cause and the Case* (London: Victor Gollancz, 1975); J. Dan Taylor, 'The Party's Over: The Angry Brigade, the Counter-Culture, and the British New Left, 1967–1972' (2015) 58 (3) *Historical Journal* 877–900.

98 Ibid., p. 895.

99 Beatrice de Graaf, 'Terrorism in the Netherlands: A History' in English (ed.), *The Cambridge History of Terrorism* 333–360, p. 348. See also Beatrice de Graaf and Leena Malkki, 'Killing it Softly? Explaining the Early Demise of Left-Wing Terrorism in the Netherlands' (2010) 22 (4) *Terrorism and Political Violence* 623–640.

100 de Graaf, 'Terrorism in the Netherlands', p. 350. The direct quote from the prime minister is taken from de Graaf, ibid.

101 Ibid., p. 352.

Chapter 3

1 Ryan D. Griffiths, *Age of Secession: The International and Domestic Determinants of State Birth* (Cambridge: Cambridge University Press, 2016).

2 See Eric J. Hobsbawm, *Nations and Nationalism since 1780: Programme, Myth, Reality* (Cambridge: Cambridge University Press, 1990).

3 Harry Hearder, *Europe in the Nineteenth Century 1830–1880* 2nd edn (London: Longman, 1988).

4 Statutes of Kilkenny 1366.

5 Poynings Law 1494.

6 There are of course many excellent histories of Ireland. A personal favourite, and covering much of the ground dealt with here, is Roy F. Foster, *Modern Ireland 1600–1972* (London: Allen Lane, 1988).

7 Martyn Frampton, 'History and the Definition of Terrorism' in Richard English (ed.), *The Cambridge History of Terrorism* (Cambridge: Cambridge University Press, 2021) 31–57, p. 39.

8 Fearghal McGarry, 'Political Violence in Ireland' in English (ed.), *The Cambridge History of Terrorism* 254–283, p. 258.

9 Ibid., p. 262. For the origins of police primacy in relation to Irish political violence see Lindsay Clutterbuck 'Countering Irish Republican Terrorism in Britain: Its Origin as a Police Function' (2006) 18 (1) *Terrorism and Political Violence* 95–118.

10 81 HC DEB 2510 (27 April 1916) (The Prime Minister). See Keith D. Ewing and Conor A. Gearty, *The Struggle for Civil Liberties: Political Freedom and the Rule of Law in Britain, 1914–1945* (Oxford: Oxford University Press, 2000), p. 339, and ch. 7 generally for a legal account of Ireland's political disorders during this time. Much of what follows in the historical account here is drawn from that work.

11 *R v Governor of Lewes Prison, ex parte Doyle* [1917] 2 KB 254, 273 per Darling J.

12 On what follows see generally Colm Campbell, *Emergency Law in Ireland 1918–1925* (Oxford: Oxford University Press, 1994). Also useful is Seosamh Ó Longaigh, *Emergency Law in Independent Ireland, 1922–1948* (Dublin: Four Courts Press, 2006).

13 Ewing and Gearty, *The Struggle for Civil Liberties* n 10 above, p. 355.

14 See ibid., pp. 360–361 (footnotes omitted). The full text of both proclamations is to be found in *R v Murphy* [1921] 2 IR 190, 198–200.

15 [1921] 2 IR 241.

16 Ibid., 264 per Sullivan CJ.

17 See Charles Townshend, *The British Campaign in Ireland 1919–1921: The Development of Political and Military Policies* (Oxford: Oxford University Press, 1975), p. 161.

18 [1921] 1 IR 265.

19 Article 1 of the Treaty; see https://www.difp.ie/volume-1/1921/anglo-irish-treaty/214/#section-documentpage (last visited 29 September 2022).

20 Government of Ireland Act 1920.

21 Ireland Act 1949 s 2.

22 Bill Kissane, 'Defending Democracy? The Legislative Response to Political Extremism in the Irish Free State, 1922–1939' (2004) 34 *Irish Historical Studies* 156–174.

23 The case was *The State (Burke) v Lennon and the Attorney General* [1940] IR 136, and the amending legislation the Offences Against the State (Amendment) Act 1940. For the Supreme Court on the amending legislation see *In the Matter of Article 26 and in the Matter of the Offences Against the State (Amendment) Bill 1940* [1940] 1 IR 470. See generally Gerard Hogan and Clive Walker, *Political Violence and the Law in Ireland* (Manchester: Manchester University Press, 1988).

24 We return to this issue of liberal challenges to anti-terrorism legislation in Part Two.

25 Conor Cruise O'Brien, *States of Ireland* (London: Hutchinson, 1972), p. 283.

26 For a dramatic account see the *Irish Times* archive at https://www.irishtimes.com/opinion/december-2nd-1972-1.684477 (last visited 29 September 2022).

27 Ewing and Gearty, *The Struggle for Civil Liberties* n 10 above, p. 373 (footnotes omitted).

28 Quoted in ibid., p. 373 (footnote omitted).

29 The experienced General Sir Frank Kitson, who had a long record of involvement in countering anti-colonial resistance across the Empire/Commonwealth, was brought into Northern Ireland as a senior army figure in the early 1970s. See David Burke, *Kitson's Irish War: Mastermind of the Dirty War in Ireland* (Dublin: The Mercier Press, 2021). Kitson's *Low Intensity Operations: Subversion, Insurgency, Peacekeeping* (London: Faber and Faber, 1971) has been an extremely influential text in the field.

30 For a good general account see Martin J. McCleery, *Operation Demetrius and Its Aftermath: A New History of the Use of Internment Without Trial in Northern Ireland* (Manchester: Manchester University Press, 2015).

31 For the general background see Laura K. Donohue, *The Cost of Counterterrorism: Power, Politics, and Liberty* (Cambridge: Cambridge University Press, 2008); Aileen McColgan, 'Lessons from the Past? Northern Ireland Now and Then, Terrorism, and the Human Rights Act' in Tom Campbell, Keith D. Ewing and Adam Tomkins (eds.), *The Legal Protection of Human Rights: Sceptical Essays* (Oxford: Oxford University Press, 2011) 177–206.

32 *Ireland v United Kingdom*, European Court of Human Rights, 18 January 1978, (1978) 2 EHRR 25. See Aoife Daly, *Torture and Human Rights in Northern Ireland: Interrogation in Depth* (Abingdon: Routledge, 2019).

33 See p. 54 above for this aspect of the German campaign by the RAF.

34 *Report of the Commission to Consider Legal Procedures to Deal with Terrorist Activities in Northern Ireland* (the Diplock Report), Cmnd 5185 (London, HMSO, 1972).

35 Thomas Leahy, *The Intelligence War Against the IRA* (Cambridge: Cambridge University Press, 2020); Aaron Edwards, *Agents of Influence: Britain's Secret Intelligence War Against the IRA* (Newbridge: Irish Academic Press, 2021).

36 *In re Attorney General for Northern Ireland's Reference (No 1 of 1975)* [1977] AC 105.

37 Chris Mullin, *Error of Judgment: The Truth About the Birmingham Bombings* (London: Chatto and Windus, 1986); Grant McKee and Ross Franey, *Time Bomb: Irish Bombers, English Justice and the Guildford Four* (London: Bloomsbury, 1988); Clive Walker and Keir Starmer (eds.), *Justice in Error* (London: Blackstone Press, 1993).

38 There are of course many histories of these events, which unfolded from the mid-1970s through to the successful conclusion of the peace process; see generally Keith Ewing and Conor Gearty, *Freedom Under Thatcher: Civil Liberties in Modern Britain* (Oxford: Oxford University Press, 1990), ch. 7.

39 Steven Greer, *Supergrasses: A Study in Anti-Terrorist Law Enforcement in Northern Ireland* (Oxford: Clarendon Press, 1995).

40 Steven Livingstone, 'The House of Lords and the Northern Ireland Conflict' (1994) 57 (3) *Modern Law Review* 333–360.

41 Niall Ó Dochartaigh, *Deniable Contact: Back-Channel Negotiation in Northern Ireland* (Oxford: Oxford University Press, 2021).

42 An excellent account, by one of the architects of the Northern Ireland peace, is Jonathan Powell, *Talking to Terrorists: How to End Armed Conflicts* (London: The Bodley Head, 2014).

43 Ludger Mees, 'Terrorism in the Basque Country' in English (ed.), *The Cambridge History of Terrorism* 173–198, p. 179. McClellan A. Davis, 'The Differences in Talk about Violence and Terrorism: A Case Study of Northern Ireland and the Basque Country' (2020)

University of Mississippi Honors Theses 1390, at https://egrove.olemiss.edu/hon_thesis /1390 (last visited 18 August 2023), is a well-sourced and nuanced discussion.

44 Mees, ibid., p. 183.

45 Ignacio Sànchez-Cuenca, 'The Dynamics of Nationalist Terrorism: ETA and the IRA' (2007) 19 (3) *Terrorism and Political Violence* 289–306.

46 Mees, 'Terrorism in the Basque Country' n 43 above, pp. 186–187.

47 Ibid., p. 188.

48 *Herri Batasuna and Batasuna v Spain*, European Court of Human Rights, 30 June 2009.

49 Cited in Mees, 'Terrorism in the Basque Country' n 43 above, p. 197.

50 The politician was Séamus Mallon. See Kimberley Moran, '"Sunningdale for Slow Learners?": Negotiating a Credible Commitment to Peace in Northern Ireland' (2012) 1 (1) *The Public Sphere: Journal of Public Policy* 54–63.

51 Beatrice De Graaf, 'Terrorism in the Netherlands: A History' in English (ed.), *The Cambridge History of Terrorism* 333–360, pp. 346–348.

52 Steve Hewitt, 'The Missing Histories of Counterterrorism' in English (ed.), *The Cambridge History of Terrorism* 503–523, pp. 519–520. See David A. Charters (1997) 'The Amateur Revolutionaries: A Reassessment of the FLQ' (1997) 9 (1) *Terrorism and Political Violence* 133–169.

53 See pp. 103–104 below.

54 Prevention of Terrorism (Temporary Provisions) Act 1974.

Chapter 4

1 UN General Assembly Resolution 181 (1947).

2 *Royal Commission of Enquiry to Palestine* Cmd 5479 (HM Stationary Office, 1937).

3 Ibid., p. 375, ch. 20, para 19.

4 Thurston Clarke, *By Blood and Fire: The Attack on the King David Hotel* (New York: G.P. Putnam's Sons, 1981).

5 UN Security Council Resolution 242 (22 November 1967).

6 Conor Gearty, *Terror* (London: Faber and Faber, 1991), p. 51. I have gone back to this book for much of the factual detail that has appeared in the opening sections of this chapter.

7 UN Security Council Resolution 248 (24 March 1968). The marauders reference is in a letter from Israel's Permanent Representative, Mr Yosef Tekoah, to the President of the Security Council, 18 March 1968: https://digitallibrary.un.org/record/519461?ln=ru (last visited 12 December 2022).

8 UN Security Resolution 265 (1 April 1969).

9 'If the world was not prepared to consider the fate of the Palestinians, then the world would not be spared the same fate which the Palestinians had suffered.' Abdallah Frangi, *The PLO and Palestine* (London: Zed Books, 1983), p. 119.

10 Gerard Chaliand, *Terrorism: From Popular Struggle to Media Spectacle* (London: Saqi Books, 1987); Alex P. Schmid and Janny de Graaf, *Violence as Communication: Insurgent Terrorism and the Western News Media* (London: Sage Publications, 1982).

11 There is a good account incorporating recent developments at '"Goodbye Everybody": The Swissair 330 Disaster', https://www.swissinfo.ch/eng/society/wuerenlingen-plane-crash_-goodbye-everybody---the-swissair-330-disaster/45563898 (last visited 13 October 2022).

12 Richard Falk, 'The Beirut Raid and the International Law of Retaliation' (1969) 63 (3) *American Journal of International Law* 415–443.

13 Julie M. Norman, 'Terrorism in Israel/Palestine' in Richard English (ed.), *The Cambridge History of Terrorism* (Cambridge: Cambridge University Press, 2021) 149–172.

14 Falk, 'The Beirut Raid and the International Law of Retaliation' n 12 above, p. 417.

15 Lisa Stampnitzky, *Disciplining Terror: How Experts Invented 'Terrorism'* (Cambridge: Cambridge University Press, 2013). Cf. Marc Sageman, *Misunderstanding Terrorism* (Philadelphia, University of Pennsylvania Press, 2017).

16 Stampnitzky, ibid., p. 51.

17 Ibid., p. 53.

18 Ibid., p. 52.

19 Ibid., p. 23, citing Ronald D. Crelinsten, 'Images of Terrorism in the Media: 1966–1985' (1989) 12 *Terrorism* 167–198.

20 Alex P. Schmid and Albert J. Longman, *Political Terrorism: A New Guide to Actors, Authors, Concepts, Data Bases, Theories, and Literature* (New Brunswick NJ: Transaction Books, 1988) xiii, quoted by Stampnitzky, *Disciplining Terror* n 15 above, p. 24.

21 Ibid., p. 30.

22 Ibid., pp. 34–35.

23 Ibid., p. 43.

24 Ibid., p. 22 has the quotes.

25 Frangi, *The PLO and Palestine* n 9 above, p. 121.

26 UN General Assembly Resolution 3034 (18 December 1972): reprinted in Ben Saul (ed.), *Terrorism: Documents in International Law* (Oxford: Hart Publishing, 2012), p. 301.

27 UN General Assembly Resolution 3034 (18 December 1972), para 10.

28 Stampnitzky, *Disciplining Terror* n 15 above, p. 27.

29 Ibid., p. 27 (footnote omitted). There was also of course some domestic subversion that gradually came to be seen in a similar light; see Daniel S. Chard, *Nixon's War at Home: The FBI, Leftist Guerrillas, and the Origins of Counterterrorism* (Chapel Hill: University of North Carolina Press, 2021).

30 Stampnitzky, *Disciplining Terror* n 15 above, pp. 65–66.

31 Ibid. (emphasis in the original).

32 Edward F. Mickolus, *The Literature of Terrorism: A Selectively Annotated Bibliography* (Westport CT: Greenwood Press, 1980).

33 Stampnitzky, *Disciplining Terror* n 15 above, p. 70. For other exchanges of this sort see pp. 69–75. The speaker quoted in the text was Representative John Buchanan.

34 See p. 55 above.

35 For a fuller account see Gearty, *Terror* n 6 above, ch. 5.

36 UN General Assembly Resolutions 3236 and 3237 (22 November 1974).

37 Arnold Mandel, 'France' (1976) 6 *The American Jewish Yearbook* 303–312, p. 305.

38 David Hirst, *The Gun and the Olive Branch: The Roots of Violence in the Middle East* 2nd edn (London: Faber and Faber, 1984).

39 Stampnitzky, *Disciplining Terror* n 15 above, pp. 122–127.

40 Marius H. Livingstone, Lee Bruce Kress and Marie G. Wanek (eds.), *International Terrorism in the Contemporary World* (Westport, CT: Greenwood Press, 1978) 19, quoted in Stampnitzky, ibid., p. 65.

41 Yonah Alexander and Edgar H. Brenner (eds.), *The United Kingdom's Legal Responses to*

Terrorism (London: Cavendish Publishing Ltd, 2003), xiii. See also Yonah Alexander and Alan S. Nanes (eds.), *Legislative Responses to Terrorism* (The Hague: Martinus Nijhoff, 1986).

42 Edward Herman and Gerry O'Sullivan, *The 'Terrorism' Industry: The Experts and Institutions That Shape Our View of Terror* (New York: Pantheon Books, 1989), p. 146. Alexander was still going in 2007; see the three-volumed Yonah Alexander and Michael B. Kraft, *Evolution of Counterterrorism* (Westport, CT: Praeger Security International, 2007).

43 Yonah Alexander, David Alexander and Joshua Sinai, *Terrorism: The PLO Connection* (New York: Crane Russak, 1989), p. ix.

44 Yonah Alexander and Eli Tavin (eds.), *Terrorists or Freedom Fighters?* (Fairfax: Hero Books, 1986).

45 Herman and O'Sullivan, *The 'Terrorism' Industry* n 42 above, p. 147.

46 Yonah Alexander and Charles K. Ebinger (eds.), *Political Terrorism and Energy: The Threat and Response* (New York: Praeger, in cooperation with the Center for Strategic and International Studies, Georgetown University, 1982), p. 45.

47 Benjamin Netanyahu, *International Terrorism: Challenge and Response* (New Brunswick NJ: Transaction Publishers, 1989, first published 1981).

48 Ibid., pp. 39–46.

49 Benjamin Netanyahu, *How the West Can Win* (London: Weidenfeld and Nicolson, 1986), p. xi. See also Benjamin Netanyahu, *Fighting Terrorism: How Democracies Can Defeat Domestic and International Terrorists* (London: Allison and Busby Ltd, 1996).

50 882 HC DEB 634 (28 November 1974).

51 354 HL DEB 1501 (28 November 1974).

52 882 HC DEB 687 (28 November 1974) (John Lee).

53 882 HC DEB 685 (28 November 1974) (Maurice Macmillan).

54 882 HC DEB 729 (28 November 1974) (Sydney Tierney).

55 354 HL DEB 1543 (28 November 1974) (Viscount Brookeborough).

56 882 HC DEB 645 (28 November 1974).

57 Prevention of Terrorism (Temporary Provisions) Act 1984 ss 12(3)(b) and 13(1)(*a*)(i).

58 Terrorism Act 2000.

59 882 HC DEB 652 (28 November 1974) (Michael Mates).

60 Göran Elwin, 'Swedish Anti-Terrorist Legislation' (1977) 1 *Contemporary Crises* 289–301.

61 Kent Roach, *The 9/11 Effect: Comparative Counter-Terrorism* (Cambridge: Cambridge University Press, 2011), pp. 314–317.

62 See ibid., pp. 365–374.

Chapter 5

1 Yair Galily, '"We Can Only Trust Ourselves": Operation Wrath of God in Perspective' (2022) 28 (4) *Israel Affairs* 589–596.

2 One of the essential aspects of the programme was 'plausible deniability . . . for both the Israeli cabinet and the public at large'. Ibid., p. 591.

3 (1979) 25 *Kessing's Record of World Events* 29648.

4 Ibid.

5 UN Security Council Resolutions 425 and 426 (19 March 1978) setting up a UN Interim Force in Lebanon (UNIFL).

6 Linda Butler, '"Mr UNIFIL" Reflects on a Quarter Century of Peacekeeping in South Lebanon: An Interview with Timur Göksel' (2007) 36 (3) *Journal of Palestinian Studies* 50–77, pp. 55, 62.

7 For the wider story see Sheila Ryan, 'Israel's Invasion of the Lebanon: Background to the Crisis' (1982) 12(1) *Journal of Palestine Studies* 23–37.

8 W. Thomas Mallison, George K. Walker, John F. Murphy and Jordan Paust, 'Aggression or Self-Defense in Lebanon in 1982?' (1983) 77 *Proceedings of the Annual Meeting (American Society of International Law)* 174–189, p. 175 (Mallison).

9 Ibid., pp. 175–176 (Mallison).

10 Brian R. Parkinson, 'Israel's Lebanon War: Ariel Sharon and Operation "Peace for Galilee"' (2007) 24 (2) *Journal of Third World Studies* 63–84, p. 64.

11 See 'The 1982 Invasion of Lebanon: The Casualties' (1983) 24 (4) *Race and Class* 340–343.

12 Laurence M. Gross, 'The Legal Implications of Israel's 1982 Invasion into Lebanon' (1983) 13 (3) *California Western International Law Journal* 458–492, p. 475.

13 Mallison et al., 'Aggression or Self-Defense in Lebanon' n 8 above, p. 177 (Mallison).

14 See Barry A. Feinstein, 'The Legality of the Use of Force by Israel in Lebanon – June 1982' (1985) 20 (2–3) *Israel Law Review* 362–396, p. 383 (n 75).

15 '[E]ven if it were possible to argue that each individual PLO strike was not of sufficient intensity to justify Israel's use of force, when considered in total, the numerous PLO acts of terrorism indeed constituted an "armed attack" of considerable magnitude.' Ibid., p. 386. For a defence of Israeli action which despite its title goes beyond law see Justus R. Weiner, 'Terrorism: Israel's Legal Responses' (1987) 14 (2) *Syracuse Journal of International Law and Commerce* 183–208.

16 For a neat illustration of the difficulties inherent in deploying proportionality in the context of future harm see Gross, 'The Legal Implications of Israel's 1982 Invasion' n 12 above, p. 487.

17 Christian Emery, *US Foreign Policy and the Iranian Revolution: The Cold War Dynamics of Engagement and Strategic Alliance* (Basingstoke: Palgrave Macmillan, 2013).

18 Remarks at the Welcoming Ceremony for the Freed American Hostages, 27 January 1981, Ronald Reagan Presidential Library and Museum: https://www.reaganlibrary.gov/archives/speech/remarks-welcoming-ceremony-freed-american-hostages-0 (last visited 20 March 2023).

19 For the early history see Matthew Levitt, *Hezbollah: The Global Footprint of Lebanon's Party of God* (Washington: Georgetown University Press, 2013), ch. 1.

20 See p. 21 n 31 above.

21 Conor Gearty, *Terror* (London: Faber and Faber, 1991), pp. 79–80.

22 Act to Combat International Terrorism 1984.

23 Anti-terrorism Act 1986.

24 *Terrorist Group Profiles* (Washington, 1988), foreword by George Bush, p. ii.

25 Ibid., p. 3.

26 Ibid., p. 129.

27 Ibid., p. iii (foreword by George Bush).

28 Samuel P. Huntington, 'The Clash of Civilizations?' (1993) 72 (3) *Foreign Affairs* 22–49, p. 22; see his *The Clash of Civilizations and the Remaking of World Order* (New York: Simon and Schuster, 1996).

29 Edward Said, 'The Clash of Ignorance' in Jason Dittmer and Joanne Sharp, *Geopolitics:*

NOTES TO PAGES 116–120

An Introductory Reader (London: Routledge, 2014), 191–194 (originally published in *The Nation* in 2001). Paul Berman, *Terror and Liberalism* (New York: W.W. Norton and Co, 2003) is more sympathetic but still sharply critical: pp. 15–18, 182.

30 For two in-depth studies see Tom Ruys, *'Armed Attack' and Article 51 of the UN Charter: Evolutions in Customary Law and Practice* (Cambridge: Cambridge University Press, Cambridge Studies in International and Comparative Law, 2010) and Nils Melzer, *Targeted Killing in International Law* (Oxford: Oxford University Press, Oxford Monographs in International Law, 2009).

31 UN Security Council Resolution 573 (4 October 1985).

32 See https://www.upi.com/Archives/1985/10/03/Prime-Minister-Shimon-Peres-today-de fended-a-raid-on/8204497160000/ (last visited 3 November 2022).

33 Ibid.

34 Kimberley N. Trapp, 'Back to Basics: Necessity, Proportionality, and the Right of Self-Defence against Non-State Terrorist Actors' (2007) 56 (1) *International and Comparative Law Quarterly* 141–156, p. 148 (footnotes omitted).

35 *Annex – HLS Pilac Catalogue of Apparent 'Article 51 Communications'* (Program on International Law and Armed Conflict, Harvard Law School: https://pilac.law.harva rd.edu/quantum-of-silence-paper-and-annex/annex-hls-pilac-catalogue-of-apparent-ar ticle-51-communications (last visited 12 December 2022). Accessible on the link is the scholarly article to which the catalogue is an annex: Dustin A. Lewis, Naz K. Modirzadeh and Gabriella Blum, 'Quantum of Silence: Inaction and *Jus ad Bellum*', Harvard Law School Program on International Law and Armed Conflict, 2019.

36 Security Council Official Records, 21st Year, 1320th Meeting, 16 November 1966; see https://digitallibrary.un.org/record/581598?ln=en (last visited 12 December 2022). The comments of the Israeli representative, Mr Comay, are at paras 49–84.

37 Security Council Resolution 228 of 1966 (25 November 1966).

38 Ibid., paras 2, 3.

39 Trapp, 'Back to Basics' n 34 above, p. 149.

40 Ibid. (footnote omitted).

41 See as an example of the concern expressed by leading terrorism scholars at the time, Paul Wilkinson and Alasdair M. Stewart (eds.), *Contemporary Research on Terrorism* (Aberdeen: Aberdeen University Press, 1987), xviii (foreword by Wilkinson).

42 Julie M. Norman, 'Terrorism in Israel/Palestine' in Richard English (ed.), *The Cambridge History of Terrorism* (Cambridge: Cambridge University Press, 2021) 149–172, p. 162.

43 Ibid., p. 163.

44 Helga Baumgarten, 'The Three Faces/Phases of Palestinian Nationalism, 1948–2005' (2005) 34 (4) *Journal of Palestinian Studies* 25–48.

45 Fatemah Alzubairi, *Colonialism, Neo-Colonialism, and Anti-Terrorism Law in the Arab World* (Cambridge: Cambridge University Press, 2019), p. 109.

46 Ibid.

47 Ibid., p. 114.

48 Ibid., p. 186, and see generally ch. 7.

49 Rory Miller, 'Terrorism, History and Regionalisation' in English (ed.), *The Cambridge History of Terrorism* 81–105, p. 93.

50 Ibid.

51 Ibid., p. 94.

52 Ibid., p. 93.
53 Dayyab Gillani, 'The History of Terrorism in Pakistan' in English (ed.), *The Cambridge History of Terrorism* 223–253, p. 228.
54 Ibid., p. 240.
55 Ibid., p. 228 (footnote omitted).
56 Miller, 'Terrorism, History and Regionalisation' n 49 above, p. 90.
57 Jason Burke, *The 9/11 Wars* (London: Allen Lane, 2011), p. 19. See the same author's *Al-Qaeda: The True Story of Radical Islam* (London: Penguin Books, 2003).
58 National Commission on Terrorist Attacks Upon the United States ('the 9/11 Commission') (Washington, 2004), pp. 59–60.
59 Ibid., p. 60.
60 Ibid.
61 Dennis Dworkin, 'Terrorism: An American Story' in English (ed.), *The Cambridge History of Terrorism* 361–386, p. 383. The antagonism to the Saudi Arabian leadership that underpinned the seizure of the Grand Mosque in Mecca in November 1979 might be seen as a forerunner of the ideas and approach of Osama bin Laden, but the event appeared at the time to be something of a militant 'one-off', especially when compared with the Iranian state radicalism of the day.
62 The 9/11 Commission n 58 above, p. 70.
63 Dworkin, 'Terrorism: An American Story' n 61 above, p. 383.
64 The 9/11 Commission n 58 above, p. 145.

Chapter 6
1 Fawaz A. Gerges, *The Far Enemy: Why Jihad Went Global* (Cambridge: Cambridge University Press, 2005).
2 The quote is drawn from a useful, if sparse, chronology to be found on the website of the US Department of Homeland Security: https://www.dhs.gov/september-11-chronology (last visited 8 December 2022).
3 Ibid.
4 National Commission on Terrorist Attacks Upon the United States ('the 9/11 Commission') (Washington, 2004), p. 4.
5 See the Report's Executive Summary, accessible at https://govinfo.library.unt.edu/911/re port/911Report_Exec.htm (last visited 8 December 2022).
6 See p. 112 above.
7 See the transcript at *PBS News Hour*: https://www.pbs.org/newshour/world/terrorism-ju ly-dec01-bush-speech_9-12 (last visited 9 December 2022).
8 For a full transcript of Blair's short statement see https://www.americanrhetoric.com/ speeches/tblair9-11-01.htm (last visited 9 December 2022).
9 For a full transcript see https://www.washingtonpost.com/wp-srv/nation/specials/attack ed/transcripts/bushaddress_092001.html (last visited 9 December 2022).
10 For Osama bin Laden's public position see his 'Letter to America' dating from November 2002 which was until recently reprinted in full in the *Observer*: https://www.theguardian .com/world/2002/nov/24/theobserver (last visited 10 December 2022). The letter is now difficult to access on account of concerns about how it was being used, including by far-right groups: https://www.wired.com/story/far-right-bin-laden-letter-to-america-con spiracies (last visited 4 January 2024).

11 See p. 112 above.
12 See p. 120 above.
13 See p. 118 above.
14 Paul Wilkinson and Alasdair M. Stewart (eds.), *Contemporary Research on Terrorism* (Aberdeen: Aberdeen University Press, 1987), xviii (foreword by Wilkinson).
15 Antony Anghie, *Imperialism, Sovereignty and the Making of International Law* (Cambridge: Cambridge University Press, 2004), p. 291.
16 For this incident and those that follow in this paragraph see the immensely valuable resource at *Annex – HLS Pilac Catalogue of Apparent 'Article 51 Communications'* (Program on International Law and Armed Conflict, Harvard Law School): https://pilac.law.har vard.edu/quantum-of-silence-paper-and-annex/annex-hls-pilac-catalogue-of-apparent-article-51-communications (last visited 12 December 2022). Accessible on the link is the scholarly article to which the catalogue is an annex: Dustin A. Lewis, Naz K. Modirzadeh and Gabriella Blum, "'Quantum of Silence: Inaction and *Jus ad Bellum*" Program on International Law and Armed Conflict' Harvard Law School, 2019.
17 See Letter dated 24 July 1995 from the Chargé d'Affaires of the Permanent Mission of Turkey to the United Nations addressed to the President of the Security Council: https://digitallibrary.un.org/record/198786?ln=en (last visited 14 December 2022).
18 Letter dated 24 August 1994 from the Permanent Representative of Tajikistan to the United Nations addressed to the Secretary-General: https://digitallibrary.un.org/record/194387?ln=en (last visited 14 December 2022).
19 Letter dated 20 August 1998 from the Permanent Representative of the United States of America to the United Nations addressed to the President of the Security Council: https://digitallibrary.un.org/record/258713?ln=en (last visited 15 December 2022). The spelling of Bin Laden as 'Bin Ladin' appears in the original text.
20 James Astill, 'Strike One', *Guardian*, 2 October 2001: https://www.theguardian.com/world/2001/oct/02/afghanistan.terrorism3 (last visited 15 December 2022). The factory owners' effort to sue the US was barred before the US courts on grounds of non-justiciability: 'courts are not a forum for second-guessing the merits of foreign policy and national security decisions': *El-Shifa Pharmaceutical Industries Company et al v United States of America* 207 F 3d 836 (2010), with the Supreme Court refusing to hear the case; see https://www.internationalcrimesdatabase.org/Case/964/El-Shifa-v-USA/ (last visited 14 December 2022).
21 Letter dated 7 October 2001 from the Permanent Representative of the United States of America to the United Nations addressed to the President of the Security Council: https://digitallibrary.un.org/record/449476?ln=en (last visited 16 December 2022). See generally Ben Smith and Arabella Thorp, *The Legal Basis for the Invasion of Afghanistan* House of Commons Library. Standard Note SN/IA/5340 (last updated 26 February 2010), 3–4: https://commonslibrary.parliament.uk/research-briefings/sn05340/ (last visited 11 December 2022). The UK notification, along broadly similar lines, is laid out at ibid., p. 4.
22 Letter dated 7 October 2001 from the US to the UN. Ibid.
23 Letter dated 17 June 2014 from the Permanent Representative of the United States of America to the United Nations addressed to the President of the Security Council: https://undocs.org/Home/Mobile?FinalSymbol=S%2F2014%2F417&Language=E& DeviceType=Desktop&LangRequested=False (last visited 16 December 2022).

24 See the Department of Justice briefing of 27 June 2018: https://www.justice.gov/opa/pr /ahmed-abu-khatallah-sentenced-22-years-prison-september-2012-attack-benghazi-libya (last visited 16 December 2022).

25 Letter dated 23 September 2014 from the Permanent Representative of the United States of America to the United Nations addressed to the President of the Security Council: https://www.securitycouncilreport.org/un-documents/document/s2014695.php (last visited 19 December 2022).

26 Letter dated 14 November 2023 from the Permanent Representative of the United States of America to the United Nations addressed to the President of the Security Council S/2023/877: https://documents-dds-ny.un.org/doc/UNDOC/GEN/N23/356/39/PDF /N2335639.pdf?OpenElement (last visited 1 December 2023).

27 Identical letters dated 5 December 2005 from the Permanent Representative of Israel to the United Nations addressed to the Secretary-General and the President of the Security Council: https://www.un.org/unispal/document/auto-insert-182708/ (last visited 18 December 2022).

28 Identical letters dated 27 December 2008 from the Permanent Representative of Israel to the United Nations addressed to the Secretary-General and the President of the Security Council: https://www.securitycouncilreport.org/un-documents/document/gaza-s20088 16.php (last visited 18 December 2022).

29 Identical letters dated 4 January 2009 from the Permanent Representative of Israel to the United Nations addressed to the Secretary-General and the President of the Security Council: https://www.securitycouncilreport.org/un-documents/document/gaza-s20088 16.php (last visited 18 December 2022).

30 *Human Rights in Palestine and Other Occupied Arab Territories. Report of the United Nations Fact-Finding Mission on the Gaza Conflict*, 25 September 2009, A/HRC/12/48: https://documents-dds-ny.un.org/doc/UNDOC/GEN/G09/158/66/PDF/G0915866.pdf ?OpenElement (last visited 19 December 2022) paras 30–31.

31 Identical letters dated 12 January 2010 from the Permanent Representative of Israel to the United Nations addressed to the Secretary-General and the President of the Security Council: https://digitallibrary.un.org/record/675045?ln=en (last visited 18 December 2022).

32 Ibid.

33 'Accord with Israel Reached in Principle on Payment for UN Property Damage in Gaza': https://news.un.org/en/story/2010/01/326052 (last visited 19 December 2022). $10.5 million was paid over: https://news.un.org/en/story/2010/01/327352 (last visited 19 December 2022).

34 Identical letters dated 7 October 2023 from the Permanent Representative of Israel to the United Nations addressed to the Secretary-General and the President of the Security Council S/2023/742 (9 October 2023).

35 Identical letters dated 20 January 2018 from the Chargé d'Affaires of the Permanent Mission of Turkey to the United Nations addressed to the Secretary-General and the President of the Security Council: https://documents-dds-ny.un.org/doc/UNDOC /GEN/N18/017/57/PDF/N1801757.pdf?OpenElement (last visited 20 December 2022).

36 An outrider was the killing of Osama bin Laden himself, which was not presented in article 51 terms: https://www.nytimes.com/2015/10/29/us/politics/obama-legal-autho rization-osama-bin-laden-raid.html (last visited 12 July 2023). And see Kai Ambos and

Josef Alkatout, 'Has "Justice Been Done"? The Legality of Bin Laden's Killing Under International Law' (2012) 45 (2) *Israel Law Review* 341–366.

37 *Guardian*, 8 September 2021, p. 33. The analysis was done by the civilian harm monitoring group *Airwars*: https://airwars.org/ (last visited 6 July 2023). A special issue of *Critical Terrorism Studies* is devoted to 'Drones and State Terrorism'; see the Introduction by the editors: Marina Espinoza and Afxentis Afxentiou, 'Editors' Introduction: Drones and State Terrorism' (2018) 11 (2) *Critical Studies on Terrorism* 295–300. There is a valuable rehearsal of the ethical issues in Tamar Meisels and Jeremy Waldron, *Debating Targeted Killing: Counter-Terrorism or Extrajudicial Execution?* (Oxford: Oxford University Press: 2020).

38 *Use of Armed Drones for Targeted Killings* A/HHRC/44/38 (15 August 2020): https://www.ohchr.org/en/documents/thematic-reports/ahrc4438-use-armed-drones-targeted-killings-report-special-rapporteur (last visited 20 December 2022).

39 Ibid., para 31.

40 Ibid., paras 67, 76.

41 Chris O'Meara, 'Reconceptualising the Right of Self-Defence against "Imminent" Armed Attacks' (2022) 9 (2) *Journal on the Use of Force and International Law* 278–323, p. 280. See the same author's *Necessity and Proportionality and the Right of Self-Defence in International Law* (Oxford: Oxford University Press, 2021).

42 An excellent example where all the literature is conveniently gathered is O'Meara, 'Reconceptualising the Right of Self-Defence'. Ibid.

43 Public Law 107–40; 115 Stat 224 (18 September 2001), section 2(a): https://www.congress.gov/107/plaws/publ40/PLAW-107publ40.pdf (last visited 4 January 2023).

44 UN Human Rights Council, *Joint Study on Global Practices in Relation to Secret Detention in the Context of Countering Terrorism*, A/HRC/13/42 (20 May 2010) ('the Joint Study'), para 99: https://digitallibrary.un.org/record/677500 (last visited 12 December 2023).

45 The Memorandum can be found at https://www.supremecourt.gov/opinions/URLs_Cited/OT2005/05-184/05-184_2.pdf para 2 (last visited 4 January 2023).

46 Ibid., para 3.

47 Joint Study n 44 above, para 100.

48 Ibid., paras 57, 58.

49 For this wider background see the Joint Study, n 44 above.

50 *Korematsu v United States* 323 US 214 (1944). There were strong dissents from three of the nine justices, Justices Jackson, Murphy and Roberts.

51 Presidential letter of apology, 1 October 1993: http://www.pbs.org/childofcamp/history/clinton.html (last visited 5 October 2022).

52 Emphasis added. The full executive order is accessible at https://georgewbush-whitehouse.archives.gov/news/releases/2001/11/20011113-27.html (last visited 6 January 2023).

53 James Martel, 'The Law of Rules: Hyperlegalism, Emergency and the Violence of Procedure' (2021) 17 (1) *Law, Culture and the Humanities* 53–70, p. 59.

54 Military Order. Detention Treatment and Trial of Certain Non-Citizens in the War Against Terrorism 13 November 2001 s 1 (e) and (f): https://georgewbush-whitehouse.archives.gov/news/releases/2001/11/20011113-27.html (last visited 6 January 2023).

55 Ibid., s 4 (a).

56 Ibid., s 2.

57 Ibid., s 3(a).

58 Ibid., s 3 (b) and (c).

59 Ibid., s 3 (d).

60 See article 3 of the agreement, the full text of which can be accessed at https://avalon.law
.yale.edu/20th_century/dip_cuba002.asp (last visited 6 January 2023).

61 Richard Norton Taylor, 'Guantánamo is Gulag of Our Time says Amnesty', *Guardian*,
26 May 2005: https://www.theguardian.com/world/2005/may/26/usa.guantanamo (last
visited 10 January 2023).

62 See p. 193 below.

63 On which see further Chapter 9 below.

64 Anti-terrorism, Crime and Security Act 2001, part 4. The scheme did not survive; see
pp. 186–189 below.

65 See p. 188–189 below.

66 Joint Study n 44 above, para 171.

67 Human Rights Council, *Summary Prepared by the Office of the High Commissioner for
Human Rights in Accordance with Paragraph 5 of the Annex to Human Rights Council
Resolution 16/21: India* A/HRC/WG.6/13/IND/3 (12 March 2012), para 66.

68 See Human Rights Council, *Report of the Working Group on Enforced or Involuntary
Disappearances* A/HRC/4/41 (25 January 2007) on China (para 126–134), Belarus (paras
94–98), and Russia (paras 346–361) among others.

69 See generally ibid.

70 In fact are arguably worse; see the horrifying story of one particular captor, detailed
in Opinions adopted by the Working Group on Arbitrary Detention at its ninety-
fifth session, 14–18 November 2022 Opinion No. 66/2022 concerning Zayn al-Abidin
Muhammad Husayn (Abu Zubaydah) (United States of America, Pakistan, Thailand,
Poland, Morocco, Lithuania, Afghanistan and the United Kingdom of Great Britain and
Northern Ireland) A/HRC/WGAD/2022/66. *United States v Husayn, aka Zubaydah et al*
595 US (3 March 2022).

71 There is a comprehensive account in the Joint Study n 44 above.

72 Dick Marty, *Secret Detentions and Illegal Transfer of Detainees Involving Council of Europe
Member States. Second Report*, Council of Europe, 11 June 2007: https://assembly.coe.int
/Documents/WorkingDocs/2007/edoc11302.htm (last visited 10 January 2023).

73 See 'Ten Years of Abu Ghraib', *The New Yorker*, 28 April 2014: https://www.newyorker
.com/news/news-desk/ten-years-of-abu-ghraib (last visited 10 January 2023).

74 For e.g. flight data; see the Joint Study, n 44 above, para 116.

75 Ibid., paras 141–158.

76 Marty, *Secret Detentions* n 72 above; Joint Study, n 44 above, paras 112–124.

77 *Nasr and Ghali v Italy*, European Court of Human Rights, 23 February 2016.

78 Joint Study n 44 above, paras 159.

79 Noam Chomsky, *Culture of Terrorism* (London: Pluto Press, 1989).

80 Joint Study n 44 above.

81 Ibid., para 165.

82 Ibid., para 167. See generally Victor V. Ramraj and Arun K. Thiruvengadam (eds.),
Emergency Powers in Asia: Exploring the Limits of Legality (Cambridge: Cambridge
University Press, 2010) and Victor V. Ramraj, Michael Hor, Kent Roach and George
Williams, *Global Anti-Terrorism Law and Policy* 2nd edn (Cambridge: Cambridge
University Press, 2012) – both invaluable comparative analyses.

83 Joint Study n 44 above, para 288.

84 Ibid., para 288.
85 *Follow-up Report to the Joint Study on Global Practices in Relation to Secret Detention in the Context of Countering Terrorism. Report of the Special Rapporteur on the promotion and protection of human rights and fundamental freedoms while countering terrorism*, Fionnuala Ní Aoláin A/HRC/49/45 (25 March 2022), para 22: https://www.ohchr.org/en/documents/thematic-reports/ahrc4945-follow-report-joint-study-2010-global-practices-relation-sec ret (last visited 11 January 2023).
86 Ibid.
87 And see her *Technical Visit to the United States and Guantánamo Detention Facility by the Special Rapporteur on the Promotion and Protection of Human Rights and Fundamental Freedoms while Countering Terrorism* (14 June 2023), calling for accountability for 'the systematic crimes of extraordinary rendition, torture, cruel, inhuman, and degrading treatment, and arbitrary detention' done to Guantánamo inmates over the years (para 66): https://www.ohchr.org/en/special-procedures/sr-terrorism/us-and-guantanamo-de tention-facility#:~:text=From%206%20February%20to%206,Naval%20Station%20Gua nt%C3%A1namo%20Bay%2C%20Cuba (last visited 12 July 2023).
88 Letter dated 19 December 2001 from the Chairman of the Security Council established pursuant to Resolution 1373 (2001) concerning counter-terrorism addressed to the President of the Security Council S/2001/1220 (19 December 2001): https://digitallibr ary.un.org/record/455939 (last visited 12 January 2022). The details of the actions taken quoted in the text below come from this report, at pp. 4–5.
89 Patriot Act ss 201–225. For Snowden see Glen Greenwald and Ewen MacAskill, 'NSA Prism Program Taps into User Data of Apple, Google and Others', *Guardian*, 17 June 2013. On covert surveillance see *Federal Bureau of Investigation and others v Fazaga and others* 595 US – (2022).
90 See p. 184 below.
91 Letter dated 19 December 2001 from the Chairman of the Security Council to the President of the Security Council n 88 above, p. 4.

Chapter 7

1 (1938) 19 *League of Nations Official Journal* 23, art 1(1). See Ben Saul (ed.), *Terrorism: Documents in International Law* (Oxford: Hart Publishing, 2012) on which I have relied for sourcing this and many of the other international instruments referred to in what follows.
2 (1938) 19 *League of Nations Official Journal* 23, art 1(2).
3 (1938) 19 *League of Nations Official Journal* 23, art 2(1).
4 Ben Saul, *Defining Terrorism in International Law* (Oxford: Oxford University Press, 2006), pp. 171–176 covers the draft Convention very well.
5 Ibid., p. 175.
6 See p. 97 above.
7 UN General Assembly Resolution 3034 (18 December 1972): in Saul (ed.), *Terrorism: Documents* n 1 above, p. 301.
8 UN Charter, art 1(2).
9 For an early critique of this approach and a call for a universal definition see J.J. Lador-Lederer, 'A Legal Approach to International Terrorism' (1974) 9 (2) *Israel Law Review* 194–220.

10 704 *United Nations Treaty Series* 219.

11 860 *United Nations Treaty Series* 105.

12 1035 *United Nations Treaty Series* 167.

13 Convention on the Safety of United Nations and Associated Personnel, adopted 9 December 1994, coming into force 15 January 1999, 2051 *United Nations Treaty Series* 363. An optional protocol followed in 2005, UN General Assembly Resolution 60/42 (2005), coming into force 19 August 2010.

14 974 *United Nations Treaty Series* 178.

15 Adopted 26 February 1988; coming into force 6 August 1989: 974 *United Nations Treaty Series* 177.

16 Adopted 17 December 1979, coming into force 3 June 1983: 1316 *United Nations Treaty Series* 205.

17 Adopted 10 March 1988, coming into force 1 March 1992: 1678 *United Nations Treaty Series* 221. An additional Protocol was adopted on 14 October 2005, coming into force 28 July 2010.

18 Adopted 1 March 1991, coming into force 21 June 1998.

19 Adopted 10 March 1988, coming into force 1 March 1992; 1678 *United Nations Treaty Series* 304.

20 Adopted 3 March 1980, coming into force 8 February 1987: 1456 *United Nations Treaty Series* 101. The quote is from the Preamble.

21 Amendment to the Convention on the Physical Protection of Nuclear Material. Adopted 8 July 2005, coming into force 8 May 2016: https://www.iaea.org/publications /documents/conventions/convention-physical-protection-nuclear-material-and-its-ame ndment#:~:text=The%20Amendment%20to%20the%20CPPNM,domestic%20use%2C %20storage%20and%20transport (last visited 16 January 2023).

22 The language was taken directly from UN General Assembly Resolution 40/61 (9 December 1985).

23 2149 *United Nations Treaty Series* 256.

24 2178 *United Nations Treaty Series* 229.

25 Ibid., art 2(1)(a) and annex.

26 Saul, *Defining Terrorism* n 4 above, pp. 184–185 (footnotes omitted).

27 Ibid., pp. 178–180.

28 Ibid., p. 184.

29 Ibid., p. 186.

30 Cited by Saul, *Defining Terrorism* n 4 above, p. 182.

31 UN General Assembly Resolution 56/1, *Condemnation of Terrorist Attacks in the United States of America* (12 September 2001).

32 UN General Assembly Resolution 56/88, *Measures to Eliminate International Terrorism* (12 December 2001).

33 Ibid., paras 15–16.

34 Ibid., para 17.

35 Saul, *Defining Terrorism* n 4 above, pp. 184–185 (footnotes omitted).

36 UN Security Council Resolution 1368, *Threats to International Peace and Security Caused by Terrorist Acts* (12 September 2001), paras 1–4.

37 Ibid., para 5.

38 UN Charter, art 1(3).

39 Arianna Vedaschi and Kim Lane Scheppele (eds.) *9/11 and the Rise of Global Anti-Terrorism Law: How the UN Security Council Rules the World* (Cambridge: Cambridge University Press, 2021). A recent stimulating study by Alice Martini, *The UN and Counter-Terrorism: Global Hegemonies, Power and Identities* (Abingdon: Routledge: 2021), emphasizes more the global hegemonies and international relations of power that have shaped the UN's perspective.

40 Ben Saul, 'The Legal Black Hole in United Nations Counterterrorism', IPI Global Observatory, 2 June 2021: https://theglobalobservatory.org/2021/06/the-legal-black-hole-in-united-nations-counterterrorism/ (last visited 12 July 2023). Saul discusses here the effort at a definition in the later UN Security Council Resolution 1566 (S/RES/1566 (2004) 8 October 2004) which has not however 'appreciably influenced national practice'.

41 UN Security Council Resolution 1373, para 5.

42 Ibid., para 6.

43 Ibid., para 7.

44 Ibid., para 8.

45 Ibid., para 9.

46 UN Security Council, Counter-Terrorism Committee (CTC) established pursuant to UN Security Council Resolution 1373 (2001), *Note by the Chairman: Guidelines of the Committee for the Conduct of its Work*, UN Doc S/AC.40/2001/CRP.1, para 1(c) (16 October 2001).

47 UN Security Council Resolution 1535 (2004) (26 March 2004), para 2.

48 UN Security Council Resolution 2617 (30 December 2021).

49 See the factsheet about the CTED at https://www.un.org/sites/www.un.org.security council.ctc/files/ctc_cted_factsheet_about_cted_may_2021.pdf (last visited 23 January 2023).

50 See https://www.un.org/en/about-us/un-charter/full-text (last visited 9 April 2023).

51 For further details see https://www.ohchr.org/en/what-are-human-rights/international -bill-human-rights (last visited 9 April 2023).

52 See https://www.ohchr.org/en/hrbodies/hrc/home (last visited 11 April 2023).

53 A comprehensive account is Olivier de Shutter, *International Human Rights Law: Cases, Materials, Commentary* 3rd edn (Cambridge: Cambridge University Press, 2019).

54 See the recent first-class account by Mark Goodale, *Reinventing Human Rights* (Stanford: Stanford University Press, 2022).

55 Benjamin Schreer and Andrew T.H. Tan (eds.), *Terrorism and Insurgency in Asia: A Contemporary Examination of Terrorist and Separatist Movements* (Abingdon: Routledge, 2019).

56 Samuel Moyn, *The Last Utopia: Human Rights in History* (Cambridge MA: Belknap Press, 2012).

57 UN General Assembly Resolution 56/1, *Condemnation of Terrorist Attacks in the United States of America* (12 September 2001).

58 UN General Assembly Resolution 56/99 (12 December 2001).

59 Ibid., para 3.

60 UN General Assembly Resolution 56/160 (19 December 2001).

61 Ibid.

62 UN General Assembly Resolution 57/219 (18 December 2002).

63 Ibid., para 3. See further UN General Assembly Resolution 58/187 (22 December 2003) where the request is repeated and to some extent toughened up.

64 UN Doc E/CN 4/Sub 2/1997/28.

65 See Saul (ed.), *Terrorism: Documents* n 1 above, pp. 646–647. The full paper by Koufa is at pp. 647–679.

66 Second Progress Report prepared by Special Rapporteur Kalliopi K Koufa, UN Doc E/ CN 4/Sub 2/2002/35 (17 July 2002), para 59.

67 Usefully set out in Saul (ed.), *Terrorism: Documents* n 1 above, pp. 679–716.

68 Commission on Human Rights Resolution 2004/87 (21 April 2004).

69 See *Protection of Human Rights and Fundamental Freedoms while Countering Terrorism. Study of the UN High Commissioner for Human Rights*, UN Doc A/59/428 (8 October 2004).

70 *Report of the Independent Expert on the Protection of Human Rights and Fundamental Freedoms while Countering Terrorism*, UN Doc E/CN 4/2005/103 (7 February 2005).

71 Ibid., para 91.

72 Resolution 2005/80 (21 April 2005) reprinted in Saul (ed.), *Terrorism: Documents* n 1 above, pp. 637–640.

73 *Promotion and Protection of Human Rights. Report by the Special Rapporteur on the Promotion and Protection of Fundamental Freedoms while Countering Terrorism*, UN Doc E/CN/4/2006/98 (28 December 2005) ('the Scheinin Report').

74 Ibid., para 27.

75 Ibid., para 58.

76 Ibid., para 59.

77 Ibid., para 60.

78 Ibid.

79 Ibid.

80 Ibid.

81 Ibid. For other examples see Fiona de Londras, *The Practice and Problems of Transnational Counter-Terrorism* (Cambridge: Cambridge University Press, 2022), pp. 134–140.

82 The Scheinin Report n 73 above, para 62.

83 Ibid.

84 Martin Scheinin, 'Impact of Post-9/11 Counter-Terrorism Measures on All Human Rights' in Manfred Nowak and Anne Charbord (eds.), *Using Human Rights to Counter Terrorism* (Cheltenham: Edward Elgar, 2018) 92–124, p. 92.

85 Jessie Blackbourn, Danis Kayis and Nicola McGarrity, *Anti-Terrorism Law and Foreign Terrorist Fighters* (Abingdon: Routledge, 2019).

86 See on drones, for example, the third annual report by Emmerson: UN Doc A/68/389 (18 September 2013). Foreign fighters are discussed in, for example, a report from the following year: UN Doc A/HRC/28/28 (19 December 2015), paras 31–53.

87 For example, *Report of the Special Rapporteur on the Promotion and Protection of Fundamental Rights While Countering Terrorism. Human Rights Impact of Counter-Terrorism and Countering (Violent) Extremism Policies and Practices on the Rights of Women, Girls and the Family*, UN Doc A/HRC/46/36 (22 January 2021).

88 Quoted by Schenin, 'Impact of Post-9/11 Counter-Terrorism Measures' n 84 above, p. 98.

89 UN Security Council Resolution 1438 (14 October 2002), UN Security Council

Resolution 1440 (24 October 2002) and UN Security Council Resolution 1450 (13 December 2002), respectively.

90 For example, UN Security Council Resolution 1455, Threats to International Peace and Security Caused by Terrorist Acts (17 January 2003).

91 UN Security Council Resolution 1456, para 6. Highly influential here was the then High Commissioner for Human Rights Mary Robinson, whose departing note to the CTC entitled 'A Human Rights Perspective on Counter-Terrorist Measures' – released on 23 September 2002 – anticipated much of what was to come; the note is in Saul (ed.), *Terrorism: Documents* n 1 above, pp. 607–610.

92 UN Security Council Resolution 1530 (11 March 2004).

93 UN Security Council Resolution 1535 (26 March 2004), para 2.

94 UN Security Council Resolution 1624 (2005), para 4. See UN Security Council Counter-Terrorism Committee established pursuant to Security Council Resolution 1373 (2001), *Policy Guidance PG 2: Conclusions for Policy Guidance Regarding Human Rights and the CTC*, 25 May 2006, in Saul (ed.), *Terrorism: Documents* n 1 above, p. 614.

95 Scheinin, 'Impact of Post-9/11 Counter-Terrorism Measures' n 84 above, p. 98, n 17.

96 See UN Security Council Resolution 1805 (2008).

97 UN General Assembly Resolution 60/288 (8 September 2006).

98 UN Security Council Resolution 1963 (2010), para 10.

99 Scheinin, 'Impact of Post-9/11 Counter-Terrorism Measures' n 84 above, p. 100.

100 *Report of the Special Rapporteur on the Promotion and Protection of Fundamental Rights While Countering Terrorism*, UN Doc A/HRC/34/61 (21 February 2017), para 59.

101 Ibid., para 62.

102 *Report of the Special Rapporteur on the Promotion and Protection of Fundamental Rights While Countering Terrorism, Fionnuala Ní Aoláin, Advancing Human Rights through the Mainstreaming of Human Rights in Counter-Terrorism Capacity-Building and Technical Assistance at the National, Regional and Global Levels*, UN Doc A/76/261 (3 August 2021), para 16. For the suggested definition see the Scheinin Report, n 73 above, paras 26–50.

103 Ní Aoláin, *Advancing Human Rights*, ibid., para 41.

104 Ibid., para 42. The state that had made the material available was Finland. For the Global Counter-Terrorism Compact, agreed on 23 February 2018, see: https://www.un .org/counterterrorism/global-ct-compact (last visited 27 April 2023).

105 *Report of the Special Rapporteur on the Promotion and Protection of Fundamental Rights While Countering Terrorism, Fionnuala Ní Aoláin*, UN Doc A/75/337 (3 September 2020), para 28.

106 Ibid.

Chapter 8

1 UN Security Council Resolution 217 (20 November 1965), paras 1 and 8.

2 UN Security Council Resolution 253 (29 May 1968).

3 *Bosphorus v Ireland*, European Court of Human Rights, 30 June 2005.

4 The term is used in the recitals to UN Security Council Resolution 1267.

5 UN Security Council Resolution 1267, para 4.

6 UN Security Council Resolution 1267, para 10.

7 UN Security Council Resolution 1363 (30 July 2001).

8 Gavin Sullivan, *The Law of the List: UN Counterterrorism Sanctions and the Politics of*

Global Security Law (Cambridge: Cambridge University Press, 2020). For a wide-ranging study of the whole area, see Nicholas Mulder, *The Economic Weapon: The Rise of Sanctions as a Tool of Modern War* (Yale: Yale University Press, 2022).

9 UN Security Council Resolution 1373 (28 September 2001), paras 1(c) and (d).

10 See UN Security Council Resolution 1390 (28 January 2002).

11 By the end of December 2002, however, the Security Council was already relenting to some extent, allowing that the regime need not apply to 'basic expenses, including payments for foodstuffs, rent or mortgage, medicines and medical treatment', but still without allowing that there was any human rights dimension to its decision-making: UN Security Council Resolution 1452 (20 December 2002), para 1(a).

12 Report of the Monitoring Group established pursuant to UN Security Council Resolution 1363 (2001) and extended by UN Security Council Resolution 1390, UN Doc S/2002/541, para 9: https://www.undocs.org/Home/Mobile?FinalSymbol=S%2F2002%2F541&Language=E&DeviceType=Desktop&LangRequested=False (last visited 30 January 2023).

13 Ibid., para 8.

14 Ibid., para 10.

15 Ibid., para 9.

16 Blocking Property and Prohibiting Transactions with Persons Who Commit, Threaten to Commit, or Support Terrorism (23 September 2001): https://www.state.gov/executive-order-13224/ (last visited 30 January 2023).

17 Letter dated 19 December 2001 from the Chairman of the Security Council established pursuant to UN Security Council Resolution 1373 (2001) concerning counter-terrorism addressed to the President of the Security Council, UN Doc S/2001/1220 (19 December 2001), p. 4: https://digitallibrary.un.org/record/455939 (last visited 31 January 2023).

18 Third Report of the Monitoring Group established pursuant to UN Security Council Resolution 1390 (2002), UN Doc S/2002/1338, para 11: https://www.undocs.org/Home/Mobile?FinalSymbol=S%2F2002%2F1338&Language=E&DeviceType=Desktop&LangRequested=False (last visited 1 February 2023).

19 Ibid., para 13.

20 Ibid., para 20.

21 Ibid.

22 Ibid., annex III para 5(a).

23 Ibid., annex III para 5(b).

24 Ibid., annex III para 5(c).

25 Ibid., annex III para 6.

26 Second Report of the Monitoring Group pursuant to Security Council Resolution 1455, UN Doc S/2003/1070 (2 December 2003), p. 4 and see further paras 16, 107, and 171: https://www.undocs.org/Home/Mobile?FinalSymbol=S%2F2003%2F1070&Language=E&DeviceType=Desktop&LangRequested=False (last visited 1 February 2023).

27 First report of the Analytical Support and Sanctions Monitoring Team appointed pursuant to Security Council Resolution 1526 (2004) concerning Al-Qaida and the Taliban and associated individuals and entities, UN Doc S/2004/679 (25 August 2004), para 5: https://www.undocs.org/Home/Mobile?FinalSymbol=S%2F2004%2F679&Language=E&DeviceType=Desktop&LangRequested=False (last visited 1 February 2023). UN Security Council Resolution 1526 (30 January 2004) was an attempt to improve processes so as to drive forward positive engagement with member states.

28 *Report of the Special Rapporteur on the Promotion and Protection of Fundamental Human Rights while Countering Terrorism*, UN Doc A/HRC/65/258 (6 August 2010), paras 35–39.

29 Ibid., para 53.

30 *The Impact of Counter-Terrorism Targeted Sanctions on Human Rights.* Position Paper of the United Nations Special Rapporteur on the promotion and protection of human rights and fundamental freedoms while countering terrorism (2021).

31 Luis Miguel Hinojosa-Martinez, 'Security Council Resolution 1373: The Cumbersome Implementation of Legislative Acts' in Ben Saul (ed.), *Research Handbook in International Law and Terrorism* 2nd edn (Cheltenham: Edward Elgar, 2020) 564–587, at p. 567, citing *Certain Expenses of the United Nations (Advisory Opinion)* [1962] ICJ Rep 151, 168. See Keith Harper, 'Does the United Nations Security Council have the Competence to act as Court and Legislature?' (1994) 27 (1) *New York University Journal of International Law and Politics* 103–157.

32 *Judgment (Grand Chamber) of 18 July 2013 in Cases C-584/10 P, C-593/10 P, C-595/10 p. European Commission, Council of the European Union and United Kingdom of Great Britain and Northern Ireland v Yassin Abdullah Kadi*, para 16 (*Kadi II*). For a study of the EU's approach see Christian Kaunert, Alex MacKenzie and Sarah Léonard, *The European Union as Global Counter-Terrorism Actor* (Cheltenham: Edward Elgar Publishing, 2022). What follows is drawn from Conor Gearty, 'In Praise of Awkwardness: *Kadi* in the CJEU' (2014) 10 (1) *European Constitutional Law Review* 15–27.

33 *Kadi II*, ibid., para 17.

34 Ibid.; the relevant legislative measure was Council Regulation (EC) No 881/2002.

35 *Kadi II* n 32 above, para 18.

36 Ibid., para 22.

37 Ibid., para 23.

38 Ibid., para 24.

39 Ibid.

40 UN Security Council Resolution 1730 (2006) (19 December 2006).

41 UN Security Council Resolution 1735 (22 December 2006), para 5.

42 Ibid., para 6.

43 UN Security Council Resolution 1822 (30 June 2008), para 13.

44 UN Security Council Resolution 1904 (17 December 2009), para 20.

45 Ibid. Annex 2 has the details.

46 UN Security Council Resolution 1989 (17 June 2011).

47 Eleventh report of the Analytical Support and Sanctions Implementation Monitoring Team established pursuant to Security Council Resolution 1526 (2004) and extended by Security Council Resolution 1904 (2009) concerning Al-Qaida and the Taliban and associated individuals and entities, UN Doc S/2011/245, para 10: https://www.undocs .org/Home/Mobile?FinalSymbol=S%2F2011%2F245&Language=E&DeviceType=Deskt op&LangRequested=False (last visited 30 January 2023). The figures in the text reflected the situation on 22 February 2011.

48 *Kadi II* n 32 above, para 28.

49 Ibid., para 31.

50 Commission Regulation (EC) 1190/2008 (28 November 2008).

51 Case T-85/09 *Kadi v Commission* [2010] ECR II – 5177 (30 September 2010).

52 This is how the Grand Chamber put it in *Kadi II* n 32 above, para 40.

NOTES TO PAGES 176–180

53 [2006] ECR II – 4665; see *Kadi II* n 32 above, para 41.

54 David Vaughan QC, Vaughan Lowe QC, James Crawford SC, Maya Lester and Professor Piet Eeckhout.

55 Not only Case T-315/01 *Kadi v Council and Commission* [2005] ECR II-3649 [*Kadi I*], but now also Joined Cases C-399/06 p. and C-403/06 p. *Hassan and Ayadi v Council and Commission* [2009] ECR I – 11393 and Case C-548/09 p. *Bank Melli Iran v Council.*

56 *Kadi II* n 32 above, para 67.

57 Ibid., para 97, citing Joined Cases C-399/06 p. and C-403/06 p. *Hassan and Ayadi v Council and Commission* [2009] ECR I – 11393, para 105.

58 TFEU is the Treaty on the Functioning of the European Union. *Kadi II* n 32 above, para 97.

59 *Kadi II* n 32 above, para 98.

60 Ibid., para 99.

61 This is the EU Charter of Fundamental Rights; see ibid., para 100.

62 *Kadi II* n 32 above, para 100.

63 Ibid., para 109.

64 Ibid., para 110.

65 Ibid., para 132.

66 Ibid., para 119.

67 Ibid.

68 Ibid., paras 151–162.

69 Ibid., paras 126–129.

70 Ibid., para 133.

71 See Commission Regulation (EC) No 1190/2008 of 28 November 2008.

72 The Brotherhood enjoyed a brief period in power in Egypt after the 'Arab Spring' before a military coup ended the country's experiment with democracy, albeit now without Mubarak; see Adam Shatz, 'Morsi's Overthrow' (2013) 35 (15) *London Review of Books*, 8 August 2013: https://www.lrb.co.uk/the-paper/v35/n15/adam-shatz/short-cuts (last visited 22 June 2023).

73 There is an enormous amount of detail at http://911research.wikia.com/wiki/Yasin_al-Qadi (last visited 22 June 2023).

74 On 5 October 2012: UN Security Council SC/10785: https://www.un.org/securitycouncil /content/sc10785 (last visited 22 June 2023).

75 *Kadi II* n 32 above, paras 128 and 129 (citations omitted).

76 Ibid., para 131.

77 For example, *Nada v Switzerland*, European Court of Human Rights, 12 September 2012.

78 *Sayadi and Vinck v Belgium*, Human Rights Committee Communication 1472/2006, 22 October 2008. See also the critical evaluation of the Committee on Legal Affairs and Human Rights of the Parliamentary Assembly of the Council of Europe: *UN Security Council and European Blacklists* (Doc 11454, 16 November 2007).

79 *Report of the Special Rapporteur on the Promotion and Protection of Fundamental Human Rights while Countering Terrorism*, UN Doc A/63/223 (6 August 2008); *Report of the Special Rapporteur on the Promotion and Protection of Fundamental Human Rights while Countering Terrorism*, UN Doc A/65/258 (6 August 2010); *Report of the Special Rapporteur on the Promotion and Protection of Fundamental Human Rights while Countering Terrorism*, UN Doc A/67/396 (26 September 2012); *Report of the UN High Commissioner for the*

Protection of Human Rights and Fundamental Freedoms while Countering Terrorism, UN Doc A/HRC/16/50 (15 December 2010).

80 For example, UN Security Council Resolutions 2083 (17 December 2012) and 2253 (17 December 2015). 'The enhanced mandate of the Ombudsperson [under 2083] further strengthens the due process afforded to listed individuals' according to the monitoring team annual report for 2013: UN Doc S/2013/792, para 49.

81 UN Security Council Sanctions: https://www.un.org/securitycouncil/sanctions/inform ation (last visited 4 May 2023).

82 UN Security Council Resolution 2610 (17 December 2021), para 48.

83 Ibid., para 63 and annex 2.

84 For example, *Report of the Office of the Ombudsman submitted pursuant to UNSC Resolution 2610*, UN Doc S/2023/133 (22 February 2023), para 50.

85 UN Security Council Resolution 2610 (17 December 2021), para 67.

86 United Nations Office of Counter-Terrorism: https://www.un.org/counterterrorism/20 23-counter-terrorism-week (last visited 8 May 2023).

87 The background is at https://www.un.org/counterterrorism/cct/background (last visited 8 May 2023).

88 UNCCT Annual Report 2021: https://www.un.org/counterterrorism/sites/www.un .org.counterterrorism/files/220825_uncct_ar_2021_web.pdf (last visited 7 May 2023), pp. 19–20.

89 Ibid., p. 84.

90 See https://www.coe.int/en/web/portal/-/council-of-europe-adopts-new-counter-terror ism-strategy-for-2023–2027 (last visited 18 July 2023).

91 For the text of the remarks see https://www.un.org/sg/en/content/sg/statement/2017-11 -16/secretary-general%E2%80%99s-speech-soas-university-london-%E2%80%9Ccounter -terrorism (last visited 7 May 2023).

92 The full programme is at https://www.un.org/counterterrorism/sites/www.un.org.counte rterrorism/files/20200710_virtual_ct_week_programme.pdf (last visited 7 May 2023).

93 The full programme is at https://www.un.org/counterterrorism/2023-counter-terrorism -week (last visited 15 August 2023).

94 *Report of the Special Rapporteur on the Promotion and Protection of Human Rights and Fundamental Freedoms while Countering Terrorism on the Role of Measures to address Terrorism and Violent Extremism on closing Civil Space and Violating the Rights of Civil Society Actors and Human Rights Defenders*, UN Doc A/77/345 (16 September 2022).

95 *Report of the Special Rapporteur on the Promotion and Protection of Human Rights and Fundamental Freedoms while Countering Terrorism on the Role of Measures to address Terrorism and Violent Extremism on closing Civil Space and Violating the Rights of Civil Society Actors and Human Rights Defenders*, UN Doc A/HRC/40/52 (18 February 2019).

96 *Report of the Special Rapporteur* n 94 above, para 14.

Chapter 9

1 I discuss this at length in my *Liberty and Security* (Cambridge: Polity Press, 2013) from which I have drawn some of the details for this chapter.

2 See Chapter 2 above.

3 See, for example, on the UK, Keith Ewing and Conor Gearty, *The Struggle for Civil*

Liberties: Political Freedom and the Rule of Law (Oxford: Oxford University Press, 2000). On the United States, see Samuel Walker, *In Defence of American Liberties: A History of the ACLU* 2nd edn (Carbondale and Edwardsville: Southern Illinois University Press, 1999). For Ireland see *in re Article 26 and the Emergency Powers Bill 1976* [1977] 1 IR 159.

4 [1942] AC 206.

5 Gyan Prakash, *Emergency Chronicles: Indira Gandhi and Democracy's Turning Point* (Princeton: Princeton University Press, 2019) ch. 5 is excellent on the strength of the government's hostility to the courts at this time.

6 *Secretary of State for the Home Department v Rehman* [2001] UKHL 47, [2003] 1 AC 153, para 50.

7 Ibid., para 62.

8 Lawyers Committee for Human Rights, *Imbalance of Powers: How Changes to US Law and Policy Since 9/11 Erode Human Rights and Civil Liberties* appeared as early as September 2002 and was updated in March 2003. The Council of Europe's *Guidelines on Human Rights and the Fight Against Terrorism* was issued after a Committee of Ministers session on 11 July 2002.

9 Kenneth Roth, 'The Law of War in the War on Terror: Washington's Abuse of Enemy Combatants' in James F. Hoge Jr and Gideon Rose (eds.), *Understanding the War on Terror* (New York: Foreign Affairs, Council on Foreign Relations, 2005) 302–311. The article appeared first in the January/February 2004 issue of *Foreign Affairs* – Roth was Executive Director of Human Rights Watch at the time.

10 Kenneth Roth and Minky Worden, *Torture: Does it Make Us Safer? Is It Ever OK?* (New York: The New Press in conjunction with Human Rights Watch, 2005).

11 Richard Ashby Wilson (ed.), *Human Rights in the 'War on Terror'* (Cambridge: Cambridge University Press, 2005); Benjamin J. Goold and Liora Lazarus (eds.), *Security and Human Rights* (Oxford: Hart Publishing, 2007); Andrew Lynch, Edwina Macdonald and George Williams, *Law and Liberty in the War on Terror* (Sydney: The Federation Press, 2007); Jordan J. Paust, *Beyond the Law: The Bush Administration's Unlawful Responses in the 'War' on Terror* (Cambridge: Cambridge University Press, 2007); Michael Welch, *Crimes of Power and States of Impunity: The US Response to Terror* (Rutgers: Rutgers University Press, 2009); David J. Whittaker, *Counter-Terrorism and Human Rights* (Harlow: Pearson Education Limited, 2009).

12 *Assessing Damage, Urging Action. Report of the Eminent Jurists Panel on Terrorism, Counter-Terrorism and Human Rights* (Geneva: ICJ, 2009); Office for Democratic Institutions and Human Rights, OSCE, *Countering Terrorism, Protecting Human Rights. A Manual* (2007).

13 Fiona de Londras, *Detention in the 'War on Terror': Can Human Rights Fight Back?* (Cambridge: Cambridge University Press, 2011).

14 *The Berlin Declaration. The ICJ Declaration on Upholding Human Rights and the Rule of Law in Combating Terrorism* (International Commission of Jurists, 29 August 2004).

15 'Salus populi suprema lex' *Michaels v Block* (1918) 34 *TLR* 438. The judge was Darling J.

16 Hallie Ludsin, *Preventive Detention and the Democratic State* (Cambridge: Cambridge University Press, 2016) is a theoretically grounded study of detention in the UK, and also the US and India.

17 See generally Part IV of the Act as originally enacted.

18 The UK Human Rights Act was enacted in 1998 but came fully into effect only in 2000.

19 Article 15(1). See the Human Rights Act 1998 (Designated Derogation Order) 2001 (SI 2001/3644).

20 *Chahal v United Kingdom*, European Court of Human Rights, 15 November 1996.

21 See [2002] EWCA 1502, [2004] QB 335.

22 *Counter-Terrorism Powers. Reconciling Security and Liberty in an Open Society. A Discussion Paper* (CM 6147, February 2004), esp. para 31.

23 Privy Counsellor Review Committee, *Anti-terrorism, Crime and Security Act 2001 Review: Report* HC 100 (18 December 2003).

24 *A and Others v Secretary of State for the Home Department* [2004] UKHL 56, [2005] 2 AC 68.

25 Showing a dramatically different approach to that which he took in *Rehman* (see pp. 183–184 above), Lord Hoffman was the exception; see [2004] UKHL 56, paras 91–97.

26 Receiving Royal Assent on 11 March 2005.

27 Royal Assent was granted on 14 December 2011.

28 See the reports of the Independent Reviewer of Terrorism Law, currently Jonathan Hall KC: https://terrorismlegislationreviewer.independent.gov.uk/ (last visited 5 June 2023).

29 See the Reviewer's *Report on the Terrorism Acts in 2021*: https://terrorismlegislationrevie wer.independent.gov.uk/terrorism-acts-in-2021/ (last visited 5 June 2023). TPIMs are at pp. 127–131.

30 See Kent Roach, *The 9/11 Effect: Comparative Counter-Terrorism* (Cambridge: Cambridge University Press, 2011), p. 310. All the details are in Shahram Dana and Ben White, 'Terrorising Innocence: Australia's Counter-Terrorism Laws Trump Freedom of Liberty' (2021) 27 (2) *Australian Journal of Human Rights* 352–375. For a valuable account from some years ago, see Andrew Lynch, Nicola McGarrity and George Williams, *Inside Australia's Anti-Terrorism Laws and Trials* (Sydney: New South Books, 2015).

31 The power is, however, coming under increased critical scrutiny. For a summary of the position at the time of writing, see Christopher Knaus and Nino Bucci, 'Law Council Joins Calls to Abolish Australia's Powers to Detain Terrorist Offenders to Prevent Future Crimes', *Guardian*, 4 April 2023: https://www.theguardian.com/law/2023/apr/04/law-council-joins-calls-to-abolish-australias-powers-to-detain-terrorist-offenders-to-prevent-future-crimes (last visited 23 June 2023).

32 See Roach, *The 9/11 Effect* n 30 above.

33 Special Immigration Appeals Commission Act 1997.

34 See, for example, Australia, Attorney-General's Department, *Control Orders*: https://www.ag.gov.au/national-security/australias-counter-terrorism-laws/control-orders (last visited 23 June 2023).

35 542 US 426 (28 June 2004).

36 542 US 426, 465.

37 *Hamdi v Rumsfeld* 542 US 507 (28 June 2004).

38 *Hamdi v Rumsfeld* 542 US 507, 554–555.

39 542 US 466 (28 June 2004).

40 The exact text is at https://www.coherentbabble.com/ss2005.htm#a200513 (last visited 7 June 2023). See Arsalan M. Suleman, 'The Detainee Treatment Act' (2006) 19 *Harvard Human Rights Journal* 257–265. Further details of the signing statement are at p. 263.

41 *Hamdan v Rumsfeld* 548 US 557 (29 June 2006).

42 553 US 723 (2008).

43 Sarah E. Mendelson, *Closing Guantánamo: From Bumper Sticker to Blueprint* (Washington: Center for Strategic and International Studies, September 2008).

44 Executive Order 13492 (22 January 2009).

45 Executive Order 13567. The quotes in the paragraph that follow are drawn from that order.

46 'Guantánamo Docket', *New York Times*: https://www.nytimes.com/interactive/2021/us /guantanamo-bay-detainees.html (last visited 5 June 2023).

47 Ibid.

48 *Opinions adopted by the Working Group on Arbitrary Detention at its ninety-fifth session, 14–18 November 2022 Opinion No. 72/2022 concerning Abd al-Rahim Hussein al-Nashiri (Afghanistan, Lithuania, Morocco, Poland, Romania, Thailand, United Arab Emirates and United States of America)*, UN Doc A/HRC/WGAD/2022/72: https://www.ohchr.org/ sites/default/files/documents/issues/detention-wg/opinions/session95/A-HRC-WGAD-2022-72-USA-Advance-Edited-Version.pdf (last visited 5 June 2023).

49 *Al Nashiri v Poland*, European Court of Human Rights, 10 July 2012.

50 And not only the United States: see Ruth Blakeley and Sam Raphael, 'British Torture in the "War on Terror"' (2017) 23 (2) *European Journal of International Relations* 243–266.

51 For a flavour of those debates in which US law professor Alan Dershowitz figured prominently, see his 'The Torture Warrant: A Response to Professor Strauss' (2003) 48 *New York Law School Law Review* 275–294.

52 On 11 July 2002; see https://www.coe.int/t/dlapil/cahdi/Source/Docs2002/H_2002_4E .pdf (last visited 7 June 2023). The relevant article is article 4.

53 For a long-view from the doyen of UK legal scholars in the field, see Clive Walker, 'Counterterrorism within the Rule of Law? Rhetoric and Reality with Special Reference to the United Kingdom' (2021) 33 (2) *Terrorism and Political Violence* 338–352.

54 Protection of Freedoms Act 2012, ss 57 and 58. For a flavour of the old controversies see Justice, *Pre-trial Detention in Terrorism cases* (Justice, 2007): https://justice.org.uk /pre-charge-detention-terrorism-cases (last visited 4 January 2024) and Joint Committee on Human Rights, *Counter-Terrorism Policy and Human Rights: 28 Days, Intercept and Post-Charge Questioning*, 19th report 2006–2007, 16 July 2007. For a valuable study of the post-11 September coordination of counter-terrorism practices in two post-colonial states, see Frank Foley, *Countering Terrorism in Britain and France: Institutions, Norms and the Shadow of the Past* (Cambridge: Cambridge University Press, 2013).

55 Eva Nanopoulos, 'European Human Rights Law and the Normalisation of the "Closed Material Procedure": Limit or Source?' (2015) 78 (6) *Modern Law Review* 913–944.

56 For the current operation of the powers in the UK see https://www.gov.uk/government /statistics/operation-of-police-powers-under-the-terrorism-act-2000-quarterly-update-to -june-2022/operation-of-police-powers-under-the-terrorism-act-2000-and-subsequent -legislation-arrests-outcomes-and-stop-and-search-great-britain-quarterly-u (last visited 8 June 2023).

57 Home Office, *Proscribed Terrorist Groups or Organisations* (November 2021): https:// www.gov.uk/government/publications/proscribed-terror-groups-or-organisations--2/ proscribed-terrorist-groups-or-organisations-accessible-version (last visited 8 June 2023).

58 Australian National Security, *Listed Terrorist Organisations* lists the twenty-nine groups affected: https://www.nationalsecurity.gov.au/what-australia-is-doing/terrorist-organisati ons/listed-terrorist-organisations (last visited 23 June 2023). See Nicola McGarrity and

George Williams, 'The Proscription of Terrorist Organisations in Australia' (2018) 30 (2) *Terrorism and Political Violence* 216–235.

59 State Department, Bureau of Counterterrorism, *Foreign Terrorist Organisations*: https://www.state.gov/foreign-terrorist-organizations/ (last visited 23 June 2023).

60 Council of the European Union, *EU Terrorist List*: https://www.consilium.europa.eu/en/policies/fight-against-terrorism/terrorist-list/ (last visited 8 June 2023).

61 See *Internationale Humanitäre Hilfsorganisation eV*: see BVerfG, Order of the First Senate of 13 July 2018. I BvR 1474/12, paras 1–167.

62 Ibid., para 125. For a particularly severe operation of this principle involving the Holy Land Foundation for Relief and Development, see *US v El Mezain HLF* US Court of Appeals Fifth Circuit, 7 December 2011: https://caselaw.findlaw.com/court/us-5th-circuit/1587675.html (last visited 19 July 2023).

63 The Proscribed Organisations Appeals Commission, established by the Terrorism Act 2000, Part 2, ss 3–13. Australia has its Independent National Security Legislation Monitor overseeing a range of security powers: https://www.inslm.gov.au/ (last visited 23 June 2023).

64 He was promptly seized and sent back to India for trial; see p. 26 above.

65 Téwodros Workneh and Paul Haridakis (eds.), *Counter-Terrorism Laws and Freedom of Expression: Global Perspectives* (Lanham: Lexington Books, 2021). On extremism, see House of Commons Home Affairs Committee, *Terrorism and Community Relations* (Sixth Report of Session 2004–05 HC 165). Radicalization programmes are well covered by Hamed El-Said, *New Approaches to Countering Terrorism: Designing and Evaluating Counter Radicalization and De-Radicalization Programs* (Basingstoke: Palgrave Macmillan, 2015). Sayeeda Warsi, *The Enemy Within: A Tale of Muslim Britain* (London: Allen Lane, 2017) is a fascinating, partly autobiographical account by a Tory insider.

66 *Global Study on the Impact of Counter-Terrorism on Civil Society and Civic Space* (21 June 2023): https://defendcivicspace.com/# (last visited 4 January 2024).

67 Ben Saul, 'United Nations Measures to Address the "Root Causes" and "Conditions Conducive" to Terrorism, and to Prevent Violent Extremism (PVE): 1972–2019' in Ben Saul (ed.), *Research Handbook on International Law and Terrorism* 2nd edn (Cheltenham: Edward Elgar, 2020), 530–549.

68 Rob Faure Walker, *The Emergence of Extremism: Exposing the Violent Discourse and Language of 'Radicalization'* (London: Bloomsbury, 2022).

69 Recep Onursal and Daniel Kirkpatrick (2021) 'Is Extremism the "New" Terrorism? The Convergence of "Extremism" and "Terrorism" in British Parliamentary Discourse' (2021) 33 (5) *Terrorism and Political Violence* 1094–1116.

70 *Holder v Humanitarian Law Project* (2010) 561 US 1.

71 BVerfG Judgment of the First Senate of 24 April 2013 1215/07 para 133: https://www.bundesverfassungsgericht.de/SharedDocs/Entscheidungen/EN/2013/04/rs20130424_1bvr121507en.html (last visited 8 June 2023). Cf. *Klass and Others v Germany*, European Court of Human Rights, 6 September 1978.

Conclusion

1 Yolande Knell and David Gritten, 'Jenin: Israeli Military Launches Major Operation in West Bank City', BBC, 4 July 2023: https://www.bbc.co.uk/news/world-middle-east-66083295 (last visited 17 July 2023).

2 'The state of Israel will act in any way necessary to protect its citizens and sovereignty from the ongoing terrorist attacks originating from the Gaza Strip and carried out by Hamas and other terrorist organizations'; see Identical letters dated 7 October 2023 from the Permanent Representative of Israel to the United Nations Gilan Erdan addressed to the Secretary-General and the President of the Security Council S/2023/742 (7 October 2023): https://www.un.org/unispal/wp-content/uploads/2023/10/N2329234.pdf (last visited 1 December 2023).

3 Conor Gearty, 'War Crimes' (2023) 45 (23) *London Review of Books*, 30 November 2023, 14–15: https://www.lrb.co.uk/the-paper/v45/n23/conor-gearty/short-cuts (last visited 1 December 2023). For the International Court of Justice proceedings see *South Africa v Israel* https://www.icj-cij.org/case/192 (last visited 4 January 2023).

4 See European Legal Support Centre, *Suppressing Palestinian Rights Advocacy through the IHRA Working Definition of Antisemitism* (June 2023). For an argument that the criticism of Israel as increasingly apartheid in its approach to the Palestinian question is damaging its medium- to long-term interests, see Ben White, *Cracks in the Wall: Beyond Apartheid in Palestine/Israel* (London: Pluto Press, 2018).

5 Darryl Li, 'Terrorism Torts and the Right to Colonize' (13 March 2023): https://lpeproje ct.org/blog/terrorism-torts-and-the-right-to-colonize/ (last visited 16 July 2023).

6 For the full speech see *The Spectator*, 24 February 2022: https://www.spectator.co.uk/ar ticle/full-text-putin-s-declaration-of-war-on-ukraine/ (last visited 26 June 2023).

7 Nadeem Shad and Robert Greenall, 'Moscow Drone Attack: Putin Says Ukraine Trying to Frighten Russians', BBC, 30 May 2023: https://www.bbc.co.uk/news/world-europe-65 751632 (last visited 26 June 2023).

8 See the Associated Press report of the first day of the hearing of the case: https://www.rf erl.org/a/ukraine-russia-un-court/32447039.html (last visited 26 June 2023).

9 As it was formally designated in the UK on 15 September 2023: https://www.gov.uk/gover nment/news/wagner-group-proscribed (last visited 1 February 2024).

10 Laura Scaife, *Social Networks as the New Frontier of Terrorism* (Abingdon: Routledge, 2017).

11 'Domestic terrorism . . . has evolved into the most urgent terrorism threat the United States faces today.' White House Fact Sheet, *Countering Domestic Terrorism*, 15 June 2021: https://www.whitehouse.gov/briefing-room/statements-releases/2021/06/15/fact-sh eet-national-strategy-for-countering-domestic-terrorism/ (last visited 4 July 2023). See Marc Sageman, *Misunderstanding Terrorism* (Philadelphia, University of Pennsylvania Press, 2017), ch. 5. The journal *Critical Studies on Terrorism* devoted a special issue to the problem in 2022, its editors lamenting the risk that 'this shift is further reifying the use of unstable and unfixed categories such as "terrorism"'; see Alice Martini and Raquel da Silva, 'Editors' Introduction: Critical Terrorism Studies and the Far-Right: New and (Re) new(ed) Challenges Ahead?' (2022) 15 (1) *Critical Studies on Terrorism* 1–12, p. 1.

12 Laura Bates, 'The Threat Posed By Incels and Why We Need to Start Calling Them What They Really Are – Terrorists', *The Stylist* (undated): https://www.stylist.co.uk/news/incels -terrorism/556131 (last visited 26 June 2023).

13 James Butler's 'A Coal Mine for Every Wildfire' and Adam Tooze's 'Ecological Leninism' (in (2021) 43 (22) *London Review of Books*, 18 November 2021, 9–12 and 13–15 respectively) are good overviews of environmental radicalism generally and Andreas Malm's climate activism in particular.

14 See p. 30 above.

15 Noam Chomsky, *Culture of Terrorism* (London: Pluto Press, 1989).

16 Michel Foucault, 'The Dangerous Individual' in Lawrence D. Kritzman (ed.), *Politics, Philosophy, Culture: Interviews and Other Writings 1977–1984* (New York: Routledge, 1990), p. 143, cited by Victoria Sentas, *Traces of Terror: Counter-Terrorism Law, Policing, and Race* (Oxford: Oxford University Press, 2014), p. 78.

17 See https://www.theguardian.com/us-news/2023/feb/15/buffalo-shooting-gunman-sentenced-life-prison (last visited 1 February 2024).

18 Not the Right, whose violence was invariably seen as over-supportive of the state. Thus, to take one example of this, until very late in the day fascism in the UK in the 1930s was perceived by the police as broadly supportive of their efforts to secure the state from what both the authorities and the Right saw as the real enemy, communism. See Keith Ewing and Conor Gearty, *The Struggle for Civil Liberties: Political Freedom and the Rule of Law in Britain, 1914–45* (Oxford: Oxford University Press, 2000), ch. 6.

19 Suggestions that the relevant footage of these celebrations was faked have been rebutted; see David Mikkelson, 'Palestinians Dancing in the Street', *Snopes Fact-Check*, 23 September 2001: https://www.snopes.com/fact-check/false-footaging/ (last visited 3 July 2023).

20 Martini and da Silva, 'Editors' Introduction' n 11 above, p. 3.

21 Ilyas Mohammed, 'Decolonialisation and the Terrorism Industry' (2022) 15 (2) *Critical Studies on Terrorism* 417–440.

22 William Shawcross, *Report of the Independent Review of Prevent* (HO 1072 (2023)).

23 Ibid., p. 3.

24 Sahar F. Aziz, 'Race, Entrapment, and Manufacturing "Homegrown Terrorism"' (2023) 111 (3) *Georgetown Law Journal* 381–463, pp. 381–382.

25 Ibid., p. 461.

26 Fatima Ahdash, 'Countering Terrorism in the Family Courts: A Dangerous Development' (2023) 86 (5) *Modern Law Review* 1197–1231.

27 Sentas, *Traces of Terror* n 16 above, p. 5.

28 Nadine El-Enany, *(B)ordering Britain: Law, Race and Empire* (Manchester: Manchester University Press, 2020), p. 10.

29 Ronan McGreevy, 'Metropolitan Rebel', *Irish Times*, 30 June 2023: https://www.irishtimes.com/opinion/an-irish-diary/2023/06/29/metropolitan-rebel-ronan-mcgreevy-on-london-and-the-making-of-michael-collins/ (last visited 4 July 2023).

30 Eithne Dodd and Cathal Ryan, 'The Times' UK Cartoon Depiction of Joe Biden Slammed for Offensive Irish Stereotype', *Irish Mirror*, 14 April 2023: https://www.irishmirror.ie/news/irish-news/times-uk-cartoon-depiction-joe-29711759 (last visited 4 July 2023).

31 Fahad Ansari, *British Anti-Terrorism: A Modern Day Witch-hunt* (Islamic Human Rights Commission, October 2005, updated June 2006). A brilliant study is Mahmood Mamdani, *Good Muslim, Bad Muslim: America, the Cold War and the Roots of Terrorism* (New York: Pantheon Books, 2004).

32 Sentas, *Traces of Terror* n 16 above, p. 37 (footnote omitted).

33 El-Enany, *(B)ordering* Britain n 28 above, p. 20.

34 Gareth Peirce, 'Was It Like This for the Irish?' (2008) 30 (7) *London Review of Books*, 10 April 2006, 3–8. See Paddy Hillyard's path-breaking *Suspect Community: People's*

Experience of the Prevention of Terrorism Acts in Britain (London: Pluto Press, 1993). The idea goes further back as well: Evan Smith and Andrekos Varnava, 'Creating a "Suspect Community": Monitoring and Controlling the Cypriot Community in Inter-War London' (2017) 132 (558) *English Historical Review* 1149–1181.

35 Taken from the excerpts from Bartolome de Las Casas, *In Defence of the Indians* (1550): https://2.files.edl.io/nFAzwPg6SRnhLGpQWsyzCZka8QfykAFWkGhRAw7OerzLRU Vk.pdf (last visited 1 February 2024).

36 Ann Laura Stoler, 'Colonial Aphasia: Race and Disabled Histories in France' (2011) 23 (1) *Public Culture* 121–156, p. 125, quoted by Deana Heath, *Colonial Terror: Torture and State Violence in Colonial India* (Oxford: Oxford University Press, 2021), p. 17.

37 Nigel Biggar, *Colonialism: A Moral Reckoning* (London: William Collins, 2023).

38 Gearty, 'War Crimes', n 3 above.

39 See Ntina Tzouvalu, *Capitalism as Civilisation: A History of International Law* (Cambridge: Cambridge University Press, 2020), esp ch. 5; and Tzouvalu, 'The "Unwilling or Unable" Doctrine and the Political Economy of the War on Terror' (2023) 14 (1) *Humanity* 19–38.

40 I write about this in Conor Gearty, 'No Golden Age: The Deep Origins and Current Utility of Western Counter-Terrorism Policy' in Richard English (ed.), *Illusions of Terrorism and Counter-Terrorism* (Oxford: Oxford University Press, 2015) 73–93.

41 *The Tablet*, 17 July 2021 p. 25.

42 Fiona de Londras, *The Practice and Problems of Transnational Counter-Terrorism* (Cambridge: Cambridge University Press, 2022), p. 8.

43 'Climate change . . . should be considered as a significant macro-level driver of terrorism.' Andrew Silke and John Morrison, 'Gathering Storm: An Introduction to the Special Issue on Climate Change and Terrorism' (2022) 34 (5) *Terrorism and Political Violence* 883–893, p. 883.

44 Mark Condos, *The Insecurity State: Punjab and the Making of Colonial Power in British India* (Cambridge: Cambridge University Press, 2017), p. 230.

Index